# Furious Hours

# Furious Hours

Murder, Fraud, and the Last Trial
of Harper Lee

## Casey Cep

ALFRED A. KNOPF | NEW YORK 2019

THIS IS A BORZOI BOOK
PUBLISHED BY ALFRED A. KNOPF

Copyright © 2019 by Casey N. Cep

All rights reserved. Published in the United States by Alfred A. Knopf,
a division of Penguin Random House LLC, New York, and distributed
in Canada by Random House of Canada, a division of Penguin
Random House Canada Limited, Toronto.

www.aaknopf.com

Knopf, Borzoi Books, and the colophon are registered trademarks of
Penguin Random House LLC.

Library of Congress Cataloging-in-Publication Data
Names: Cep, Casey N., author.
Title: Furious hours : murder, fraud, and the last trial of
Harper Lee / Casey Cep.
Description: First Edition. | New York : Knopf, 2019. |
Includes bibliographical references.
Identifiers: LCCN 2018043337 | ISBN 9781101947869 (hardcover) |
ISBN 9781101947876 (ebook)
Subjects: LCSH: Serial murders—Alabama. | Murder—Investigation—
Alabama. | Trials (Murder)—Alabama. | BISAC: BIOGRAPHY &
AUTOBIOGRAPHY / Literary. | TRUE CRIME / Murder / Serial Killers. |
HISTORY / United States / State & Local / South (AL, AR, FL, GA, KY, LA,
MS, NC, SC, TN, VA, WV).
Classification: LCC HV6533.A2 C47 2019 | DDC 364.152/32092—dc23
LC record available at https://lccn.loc.gov/2018043337

Jacket photograph by BJ Ray / Shutterstock; (torn newspaper) by
StillFx / Getty Images
Jacket design by Jenny Carrow

Map by Mapping Specialist, Ltd.

Manufactured in the United States of America

First Edition

*For my father and my mother,*
*who gave me a pocket watch,*
*then taught me to tell time*
*and everything else*

We are bound by a common anguish.

—*Harper Lee*

TENNESSEE

GEORGIA

ALABAMA

MISS.

Anniston

Birmingham

Tuscaloosa

Coosa

See inset
below

Alexander
City

River

Lake
Martin

Tallapoosa

Selma

Montgomery

River

Eufaula

Alabama

Monroeville

New Site

Tallapoosa River

Coosa
County

Kellyton

Alexander
City

Tallapoosa
County

Rockford

Cottage
Grove

Nixburg

Lake
Martin

Dadeville

Camp Hill

Elmore
County

Eclectic

Auburn

Gulf of Mexico

Coosa

River

Tallapoosa River

Elmore

Wetumpka

N
W        E
S

0        25        50
Scale of Miles

# | Contents |

# Furious Hours

# | Prologue |

Nobody recognized her. Harper Lee was well known, but not by sight, and if she hadn't introduced herself, it's unlikely that anyone in the courtroom would have figured out who she was. Hundreds of people were crowded into the gallery, filling the wooden benches that squeaked whenever someone moved or leaning against the back wall if they hadn't arrived in time for a seat. Late September wasn't late enough for the Alabama heat to have died down, and the air-conditioning in the courthouse wasn't working, so the women waved fans while the men's suits grew damp under their arms and around their collars. The spectators whispered from time to time, and every so often they laughed—an uneasy laughter that evaporated whenever the judge quieted them.

The defendant was black, but the lawyers were white, and so were the judge and the jury. The charge was murder in the first degree. Three months before, at the funeral of a sixteen-year-old girl, the man with his legs crossed patiently beside the defense table had pulled a pistol from the inside pocket of his jacket and shot the Reverend Willie Maxwell three times in the head. Three hundred people had seen him do it. Many of them were now at his trial, not to learn why he had killed the Reverend—everyone in three counties knew that, and some were surprised no one had done it sooner—but to understand the disturbing series of deaths that had come before the one they'd witnessed.

One by one, over a period of seven years, six people close to the

Reverend had died under circumstances that nearly everyone agreed were suspicious and some deemed supernatural. Through all of the resulting investigations, the Reverend was represented by a lawyer named Tom Radney, whose presence in the courtroom that day wouldn't have been remarkable had he not been there to defend the man who killed his former client. A Kennedy liberal in the Wallace South, Radney was used to making headlines, and this time he would make them far beyond the local *Alexander City Outlook*. Reporters from the Associated Press and other wire services, along with national magazines and newspapers including *Newsweek* and *The New York Times,* had flocked to Alexander City to cover what was already being called the tale of the murderous voodoo preacher and the vigilante who shot him.

One of the reporters, though, wasn't constrained by a daily deadline. Harper Lee lived in Manhattan but still spent some of each year in Monroeville, the town where she was born and raised, only 150 miles away from Alex City. Seventeen years had passed since she'd published *To Kill a Mockingbird* and twelve since she'd finished helping her friend Truman Capote report the crime story in Kansas that became *In Cold Blood*. Now, finally, she was ready to try again. One of the state's best trial lawyers was arguing one of the state's strangest cases, and the state's most famous author was there to write about it. She would spend a year in town investigating the case, and many more turning it into prose. The mystery in the courtroom that day was what would become of the man who shot the Reverend Willie Maxwell. But for decades after the verdict, the mystery was what became of Harper Lee's book.

# PART ONE

# The Reverend

| 1 |

# Divide the Waters from the Waters

ENOUGH WATER, LIKE ENOUGH TIME, CAN MAKE ANYTHING disappear. A hundred years ago, in the place presently occupied by the largest lake in Alabama, there was a region of hills and hollers and hardscrabble communities with a pretty little river running through it. The Tallapoosa River forms where a creek named McClendon meets a creek named Mud, after each of them has trickled down from the Appalachian foothills of Georgia. Until it was dammed into obedience, the Tallapoosa just kept on trickling from there, lazing downward until it met its older, livelier sibling, the Coosa River, near the town of Wetumpka, where together the two streams became the Alabama River, which continued westward and southward until it spilled into Mobile Bay, and from there into the Gulf of Mexico. For 265 miles and millions of years, the Tallapoosa carried on like that, serenely genuflecting its way to the sea.

What put an end to this was power. Man's dominion over the earth might have been given to him in Genesis, but he began acting on it in earnest in the nineteenth century. Steam engines and steel and combustion of all kinds provided the means; manifest destiny provided the motive. Within a few decades, humankind had come to understand nature as its enemy in what the philosopher William James called, approvingly, "the moral equivalent of war." This was especially true in the American South, where an actual war had left behind physical and financial devastation and liberated the enslaved men and women who had been the region's economic engine. No longer legally able to subjugate other people, wealthy white southerners turned their attention to nature instead. The untamed world seemed to them at worst like a mortal danger, seething with disease and constantly threatening disaster, and at best like a terrible waste. The numberless trees could be timber, the forests could be farms, the malarial swamps could be drained and turned to solid ground, wolves and bears and other fearsome predators could be throw rugs, taxidermy, and dinner. And as for the rivers, why should they get to play while people had to work? In the words of the president of the Alabama Power Company, Thomas Martin, "Every loafing stream is loafing at the public expense."

By the turn of the century, hydroelectric power had become the hope of the South as factories that had run off men and mules were mechanized and lightbulbs flickered on in homes that had known nothing but candlelight and kerosene. Suddenly every river below the Mason-Dixon Line was being eyed in terms of cubic feet per second and kilowatts per hour. In 1912, some scouts from Alabama Power borrowed a Winton Six automobile from a local woman and drove with her around the Tallapoosa River basin, searching for a site that could accommodate a large-scale dam. They settled on Cherokee Bluffs, a gorge lined by two-hundred-foot cliffs of gneiss and granite, with the same solid rock laid down along the riverbed. So ideal was the location that other power companies had already tried to build a dam there, twice. The first attempt, in 1896, was thwarted by an outbreak of yellow fever, which made financiers afraid to visit; the second, in 1898, by the outbreak of the Spanish-American War, which left investors unwilling to gamble their money on an infrastructure project at the back of beyond. But Alabama Power arrived at Cherokee Bluffs during the boom years of the early twentieth century, when there was finally enough financial backing to begin buying up the land around it.

Some people in the area sold willingly. Convinced that the lake would come anyway and worried about the diseases that might fester in it, they were happy to take the twelve dollars an acre the company was offering and start new lives in nearby towns. But others fought the dam, including businesses downstream, and by 1916 they had taken their battle all the way to the U.S. Supreme Court. In *Mt. Vernon–Woodberry Cotton Duck Co. v. Alabama Interstate Power Co.,* the high court upheld the state's right to seize land from private owners for public use through eminent domain, including by transfer to power companies. "To gather the streams from waste and to draw from them energy, labor without brains, and so to save mankind from toil that it can be spared," wrote the celebrated justice Oliver Wendell Holmes in the Court's unanimous opinion, "is to supply what, next to intellect, is the very foundation of all our achievements and all our welfare."

For the power company, it was a good outcome with bad timing. Shortly after the verdict, the United States entered World War I, and the Cherokee Bluffs project was once again delayed as men and money went abroad. Alabama Power would not resume work on the dam until after the armistice, and construction did not begin until 1923. That year, a hundred carpenters came to build the camp where the burners, cooks, engineers, loggers, masons, mechanics, sawyers, skidders, and superintendents would live while readying the basin and building the dam. When they were done, nearly three thousand employees moved in with their families, temporarily transforming Cherokee Bluffs into one of the largest settlements in the region. In addition to the segregated housing for black and white laborers, there was a bakery, a barbershop, a cafeteria, an ice plant, a school, a recreation hall for movies and religious services, and a hospital where dentists pulled teeth, surgeons took X-rays, and babies were born.

The town was big for Alabama, but the dam was huge by any standard. When it was finished and the floodgates were closed, the waters that filled in behind it would cover some forty-four thousand acres—at the time, the largest man-made lake in the world. By federal regulation, every one of those acres had to be cleared of any trees that would break the high-water line, and by company policy they had to be cleared of everything else, too: every last stick and brick that got there by force of nature or act of man before the power company came along. The three thousand workers set about moving houses, breaking down barns, relocating gristmills, digging up hundreds of bodies from a dozen cemeteries and reinterring them elsewhere. Mostly, though, they cut down trees: shortleaf pines, longleaf pines, loblollies, hickories, and oaks. Whatever they couldn't fell, they burned.

Mule teams, steam shovels, and a railroad line followed. By December 1923, the crew had built their first coffer, and pumps started pulling water from the gorge so that masons could build the foundations of the dam. When its final cornerstone was laid almost two years later, in a ceremony attended by thousands of people, the dam stood 168 feet tall and 2,000 feet long, a concrete raptor with a wingspan as wide as Cherokee Bluffs. It was christened Martin Dam, for the man who had said that streams should stop loafing and get to work.

The next year, on June 9, 1926, the men and women who had flocked to that earlier ceremony came back to watch as the floodgates on the dam were closed for the first time and the river began to fill the land behind them, forming the reservoir that would be known as Lake Martin. Water ran into wagon ruts and wheel tracks, sinkholes and stump holes, ditches and streams; it rose above blades of grass, tips of weeds, cornstalks, fence rails, fence posts, and finally the tops of those few trees that had been left, destined to sink so deep in the lake that no hull would ever brush against them.

All of this happened slowly, less deluge than drip, billions of gallons of water rising over tens of thousands of acres all day and all night for weeks. Moonshiners had time to move their stills from hollows to higher ground, and families who had decided to hold on to their land kept dragging their lives above the waterline. People fished the reservoir as soon as it was deep enough to stock with bass and bream, and children swam in it, emerging slick with the red clay loosened by the rising waters. Farmers watched watermelons float away; boaters out for a day trip on the new lake could not find the landing where they had put in, so constantly did the shoreline change. Bed nets and quinine tablets were handed out to anyone within a mile of the backwater, and twenty mosquito boats cruised the new inlets and bays spraying insecticide. Months passed like this. And then one day, where there had once been cabins and dogtrots, fields and farms, churches and schoolhouses, general stores and graves, there was nothing but water.

THERE WAS WICKEDNESS IN THE WORLD BEFORE THIS PARTICU-
lar flood and wickedness after it, but the future Reverend Willie Maxwell was born right in the middle, in May of the year that Alabama
Power laid the cornerstone for Martin Dam. His mother, Ada, was
a housekeeper; his father, Will, was a sharecropper, working a patch
of land on what was rapidly becoming, when Willie was born, the
western shore of Lake Martin. He was the sixth of their nine children,
the second of their five sons. Born in an age of political and environ-
mental upheaval, he never saw the Tallapoosa River in its meandering
days, never knew its watershed before it was transformed by hydro-
power or its culture before it was transformed by Jim Crow. His childhood years were bad ones for the state. The boll weevil came north
from Mexico and destroyed the cotton crop; the Communist Party
came south to organize sharecroppers, and horrific violence followed
in its wake. The Great Depression came from Wall Street and stayed
in Alabama for a long, long time, longer than the boys who traveled
to the local C.C.C. camp for a spell before returning to New Jersey
or New York.

Many of those young men who came down barely knew where
they were going; nearly forty years would pass before the Reverend
Martin Luther King Jr. and Governor George Wallace put Alabama on
the map for most Americans. The state sits like a headstone between
Mississippi and Georgia, its top flush against Tennessee, its base resting mostly on the panhandle of Florida, but dipping at its tip into the
Gulf of Mexico. For its part, Lake Martin is a little too far east and
a little too far south to be the dead center of Alabama, and its own
center is hard to find, because its arterial edges make it look less like a
reservoir than a Rorschach blot, flowing into the countless folds and
gullies and valleys of three counties: Coosa, Tallapoosa, and Elmore.
The largest town in the region is Alexander City, just to the north of
the lake; Wetumpka, the second largest, sits to the south. Most of the
other towns around Lake Martin are much smaller, barely big enough
for a post office or a service station.

Willie Maxwell and his siblings were born in Kellyton, one of those map-dot towns just west of Alex City, and raised in Crewsville, an unincorporated community too tiny to even count as a village—only a few homes, a couple of stores, and at least that many churches, since white and black believers required separate sanctuaries and the Methodists and the Baptists wouldn't worship together, either. There was traffic, but it never did more than pass through. In those days, it consisted mostly of horses and mule teams, though a few Model Ts found their way over from the Walker Ford Company in the next county, and the horns were loud enough when they did to make some of the people and most of the livestock jump. When the trains began coming through, children learned to recognize the different locomotives by the sound of their whistles. Otherwise, it was so quiet in that part of Alabama that you could hear birdsong all morning and bullfrogs all night. There were only twelve thousand people in the whole of Coosa County at the time, and enough pine trees that a boy playing Tarzan could practically swing from one end of it to the other without touching the ground. What little crime there was ran to bigamy, bastardy, hoboing, failing to honor the Sabbath, and using vulgar language in front of women.

Certain crimes, however, ran so deep in the veins of the South that those in power failed to register them as criminal. Many of the white residents of Coosa County and nearly all of the black ones were tenant farmers, victims of a brutal system that left those trapped within it barely able to eke out a living. Because they had to buy their seeds and fertilizers in the spring, sharecroppers were said to eat their crops before they planted them, and much of whatever they could later coax out of the ground went straight to the landowner. The terms of the loans a sharecropper could get were often unfavorable, the yields inadequate to feed and clothe a family, and the work itself backbreaking—sunrise to sundown, six days a week. Any child born into such circumstances was expected to help from the time he could walk.

In 1936, when Walker Evans and James Agee documented the gaunt faces and careworn lives of white tenant farmers in western Alabama, in what would later become *Let Us Now Praise Famous Men*,

Willie Maxwell was eleven, living on the other side of the state and the other side of the color line. Although his later years would leave documentation in courthouses around Alabama and make headlines around the nation, little is known of his early life, a silence characteristic of the historical record for African Americans in that time and place. Maxwell attended school, but around the harvest seasons, since life in Coosa County was organized chiefly by the rhythm of what went into the ground and what came out of it. Sharecroppers there grew corn, cotton, wheat, and oats in rotation, and, if they could, peanuts, peaches, or watermelons. There were baptisms and cemetery cleanings in the spring, quilting and corn shucking in the fall. Boys like Willie planted, hoed, picked fruits and vegetables, scared crows off the corn and rabbits out of the lettuce while learning to shoot, and fished for whatever they could catch in the Beau, the Hatchet, the Socapatoy, and Jacks Creek, the streams that bounded Crewsville.

Around the edges of all that, Willie got seven years of formal education. After school, in the summer of 1943, he joined two million other African American men in registering for the draft. At eighteen, he reported for basic training at Fort Benning, a base, named for a Confederate general, that straddles the state line with Georgia. He was issued a uniform, and his hair was shaved to the tight trim he would maintain for the rest of his life. Although he went through combat training, the army assigned Maxwell to an engineer aviation battalion at Keesler Field in Mississippi, and then to Camp Kearns in Utah.

Before the war, Camp Kearns was five thousand acres of wheat fields. Stripped of its crops, the wartime version was a gritty, filthy place. Military vehicles ran their headlights during the day to see through the clouds of dust, and soldiers woke most mornings under a layer of dirt that had blown in through the plywood and tar-paper windows. The men were packed into barracks so tightly that they called their quarters chicken coops; respiratory infections spread like rumors of deployment. Maxwell lived there for two years, until November 1945, when he was discharged with $413.80 and, in common with millions of other servicemen, a Victory Medal to mark the end of World War II. Instead of returning to Alabama, however, he chose to reenlist and was sent to California to join the 811th Engineer Aviation Battalion, one of forty-eight black units that constructed and maintained airfields around the world. From there, he went to the Pacific theater and drove trucks for the U.S. Army Corps of Engineers.

At the time, the military was almost as divided as the Deep South that Willie Maxwell had left behind, an injustice that became even more glaring after the United States joined the fight against the Nazis. "Our local Nordics have a mass psychosis, too," wrote Langston Hughes: "As the Hitlerites treat the Jews, so they treat the Negroes, in varying degrees of viciousness." The same prejudice that kept civilians separated by race in schools and churches and soda shops kept soldiers segregated in camp bunks, mess halls, and on the front lines. The army would finally begin to integrate in 1948, but that was too late for Sergeant Maxwell. In January 1947, after returning to America with a Good Conduct Medal, he was voluntarily discharged. By early May, he was headed home.

Back in Coosa County, Maxwell settled in Kellyton, the town where he was born. Now twenty-one years old, he was six feet two and 180 pounds—tall enough to see over almost any man and slim enough to pass between any two. His brown eyes were always watchful, his face handsome and lean; a narrow mustache sat like an officer's chevron above his lips. His speech was elegant, almost formal, and the charm most young men could spare only for their steadies he offered to everyone he met, leaving "sirs" and "ma'ams" like fingerprints wherever he went. "There wouldn't be anybody nicer to you, conversation-wise," people said of him. "You'd think that man came from heaven he was so smooth."

Sometime after his return home, Maxwell traded his uniform for a job with the company that had made it: Russell Manufacturing, Alexander City's largest textile mill. The handsome young army vet also met a quiet local girl named Mary Lou Edwards. Born and raised in Cottage Grove, another one of Coosa County's tiny towns, Mary Lou was two years younger than Willie and still living with her parents when he gave her an engagement ring. They got their medical certificate the last week of March and were married at the probate court in the county seat of Rockford on April 2, 1949. It was the first but not the last marriage of the future Reverend Willie Maxwell, and whatever else can be said about it, this much is true: it lasted, as he promised that day that it would, until death did them part.

# 2

# Minister of the Gospel

Mary Lou Maxwell was shelling peas. It was the first week of August, after the summer storms had battered the bird nests and wildflowers, when the cicadas were loud in the trees and the ticks were wild in the grass. Once the corn grew heavy on the stalk and other vegetables sat fat and sedate on the vine, the pea pods were ready and could be plucked by their bonnets off the plants and shelled one at a time by the hundreds. Women and children pressed their thumbs against the pods, popping the creases and sending peas pinging into a colander. Over the course of slow summer hours, bushel baskets full of tangled greens were reduced to bowls of peas, ready for washing and blanching and packing away in the freezer.

Mary Lou had been shelling since she got home from her shift at Russell Mills—her second job, on top of working from home as a laundress and seamstress, taking in clothes and linens from her neighbors. Shelling was a peaceful, mindless task, good for gossip if you had company and contemplation if you did not. But when one of her sisters came by the house that evening, she found Mary Lou sweating and anxious. Earlier that day, Willie Maxwell had been dismissed from his own job at the mill. It was not the first time he had been fired, and it was unwelcome news for the couple financially, but Mary Lou hadn't been able to discuss it with her husband yet, because he had a second job, too, and he had to go straight to it that night: the Reverend Maxwell, as he was universally known by then, was scheduled to preach at a revival near Auburn.

Back then, as today, southern revivals were all fire and brimstone, and they could go on for hours inside tents raised especially for the occasion. Even in the evening, the heat was so tremendous under the pavilions that attendees could be forgiven for thinking the setting had been designed to remind them of what awaited if they didn't repent. But people flocked to them anyway, sometimes by the thousands, and churches kept hosting them, for the simple reason that they worked: it was partly thanks to the state's vibrant revival culture that by 1970 one in four Alabamians was Baptist. Sometimes churches came together to host a collective revival, but generally they staggered them, so that summer was one long season of spiritual improvement where salvation was always within driving distance.

Maxwell had been invited to this particular revival by the Reverend and Mrs. Reese of Macedonia Baptist Church, but Mrs. Maxwell did not want to come along. In a small town, a preacher's wife faces more scrutiny than almost anyone. Where she goes and what she wears, how she talks and whom she talks to and what she says: everything she does is noticed, noted, weighed, and judged. Charity begins at home, but so does humility, modesty, patience, piety, and respectability, and a preacher's wife is under pressure to embody them all—even more pressure, sometimes, than the preacher himself. It is easy to see why a woman in such a position might keep to herself when she could, and that night, August 3, 1970, Maxwell agreed to go preach without his wife, but asked her to leave the phone line clear so that he could stop somewhere to call her on his way back home.

The Reverend headed out for the revival a little before six o'clock. Mary Lou's sister left soon afterward, and later that evening Mary Lou got in her car and went to visit a different sister, Lena Martin. When she got back home, she stopped to talk with her next-door neighbor, Dorcas Anderson. Her husband, Mary Lou mentioned, was out at a revival and had asked her to stay off the telephone so he could reach her. They talked for a few minutes, and then Mary Lou went back to her house to wait out the rest of what she assumed would be a long, lonely night; she'd had enough experience of revivals by then to know that the one over in Auburn would likely carry on until well after dark, and enough experience of her husband to be used to passing evenings alone.

TO HEAR HIM TELL IT, HOURS LATER AND FOR THE REST OF HIS life, that was the night the Reverend Willie Maxwell became Job. On his way back from the revival, he pulled in to a service station in the town of Camp Hill to buy a Coca-Cola and call his wife. Forever after, he would insist that she didn't answer and that when he got home to Nixburg, just before eleven, she wasn't there. He would swear that, worn out by a long and difficult day, he'd fallen right to sleep. It was not until he woke up around two in the morning and realized his wife still had not come home that he called his mother-in-law, who said she hadn't seen her daughter that day; his neighbor, who had seen her but much earlier; and then one of Mary Lou's sisters, who said she had come by the house to visit but left hours before. It was only then that Maxwell called the police.

After the officers who were dispatched to Nixburg spoke to Maxwell, they went next door to talk with Dorcas Anderson. She had been woken earlier that night by the Reverend's telephone call and had gone over to talk with him about his missing wife, but when the police came knocking, she told them something she hadn't told the Reverend himself: Mrs. Maxwell had come to her house not once but twice that evening. The first time was after visiting her sister Lena, when Mary Lou mentioned something peculiar about how her husband wanted her to leave the phone on the hook; the second time was after ten, when she was excited and agitated. "The Reverend has been in a bad accident and I'm going to get him," she had told Dorcas, explaining that Maxwell had called to say he'd wrecked his car up near New Site.

That was the last thing that Mary Lou had ever said to Mrs. Anderson. As for Maxwell's claim to have gotten home around eleven, Anderson told the authorities that to the best of her knowledge he had been out all night. If he had come home earlier and fallen asleep, she had neither seen nor heard him. The earliest she could be sure that the

Reverend was home was when he called her, at well past two o'clock in the morning, to ask if she knew where Mary Lou was. Right after that, Mrs. Anderson said, she walked to her back door and looked across at the Reverend's garage, where she could see his car. "I went back to the bedroom," she said, "and told my husband there was something wrong because his car wasn't torn up."

The Reverend insisted that there must have been some kind of misunderstanding. He had not been in any kind of accident, and when he called home from Camp Hill, Mary Lou hadn't answered the telephone. He felt certain that it must have been his wife who had been in a wreck, and he urged the police to look for her car on Highway 22, the route that would have taken her home from her sister Lena's house and had also taken the Reverend home from New Site.

A highway in name only, 22 is a sleepy, two-lane road that crosses Hillabee Creek. At night, when the air grows colder than the water, fog rises up off the creek and hangs over the pavement like breath in winter. When the police finally found Mary Lou's 1968 Ford Fairlane along Highway 22, it was on the shoulder, twelve feet from the asphalt beside a stand of trees, but it had not actually hit any of them. There was a little damage, none of it serious; all told, it would cost only a few hundred dollars to repair. Far from looking wrecked, the car looked as if it had been parked. Its engine was running, and its headlights stared blankly out into the darkness. Mrs. Maxwell was inside, already dead.

FOR THE FIRST FIVE YEARS OF THEIR MARRIAGE, THE MAXWELLS worked as sharecroppers for a man named Mac Allen Thomas, then a county commissioner and later a probate judge, who owned a plantation just outside of Rockford. As commissioner, Mac was the kind of glad-handing, strong-arming good old boy who knew how to get bridges built and roads improved and didn't mind when people joked that he'd paved every pig trail in the county. As judge, he wasn't a stickler for details, and happily obliged law enforcement officers by pre-signing warrants for them to keep in their cars in case they came across any bootleggers. Mac took a shine to the soft-spoken, sweet-talking newlywed tilling his fields and remained friendly with the

Reverend long after pretty much every other lawman in three counties had developed a different opinion.

When Maxwell wanted to, he could be both charming and persuasive, but he did not always want to, and his self-control, such as it was, had limits. At Russell Mills, for instance, his reputation for hard work was marred by a record of absenteeism, and in 1954, two years after Hank Williams got arrested for public drunkenness and disorderly conduct and was famously photographed stumbling shirtless out of a cell in the Alexander City Jail, Maxwell was fired from the mill for failing to show up for work. Around the same time, the Maxwells stopped sharecropping for Mac Thomas, leaving them short on money. But as would later become abundantly clear, Maxwell was an entrepreneurial man, and he soon began working the series of jobs he would have in rotation for the rest of his life: powdering, pulpwooding, and preaching.

The powdering took place at a rock quarry in Fishpond, a smidge of a town near the county line. It was a difficult, dangerous job, and Maxwell excelled at it. "He was one of the most outstanding, dependable employees I had in every way," recalled his supervisor, Jack Bush, who would later be elected Alexander City's first full-time mayor. The work entailed drilling holes several feet down into the rock so that blasting caps or fertilizer blasts could bust the rock into smaller bits and a crusher could break them down. Each explosion covered the quarry and everyone in it with powdered rock, so that by the end of the day the laborers looked like they had been dusted with flour from head to toe.

Unlike his co-workers, however, Maxwell never stayed dusty for long. At the quarry as elsewhere, he excelled at erasing the evidence of what he had done. "When we cleaned up," Bush said, "he was immaculate." Maxwell didn't just brush off the powder and mop off the sweat, and he did not truck any more than necessary in work clothes; instead, he fashioned himself into one of the most dapper men in eastern Alabama. His shoes were always polished, his suits were always black, and a tie almost always accentuated his crisp white shirts. Later, people took to saying that his clothing must've been handmade for him by the Devil, and the men who watched him deliver pulpwood to wood yards in three-piece suits still talk about it today.

Pulpwooding was cleaner work than powdering, but not by much, and only because the Reverend Maxwell ran a crew instead of working on one. America's pulp and paper industry had moved south in the early decades of the twentieth century, after New England's forests were depleted and a Georgia chemist figured out how to make newsprint from southern pine despite its high resin levels. In short order, the gristmills and sawmills that had dotted rural counties around the South were overtaken by pulp mills, and many of the crews that had cut and hewed ties for the railroad industry and planed lumber for construction turned their energies to pulping wood. A war waged briefly over supply, as lumbermen fought pulpwooders over millions of acres of forests—the South's version of the farmer-versus-rancher battles in the West. In Alabama, International Paper established its headquarters in Mobile, while the Gulf States Paper Corporation landed in Tuscaloosa; those giants and many other smaller companies depended on leases with private landowners and arrangements with private crews to supply their mills.

As head of one of those crews, Maxwell worked the way most pulpwooders did: with a single-axle truck, chain saws, axes, and a team of anywhere from two to six men. When he had a full crew, one or two of the men ran the saws, a limber followed along behind removing branches, a bucker cut the delimbed logs into sections, a loader moved them onto the truck, and a driver delivered them. A crew like that could expect to harvest eight cords of short wood per day. At the mills, that wood was fed into chippers, the chips were cooked into pulp, and the pulp was pressed and dried into paper. The mills reeked of ammonia and sulfides and discharged those chemicals whenever they ran, but they gave Alabama one of its few flourishing industries and gave the country countless essential and inessential goods: newspapers, notebooks, towels, lunch bags, liquor store bags, birthday cards, tissues, milk cartons, novels.

For Maxwell, pulpwooding was a way into the lucrative logging business. It did not require a lot of overhead—just a few hundred dollars to cover saws, chains, tires for the trucks, and gas for everything with an engine. The companies that contracted men like him to bring them wood would often handle the leases and send a timber specialist in ahead of a crew to mark trees, but Maxwell did not need much help. As reliable in the woods as in the quarry, he never missed a marked tree and never cut one a client wanted standing. "I'd see after it all," said one mill manager for the Montgomery-based company Bama Wood. "Only thing was, with Maxwell, I'd just mark a small place. He'd cut it just like I told him to. I would go out there and mark about an acre of it and I'd tell him, 'Okay, Preacher, this is the way I want it to look, I want it all this way,' and he would just do it."

For Maxwell, though, both pulpwooding and powdering were side jobs. As he would later testify under oath, he always considered his real vocation to be "minister of the gospel." He was ordained in 1962, at Philippi Baptist Church in Keno, which had been Philippi Methodist Church until all of its white congregants died or moved away. The church was named for the Roman city in Macedonia that Saint Paul visited during his second missionary journey; years later, Paul would write the Philippians a letter from prison warning them to beware of false preachers. Maxwell surely knew that passage of the New Testament, given how much his parishioners admired his thorough grasp of scripture. "He could pray a prayer that could make this house move," one of them said. "He could sing and he could pray, and when it came to discussing the Bible, he knew it."

From ordination on, the Reverend Maxwell was known by that title whether or not he was in the pulpit. Legally, he was Willie Junior Maxwell; less legally, he signed official paperwork as W. J. Maxwell and W. M. Maxwell and Will Maxwell and Willie Maxwell and William with no middle initial Maxwell, but most everyone called him Preacher or Reverend. His sartorial excess, out of place in a quarry and wood yard, suited a sanctuary, and his unmistakably strange way of speaking, too antique and elegant for everyday life, earned him renown in pulpits around Alabama—at Mount Zion West Baptist Church in Our Town, Union No. 2 Baptist Church in Eclectic, Mount Gilead Baptist in Newell, Reeltown Baptist in Notasulga, and Holly Springs Baptist Church in Springhill.

As the demand for his preaching grew, Maxwell began taking seminary classes at a branch of Selma University. A black Bible college that opened in 1878, Selma trained thousands of ministers for the Alabama State Missionary Baptist Convention, while its extension school offered courses for those like Maxwell who were already serving in the ministry. Those classes convened fifty miles southwest of Alex City in the basement of Montgomery's Holt Street Baptist Church—the church where, fifteen years before, inspired by Rosa Parks, the Reverend Martin Luther King Jr. called for a boycott of the city's segregated bus system.

The Reverend Willie Maxwell was awarded a certificate of theological study from Selma University in 1970, but however much it improved his sermons, it did not improve his financial situation. The Baptists became the largest denomination in Alabama partly thanks to ministers like Maxwell—bivocational men who were willing to do other work during the week when rural parishes could not support full-time clergy. Yet even in combination with his other jobs, the Reverend could not afford his lifestyle, whose excesses went further than fancy suits. The Reverend and Mary Lou Maxwell had moved into a brick house in Nixburg, a town southwest of Alex City along Highway 9, and he owed tens of thousands of dollars to the Bank of Dadeville, another few thousand to Citibanc of Alabama, and a few thousand more to Security Mutual Finance. He was heavily mortgaged, behind on his car payments, and in arrears on the many personal accounts he had opened at mom-and-pop stores all around Lake Martin.

It was to help alleviate those debts that Mary Lou had gone to work with her husband at Russell Mills. The additional money was welcome but it didn't resolve the tensions in the Maxwell home. By then, the couple had been married for two decades, and the strain of those years was showing. Mary Lou had grown heavier, in every way; those closest to her could tell that she was unhappy, and although there was no sign of physical abuse, it was clear that her husband had found other means of hurting her. She wasn't one to complain, but what little she confided to others was enough. "She would often talk to me about the telephone calls that he would receive from different ladies," Dorcas Anderson said. "They would call asking her about the Reverend Maxwell. They would want to speak with him and she would say he's not home, and they would think she was just trying to keep them from talking to him."

Men of the cloth may have more cause than most to avoid indiscretions, but they also have more opportunities to commit them. The Reverend's parishes were far enough apart that he had reason to be away from his wife for long stretches of time, and the respect afforded the relationship between preacher and parishioner meant that, unlike most men, he could be alone with almost any woman in her home. Nor were telephone calls at all hours of the day and night unusual for a member of the clergy ministering to his flock. Maxwell was not the first preacher to take advantage of his position or to use it for cover, but Mary Lou wearied of it all, and whatever she knew or suspected of her husband's affairs before 1970, incontrovertible evidence of them arrived at the beginning of that year. On January 21, the Reverend Maxwell went before the Tallapoosa County Probate Court to legitimate a six-week-old child: to "recognize the said child as my own, capable of inheriting my estate, real and personal, as if born in wedlock," and to replace the girl's surname with his own.

However unhappy Mary Lou was about this development, however unhappy she was in general, she wasn't likely to do anything about it. "When she married, she married," one of her sisters said. Neither adultery nor insolvency could make Mary Lou reconsider her husband; if anyone was going to end the Maxwells' marriage, it would not be her.

WHEN THE POLICE OPENED THE DOORS OF THE FORD FAIRLANE that August night, they found a horrifying scene. The red polka dots on Mary Lou Maxwell's white cotton dress were barely visible for all the blood. Her hands, arms, head, and chest were covered in it, and more ran down the backs of her legs. She was swollen and bruised, her face covered with lacerations, her jawbone chipped, her nose dislocated; she was missing part of her left ear, which the police eventually found on the floorboards of the backseat. There was blood on the outside of the car, too—on the passenger door, the windshield, and the rear window. From what the police could determine, Mary Lou had been beaten to death, probably sometime before her car was parked on the side of Highway 22.

The Alexander City Police were technically outside their jurisdiction, so they handed off the case to the Tallapoosa County Sheriff's Department and the Alabama State Troopers. Some of the officers went down the road to talk with the Reverend Maxwell, while others stayed to investigate. They searched the car for any evidence of an attacker, collected fibers from the interior, and removed an empty Kleenex box and claw hammer from the backseat. Then they walked the shoulder of the road looking for footprints or signs of a struggle. At a church not too far from the car, they found drops of blood in the driveway and collected samples of those, too. Meanwhile, other officers had taken Mary Lou Maxwell's body to the Armour Funeral Home.

Violence has a way of destroying everything but itself. A murdered person's name always threatens to become synonymous with her murder; a murdered person's death always threatens to eclipse her life. That was especially true of an economically marginal black woman in Alabama. Loved ones would remember Mary Lou's talent for sewing, her devotion to her husband, her patience, her faith, and her fortitude, but apart from her birth, marriage, and death certificates, the only official record of her existence is a disturbingly thorough description of the condition of her body at the time of her death.

In addition to the lacerations and swelling that the police had already noted, the coroners found a half-inch dark bruise around Mary Lou's neck and accompanying ligature marks, as well as grains of sand and bits of leaves in her mouth. More sand and leaves were caked into the bloodstains on her dress, and there were grease spots at its midline and along the hem. The coroners concluded that Mrs. Maxwell had been beaten to death, after someone had failed to strangle her with something coiled like a rope, and that she had struggled with her attacker before falling to the ground. When the autopsy was finished, the investigators sent their findings, together with the evidence from the scene, to the Alabama Department of Toxicology and Criminal Investigation at Auburn University.

For thirty-five years, the Department of Toxicology had been Alabama's leading laboratory for forensic science. It had grown out of an incident in the state that quickly turned into one of the most infamous miscarriages of justice in American history. In March 1931, nine black boys—the youngest one just thirteen years old, and none of them older than nineteen—were falsely accused of raping two white women on a train. In three rushed trials held in Scottsboro, Alabama, all nine were convicted and eight were sentenced to death, despite the absence of any credible evidence against them and the fact that one of the accusers later recanted her testimony. For the next six years, while the boys waited in prison—in most cases, on death row—the case wound its way through the justice system, via a series of hung juries, mistrials, retrials, and two trips to the U.S. Supreme Court. In 1937, charges were dropped against some of the defendants; eventually, all of the Scottsboro Boys were released, and decades later the last three were posthumously pardoned.

It was in the middle of this debacle that the state attorney general, Thomas Knight, contacted some toxicologists at what was then Alabama Polytechnic Institute but would later become Auburn University. Knight felt that the mishandling of the Scottsboro Boys case might have been avoided had the authorities gathered and assessed the evidence scientifically. By way of a counterexample, he pointed to the scrupulous methods used in another of the era's most notorious criminal cases: the 1935 conviction of Bruno Hauptmann for the abduction and murder of the infant son of Charles and Anne Morrow Lindbergh. That latter case set a standard the state should strive for, Knight felt, and he encouraged prosecutors and law enforcement officers around Alabama to send evidence to Dr. Hubert Nixon, a professor in the agricultural laboratory, and Dr. Carl Rehling, a professor of chemistry. Within a few years, the Alabama Legislature had officially allocated funds for a special forensic laboratory. "It is not our purpose to prove guilt or innocence," Dr. Rehling said of the lab, "but to present the facts."

By the 1970s, the Department of Toxicology and Criminal Investigation was consulting on almost six thousand cases a year, offering assistance with autopsies, ballistics, fingerprinting, handwriting analysis, microscopy, and photography. Evidence from any crime committed in the state of Alabama could be sent to the department, to be studied by its team of chemists, coroners, criminologists, microbiologists, technicians, and toxicologists. Rehling called himself the "crime doctor," and his colleagues the "crime crew." Their reports routinely spared innocent suspects prison terms or the death penalty and brought closure to families whose loved ones had died under circumstances that only forensic analysis could clarify.

But the crime doctor and his crew failed to do either in the case of Mary Lou Maxwell. When the scientists at Auburn began processing the evidence from her case, they concurred with the findings of the local coroner and the investigators at the scene: she had been strangled and beaten outside her car, probably in the driveway of the church, since the blood found there matched her type. But none of the police, sheriff's deputies, or state troopers ever found the rope that the forensics team was sure had been used to strangle her, and when investigators went back to search the Reverend Maxwell's home, they discovered that he had recently burned his trash. The technicians who analyzed the burn barrel contents could identify nothing more than a cotton cloth with a seam and the remains of something with a basket-weave pattern, such as a straw hat or handbag. They suspected it was more of Mrs. Maxwell's clothing, or perhaps the Reverend's own clothes from the day of her murder, but there was no way to know for sure.

Short on physical evidence, the state investigators started asking around about the Reverend Willie Maxwell. His neighbor's testimony made him the likeliest suspect, and her comment about women calling the Maxwell house all the time gained credence when they identified several of the Reverend's "lady friends," including one on the old Kellyton Road who was driving a brand-new car for which he was making the payments—or failing to make them, since the police also uncovered Maxwell's considerable debt. Like more than a few preachers', they learned, his private life bore little resemblance to the one his parishioners thought he was living, and no resemblance at all to those he extolled in his sermons.

While the police were investigating him, the Reverend, newly unemployed and newly widowed, set about doing the kinds of things you do after the death of a spouse. His lawyer, Tom Radney, helped make the arrangements for his wife's funeral, and Maxwell buried her in the cemetery at the Peace and Goodwill Baptist Church, not far from their house in Nixburg. There was not much in the way of an estate to settle, because Mary Lou had died with no will and just a hundred dollars to her name, but he went to the probate court of Tallapoosa County to petition for the right to collect her last paycheck from Russell Mills. After that, he gathered up the sewing projects she had been working on and returned them, in their various stages of unfinishedness, to the customers who had dropped them off.

When all of that was done, Maxwell sat down and wrote a letter. "Dear Sir," it began, "I wish to advise you that (Mary L. Maxwell) were found kill [*sic*] in an automobile accident on August 3 / 1970." He included a policy number, signed the letter "Rev. W. M. Maxwell," and sent it off to the Old American Insurance Company. The policy in question had a fifteen-thousand-dollar death benefit, and the Rev. W. M. Maxwell was its sole beneficiary. He had purchased it for twenty-five cents shortly before his wife's death—shortly enough, in fact, that he never had to pay the twelve dollars required to renew it. The letter that the Reverend wrote to Old American to request payment was dated August 19, 1970, by which time, though he failed to mention it, his wife's death had been declared a homicide, and he had been indicted for her murder.

# 3

# Death Benefits

B EFORE LIEUTENANT HENRY FARLEY FIRED THE FIRST TEN-
inch mortar at Fort Sumter, there was not much of a life insurance industry in the United States. There was property insurance, of
course, for ships and warehouses, and, appallingly, for slaves, but even
the most entrepreneurial types in an entrepreneurial young nation
had not figured out a way to make money from insuring lives. To
know how much to charge people until they died, you had to know
how long they were likely to live, which was impossible because companies lacked actuarial data; to maintain consumer confidence, you
had to have enough money on hand to cover all death benefits, no
matter how early or unexpected someone's demise, which was difficult
because capital was hard to raise. The Civil War solved both of those
problems, changing not only the way Americans died but how they
prepared for death. By the time that Union soldiers had taken all the
souvenirs they could from the house at Appomattox where General
Lee surrendered, Americans were insuring their lives at record rates.

Although it took hold in the United States over the course of
four short years, the life insurance industry was, by then, thousands
of years old. Its earliest incarnation, however, looked less like companies selling policies than like clubs offering memberships. During
the Roman Empire, individuals banded together in burial societies,
which charged initiation and maintenance fees that they then used
to cover funeral expenses when members died. Similarly, religious
groups often took up collections for grieving parishioners to cover

the costs of burial and to provide aid to widows and orphans. It was centuries before these fraternal organizations came to operate like financial markets, and it took one city burning and another one crumbling for them to do so.

The city that burned was London. One Sunday morning in 1666, at the end of a long, dry summer, a bakery on Pudding Lane went up in flames. The houses around it caught fire one after another, like a row of matches in a book, and strong winds carried the blaze toward the Thames River, where it met warehouses filled with coal, gunpowder, oil, sugar, tallow, turpentine, and other combustibles. By Monday, flames and embers were falling from the sky; by Tuesday, the blaze had melted the lead roof of St. Paul's Cathedral and the iron locks of the city gates. On Wednesday, the winds shifted, and the breaks made by demolishing buildings at the edges of the disaster finally held. By then, though, the Great Fire of London had destroyed more than thirteen thousand structures and left one hundred thousand people homeless.

One of the men who made a fortune rebuilding the city after the blaze was a medical doctor turned developer with the appropriately fiery name of Nicholas If-Christ-Had-Not-Died-for-Thee-Thou-Hadst-Been-Damned Barebone. (The hortatory name had been given to him by his father, the millenarian preacher Praise God Barebone.) With his considerable profits, Dr. Barebone founded an "Insurance Office for Houses" that employed its own team of firefighters to protect the buildings on which it held insurance—five thousand of them, eventually. In an apt abridgment, the doctor became known around London as "Damned Barebone," not only because of the ruthlessness with which he ignored housing regulations and local opposition to his construction projects, but also because of the soullessness with which his firefighters responded exclusively to fires in homes where a small tin plaque indicated that the owners were clients. Barebone's "fire-marks" soon proliferated in first-floor windows around the city, and the practice of paying a little money now to insure against larger risks later became more popular. Within a decade, Barebone had come up with another innovation in the field, one that paved the way from fire insurance to life insurance: he created a joint-stock company to finance his policies. The first of its kind, it allowed investors to buy and own stock in an insurance company, the way they already could in mills, mineral mines, and spice trades.

Newly able to attract investors, insurance companies could finally raise capital. But the value of any given life was uncertain—far more so, even, than the fluctuating prices of saffron or gold. Say a banker in Dover bought a policy and then lived another four decades; by the time he died, he would have paid premiums for forty years, and his policy would have matured enough for the insurer to provide the full benefit to his widow and still make a profit. But say the same banker went straight from buying his policy to visiting the White Cliffs and promptly drowned in the English Channel. In that case, the banker's wife would get the full benefit at a fraction of the cost, while the insurer, far from making a profit, would take a substantial loss. The success of insurance companies depended on being able to guess which scenario was more likely, dying of old age or falling off a cliff—in the utter absence of any actual information about aging, falling, or all the other myriad ways that people die.

Part of the reason that information didn't exist was theological. Devout Christians were not meant to concern themselves with the details of their deaths. Like the timing of the Second Coming, as Christ proclaimed in the Gospel of Matthew: "Of that day and hour knoweth no man, no, not the angels of heaven." God, who kept watch even over the sparrow, would provide, and to doubt those provisions by making one's own end-of-life preparations was thought to reveal a lack of faith. Thus was the life insurance industry caught between a math problem and God.

To make matters worse, the overall reputation of the insurance industry had been tarnished by the sale of speculative policies, a practice barely distinguishable from betting. You could buy speculative policies with payouts contingent on everything from whether a given couple got divorced to when a particular person lost his virginity—or, in one infamous case, if a well-known cross-dressing French diplomat was biologically a man or a woman. Such policies could be purchased in secret, and the purchaser did not need to have any connection to the "insured." These seedy practices, along with the obvious incentive to murder someone whose life you had insurance on, had led France, Germany, and Spain to ban life insurance outright. England, meanwhile, created the insurable interest standard, which mandated that an insurance policy could be sold only to the person being insured or someone who had an "interest" in his life—that is, an interest in his remaining alive. But not even those advances cleaned up the industry. They only encouraged a new kind of speculation, in which elderly, indigent, or ill policyholders auctioned their insurance policies to investors who bid based on how long they thought the seller would live.

Of these various obstacles to establishing a life insurance industry—spiritual, mathematical, reputational—the mathematical one was solved first. Everyone knew that death, while uncertain, was also inevitable, yet before the seventeenth century no one had even tried tracking it, let alone measuring life spans in particular populations or for specific professions. The closest thing to an actuarial table at the time was a Bill of Mortality, a grim British innovation that listed plague victims in various parishes around the country. In 1629, a quarter century after he commissioned a new translation of the Bible, King James I instructed his clergy to start issuing those bills for all deaths, not just the ones caused by plague. Later, around the time of the Great Fire, John Graunt, a London haberdasher who dabbled in demography, organized those bills, arranging twenty years' worth of death into eighty-one causes and making it possible to see when people were most likely to die and what was most likely to kill them.

Armed with population information for the first time, insurance companies began to get a handle on probability calculations, and soon enough a natural disaster helped ease their difficulties with religion. On the feast of All Saints in 1755, just before ten in the morning, one of the deadliest earthquakes ever recorded struck the city of Lisbon. When the shaking finally stopped—fully six minutes later, some records say—tens of thousands of people had died as homes and churches collapsed, and fissures up to sixteen feet wide gaped open in the earth. Not long after, the waters along the coast of Portugal drew back in a sharp gasp, exposing the bottom of the harbor. Throngs of amazed onlookers had flocked to see old shipwrecks newly revealed on the seabed when, nearly an hour later, the ocean exhaled and a tsunami washed over the city, killing thousands more. The scale of the tragedy was so vast that existing theodicies seemed inadequate, and all of Europe struggled to answer the existential questions raised by the Lisbon catastrophe.

In the course of that struggle, theologians found themselves competing with Enlightenment philosophers, who seized on the earthquake to offer a rival account of the workings of the natural world. If earthquakes were not divine punishments but geological inevitabilities, then perhaps insuring oneself against death was not contrary to God's plan but a responsible and pious way to provide for one's family. By the end of the eighteenth century, that idea had gained legitimacy throughout Europe. Once it took hold, religious groups, initially opposed to the entire notion of life insurance, became some of its strongest advocates, in some cases even starting denominational funds to sell policies to their members.

That practice eventually spread to the United States, where even today millions of Americans buy their life insurance through religiously affiliated companies like Catholic Financial Life and Thrivent Financial for Lutherans. But such developments were a long time coming. Unlike Europe, which had decades' worth of mortality tables by the eighteenth century, colonial America had little reliable information on life expectancy, making it difficult for insurers to set prices and underwrite policies. When companies did try to offer life insurance, there were often too many beneficiaries attempting to make claims at once and rarely enough money to cover them.

In addition, although most states required insurable interest, the American life insurance industry remained exceptionally vulnerable to fraud. Some policyholders lied from the start, fibbing about their age or forging their medical history. Others lied as they went along, violating the terms of their policies by traveling to restricted places (the malarial South, for instance) or by restricted means (by railroad, without the appropriate rider). Still others lied at the end, faking their own deaths or disguising their suicides as accidents. But calling out such lies was tricky. Contesting any claim was expensive, and litigation rarely resulted in denial of coverage, since jury members were far more likely to want to see their own policies honored than care about the profit margins of insurance companies. Moreover, whenever a company preserved its profits by denying a fraudulent claim—say, a father who had failed to disclose an illness, or a husband who had purchased arsenic a few days before he died—it risked damaging its reputation in the eyes of a skeptical public, who worried that their own heirs might be cheated, too.

As companies attempted to grow, they exposed themselves to even more fraud through their own lapses in judgment. Some of their agents approved policies too freely in an effort to earn larger commissions, while some managers invested assets too dangerously in an effort to earn larger returns. Spreading into new territories meant recruiting new agents, not all of whom were scrupulous, and the more geographically diverse a company became, the less it knew about the background, life, and likely death of its would-be customers, making arbitrage of any kind difficult. The expansion of the postal service in the second half of the nineteenth century enabled mail-based sales but also mail-based fraud, on both ends: nonexistent companies could market nonexistent policies by mail, while unscrupulous clients could send away for policies they might never have qualified for in person.

Individual states tried to protect consumers by setting deposit requirements for companies and restricting their investments. But those same protections slowed sales, because they required more due diligence at every stage of the process, and decreased investment returns, because they left firms with less freedom to take the kinds of risks that could make their stocks rise. Unable to sell as many policies, companies had to pool risks across a smaller population, which left them struggling to remain profitable. Eventually, however, an industry shift from stock companies, which were owned by investors, to mutual companies, which were owned by policyholders themselves, allowed insurance companies to free themselves from the capital game; instead of attracting investors, they needed only to recruit customers. That became possible due to the carnage of the Civil War, which did for the United States what earthquakes and fires had done for Europe: spread a sense of both dread and obligation around the country, creating a massive demand for life insurance.

The total value of policies increased from $160 million in 1862 to an incredible $1.3 billion in 1870. Within fifty years there were almost as many life insurance policies as there were Americans.

THAT GROWTH IN SIZE PROMPTED A GROWTH IN FRAUD. BY THE time the Reverend Willie Maxwell began buying life insurance, the industry was wild the way the West had been: large, lawless, and lucrative for undertakers. Term policies were advertised in newspapers and magazines, flight policies were available for a few quarters from vending machines in airports, and local agents went door-to-door selling policies for premiums that could be paid on installments with pennies and dimes. With such low costs and so many ways to purchase life insurance without proper scrutiny, scams proliferated. Medical examinations were rarely undertaken at the start, and autopsies were not required at the end. All this left the industry open to every possible chicanery, from fudging the details of someone's health to forging their signature on a policy to faking a death—or, worse, committing murder. Although *Double Indemnity* (1944), *The Postman Always Rings Twice* (1946), and *The Killers* (1946) were not documentaries, they did reflect crimes that were common enough at the time: agents turned accomplice in the killing of policyholders, beneficiaries turned murderers, and insurance investigators turned detectives solving homicides alongside the authorities.

Newspapers around the country were filled with such stories. Insurance fraud was so widespread that another Willie Maxwell, born the same year as the Reverend but living in Florida, made headlines after a man he confessed to killing was found alive a few weeks later. It turned out that three people were working a grift whereby a skeleton was left along the coast so that this other Maxwell could confess to murder; then the "dead" man's cousin could collect on insurance policies, after which the ostensible victim could quietly be resurrected. Similarly, a funeral director right in Alexander City was convicted of first-degree murder in 1957, after an elderly man on whom he held insurance was found burned to death. Fred Hutchinson, who owned House of Hutchinson, one of the black funeral homes in town, became a suspect in the case when he hurriedly buried James Hunt's body the same day it was recovered. Later, one of the funeral home employees confessed to getting Hunt drunk before setting fire to his house, in exchange for some of the seven thousand dollars that Hutchinson stood to gain from the policies he had taken out on Hunt three weeks earlier.

As that suggests, it was stunningly easy to take out insurance on other people without their knowledge, and somewhere along the line the Reverend Willie Maxwell started making a habit of it. By 1970, he had policies on, among others, his wife, his mother, his brothers, his aunts, his nieces, his nephews, and the infant daughter he had only just legitimated. Although the names on the policies differed, the address was always the same, as was the beneficiary: the Reverend Willie Maxwell. One of the local insurance agents in Alex City was a regular visitor to Maxwell's house, but the Reverend also ordered policies by mail, completing the forms that arrived tucked into the pages of magazines and newspapers, then sending them away to Kansas, California, Florida, Nebraska, Pennsylvania, and cities all around Alabama, with checks made out for the initial payment—typically less than a dollar. The policies ranged in size from a few hundred dollars to tens of thousands and were held by, among others, Imperial Casualty & Indemnity Company, Bankers Life and Casualty Company, Old American Insurance Company, Fidelity Interstate Life Insurance Company, Allstate Life Insurance Company, Pennsylvania Life Insurance, Beneficial Standard, Booker T. Washington, Minnesota Mutual Life, United of Omaha, and Independent Life and Accident Insurance Company.

Many of these companies had policies on the Reverend's wife, and when he began contacting them after she died, he was met with more than the usual bureaucratic resistance. Mary Lou Maxwell's death had been declared a homicide, and insurance companies, like law enforcement, treat spouses as suspects—especially a husband who takes out sizable policies on his wife a few weeks before her murder. But if Maxwell was in a difficult position, the insurance companies soon found themselves in a worse one: not long after the Reverend was arrested for his wife's murder, the charges were dismissed for lack of evidence.

As was so often the case, Maxwell had perfect timing. He had been arrested on Monday, August 10, and five days later a grand jury returned an indictment of first-degree murder. As it happened, though, the district attorney who brought the charges had been battling alcoholism for years, was about to be charged for illegal spending of state funds, and had already been defeated in his reelection campaign earlier that year. All in all, it might have been the best time in history to come before the Fifth Judicial Circuit in Alabama, because DA Thomas F. Young had no incentive to do more than a perfunctory job. To make matters worse, the Maxwell case was particularly easy to dismiss, in both senses, because the judicial system at the time was not especially interested in domestic violence or black-on-black crime.

Some of the lawmen, though, remained interested, especially Herman Chapman, the Alabama Bureau of Investigation agent whose doggedness had earned him the nickname "Bear Tracker." Chapman, the son of a one-armed police chief from Clay County, already had twenty years of experience in law enforcement, first as a military policeman during World War II and then as a trooper with the Alabama Highway Patrol, and he didn't like to leave a case unsolved. While the court dithered, Chapman and another ABI agent, Byron Prescott, who would go on to lead the state's Department of Public Safety, kept investigating, gathering more material from the scene and more testimony from those who knew the Reverend. Based on the additional evidence they supplied, the crime lab at Auburn filed another report at the beginning of October.

When Charles Aaron took over as district attorney in January 1971, he tried right away to bring new charges against Maxwell, but the grand jury of Tallapoosa County failed to return an indictment. Although that was welcome news for Maxwell and Tom Radney, they had better things to do than celebrate. They knew that it was only a matter of time before *State of Alabama v. Willie J. Maxwell* would be back on the docket, and in the meantime they had a lot of death benefits to collect.

While the authorities continued to build their case, the Reverend and Radney set about filing civil suits against those companies that were refusing payment, hoping to force a reckoning before another grand jury could hear evidence against Maxwell. Grieving widowers, they both knew, made for better plaintiffs than indicted murderers. Radney filed complaints against Fidelity, Beneficial Standard, and Independent Life and Accident. The lawyer for Independent demurred in May, insisting that Mary Lou Maxwell's death had not been accidental and that therefore the accidental death provision of her insurance policy was not applicable. The lawyer for Fidelity filed a motion of continuance in July, claiming that the new district attorney had intimated to him that a grand jury would be impaneled during the first week of August to try once again to indict the Reverend for murder. In front of a circuit court judge, the Fidelity lawyer argued that the policy would soon be invalidated because its beneficiary was about to be convicted of murder. Unconvinced, the judge denied Fidelity's motion, and a jury then sided with the Reverend, awarding him the full accidental death benefit.

Fidelity might have lost in July, but its lawyer was proven partly right three weeks later: on August 6, 1971, almost a year to the day after his wife was found dead on the side of Highway 22, a grand jury indicted the Reverend Willie Maxwell on charges of first-degree murder. Tom Radney handled the arraignment and plea hearing, and one other matter as well: he agreed to represent one of Maxwell's "lady friends" who was also being charged in conjunction with the murder, a woman by the name of Ophelia Burns. She was alleged to have helped ambush the Reverend's wife at the church, or at least to have helped him move his or his wife's car that night. In the end, though both were indicted, only the Reverend Maxwell faced a jury, and his trial began just over a week later, in the sweltering heat of August in Alabama. Twelve jurors were selected from the hundred or so residents who had received summonses. The state subpoenaed twenty-two witnesses, and the defense subpoenaed seventeen. But the trial did not last a day.

If the prosecution had ever stood a chance, it vanished entirely when the Reverend's neighbor Dorcas Anderson took the stand. In her earlier testimony, Anderson had sworn to two things. The first was that on the night of the murder Mary Lou Maxwell had received a telephone call from the Reverend saying that he had been in an accident and had left home to pick him up. The second was that the Reverend had returned home alone very late that night without any damage to his car. But as Captain Chapman later lamented, Anderson "told an altogether different story in court."

Under oath at the trial, Dorcas Anderson claimed not to recall any of her out-of-court statements. Instead of testifying that she'd seen a frightened wife rush out of her home after a frantic telephone call from her husband, or describing the Reverend's absence that night and the pristine condition of his car when he finally returned, Anderson provided an alibi for her neighbor. To the bafflement and fury of those law enforcement agents who had taken her original testimony, Anderson now swore that the Reverend couldn't have been the one who met his wife on that dark highway because he had not been anywhere near the scene of her brutal murder. Armed with her revised—or, as the police said, perjured—testimony, and absent any physical evidence against him, Maxwell listened as one of his neighbors read aloud the jury's verdict of not guilty, and once again District Attorney Aaron watched as the Reverend walked away a free man.

AFTER THE ACQUITTAL, TOM RADNEY GOT BACK TO WORK ON the civil cases. The Reverend had agreed to pay him half of any judgment he recovered, so the lawyer went after every one of the companies that had insured the life of Mary Lou Maxwell. He secured payment on policy after policy, partly because of his talents as a lawyer but also because the facts, at least as far as the courts were concerned, were on his side. Lacking a conviction, the insurance companies got nowhere with insinuations that Maxwell had killed his wife, and their argument that murder was not a form of accidental death found even less favor with juries.

By October 1971, Radney was left with only three unpaid policies, all held by Independent Life and Accident, which was still refusing to pay, because the Reverend had purchased the policies only a few days before his wife had been murdered. Radney wanted to take

Independent to court, too, but his customary strategy had hit a snag. Facing an unusual limiting factor in the life of a lawyer, he wrote to a friend and fellow attorney to ask for help. That friend practiced in the state capital, and Radney wondered whether he might not sue the insurance company for him in Montgomery County, because, Radney confided, "I have just about worn out the Tallapoosa County juries with the Reverend Mr. Maxwell."

# | 4 |

# Seventh Son of a Seventh Son

A MAN ACCUSED OF KILLING HIS WIFE IS NOT LIKELY TO FIND another. The lofty reputation Willie Maxwell enjoyed around Lake Martin before Mary Lou's death collapsed after he was charged with her murder, and the well-spoken, uncommonly elegant man of God came to seem suspect and sordid. He was dismissed from all four of the churches where he had been pastoring, and when he was invited to preach again all the way over in Pike County at Holly Springs Baptist, people closer to home assumed that the parishioners there hadn't heard about what happened. It was just as possible, though, that a man who could persuade a jury of his innocence could also persuade a parish and that, absent a conviction, the congregation preferred to believe that a man of the cloth could not be a murderer. What was certain, though, was that the Reverend had persuaded at least one person of his innocence. In November of 1971, barely fifteen months after Mary Lou's body was found and only four months after he was acquitted of her murder, the Reverend Maxwell took another wife: his neighbor, and the state's would-be star witness, Dorcas Anderson.

Born Dorcas Duncan in Tallapoosa County in 1944, the second Mrs. Maxwell had known her new husband, or known of him, for quite a while. By the time she was a teenager, the Reverend's preaching was already renowned around Lake Martin, so she'd heard of him long before she and her first husband moved in next door to the Maxwells in Nixburg. Like the Reverend, Abram Anderson had been born and raised in Coosa County, served in the army, and then returned home to Alabama to take a job in a textile mill. The money he earned there was meant to support his wife and two young children, but his life, as well as theirs, was tragically derailed when he was diagnosed with amyotrophic lateral sclerosis, or ALS. Still in her early twenties, with two small boys at home, Dorcas became Abram's full-time caregiver.

That experience brought its own kind of grief, and after Mary Lou Maxwell was murdered, Dorcas and the Reverend began talking more and more. Although she was eighteen years his junior, they had a lot in common. She had two young sons; he had a little daughter, albeit not by Mary Lou. He had lost his wife, while she was watching ALS ravage her husband's body; the disease had already forced him into a wheelchair, and it would keep wasting his muscles until he died. The doctors thought Abram would live at least a few more years, but he went into the Veterans Administration hospital in Tuskegee on the last day of February 1971, not long after the grand jury convened to hear the charges against the Reverend, and died there three months later, at the age of thirty-five. Abram's death certificate listed the cause as pneumonia, but no autopsy was performed, and when the Reverend married Dorcas later that same year, people began to talk.

Some of it was the age difference (Dorcas was twenty-seven and the Reverend was forty-six), and some of it was the alacrity with which both widower and widow got over their grief (Maxwell had barely been widowed a year, Dorcas only a few months). Mostly, though, it was the convenient timing of Abram's death that made people suspicious. Some claimed that Maxwell had poisoned the man with antifreeze or embalming fluid, but most people had a different theory. It was after the death of Abram Anderson that the voodoo rumors started to spread.

THE WORD "VOODOO," LIKE THE PRACTICE, GOT TO THE SOUTH the long way, over land from port cities like Mobile and New Orleans and before that over sea from Togo and Benin, where, in the Fon language of the kingdom of Dahomey, it means "spirit" or "deity." It traveled to Europe chiefly in the newspaper dispatches and travelogues of early explorers—mangled variously as "veaudeau," "vaudoux," "vudu," "voudoo," "voudon," and "vodoun"—but it came to America via its practitioners: men and women from the African continent brought to the United States in chains, sometimes after a generation or two of slavery in the Caribbean. No one knows when exactly it arrived, because its early history in America was effectively erased by a dominant culture that forbade enslaved people from practicing their indigenous religions, subjected them to forced conversions, and punished them for any spiritual activity deemed aberrant.

As early as 1782, voodoo was so feared that Louisiana's governor, Bernardo de Gálvez, banned the purchase of slaves from Martinique, on the grounds that they "are too much given to voodooism and make the lives of the citizens unsafe." By then, voodoo was already well on its way to becoming a pejorative, and its beliefs and practices—also known as, although somewhat distinct from, hoodoo, obeah, conjure, folk doctoring, and root working—were being steadily delegitimized and criminalized. By the nineteenth century, voodoo had become a cultural bogeyman, shorthand for everything from orgies to human sacrifice; by the twentieth, it had become a cinematic grotesque, reduced to torture dolls and zombies. Many of its rites remained illegal long after emancipation, and the hostility of law enforcement officers to its believers and practices persists even today.

Most early anthropologists and historians shared the biases of the culture at large, leaving them uninterested in or even antagonistic to African spirituality in general and voodoo in particular. One of the first scholars to take it seriously was a graduate student at Columbia who had been born and raised in the South and longed to return there to document its folklore: the writer Zora Neale Hurston, best known for the novels she would publish years later, including *Their Eyes Were Watching God*. In the winter of 1927, Hurston boarded a train in New York City and headed for Mobile, where she began a tour of black towns and villages throughout the South.

Driving a Nash that she called Sassy Susie and carrying a chrome-plated pistol in her suitcase, Hurston followed what she called "the map of Dixie on my tongue" and recorded in the vernacular of her sources their best stories, recipes, sayings, songs, and customs. Hurston was frank about the obstacles to studying her chosen subject.

"Nobody knows for sure how many thousands in America are warmed by the fire of hoodoo," she wrote, "because the worship is bound in secrecy. It is not the accepted theology of the Nation and so believers conceal their faith. Brother from sister, husband from wife. Nobody can say where it begins or ends. Mouths don't empty themselves unless the ears are sympathetic and knowing."

One sign of the silences surrounding voodoo was the extremes to which even Hurston had to go before her subjects were willing to talk to her. Before he agreed to share any of his secrets with her, one practitioner required her to undergo a series of tests, including bringing a gift of three snake skins, draining the blood of one of her fingers into a cup with the blood of five other novitiates, and helping to slaughter a black sheep. Father George Simms, whose clients knew him as the Frizzly Rooster, sold Hurston his powders and potions but would tell her how to use them only after she underwent a candlelit initiation. As Hurston quickly learned, outsiders had viewed voodoo with fear and suspicion for so long that insiders now returned the favor.

The resulting secrecy deterred most scholars, but a few years after Zora Neale Hurston headed south, a white Episcopal priest named Harry Middleton Hyatt took a similar tour, gathering material for what would become his five-volume *Hoodoo—Conjuration—Witchcraft—Rootwork*. Hyatt spent years driving around Alabama, Arkansas, Florida, Georgia, Illinois, Louisiana, Maryland, Mississippi, North Carolina, South Carolina, Tennessee, and Virginia recording more than a thousand subjects on Edison and Telediphone cylinder cutters. When transcribed, those interviews ran to five thousand pages and covered everything from the spiritual talents of children born with cauls to the poisonous possibilities of graveyard dirt.

Between them, Hyatt and Hurston produced some of the earliest records of voodoo in America and documented three of the least appreciated aspects of the belief system. First, voodoo in this country was always syncretic, incorporating saints and feast days and enlisting pastors and priests of countless Christian denominations; a Baptist minister might overlay his Christian theology with voodoo practices, preaching the gospel in public worship but conjuring in private settings for a parishioner who lost his job or wanted to find a wife. Second, voodoo was in part a flourishing alternative medical system that served much of the South, including through drugstore clerks and pharmacists who sold essential ingredients like dragon's blood, goofer dust, eagle eyes, and John de Conqueror root, which were marketed as cures for everything from indigestion to infertility. The healing aspects of voodoo were essential for a population routinely unable to access health care because of their race, socioeconomic standing, or distance from doctors and hospitals; the incorporation of elements of other religions was, as with many syncretic faiths, a product of forced migration, social coercion, and cultural appropriation. Finally, voodoo had tremendous interracial appeal. Almost from the time that voodoo arrived with enslaved Africans, it had white clients, practitioners, and suppliers.

The role of voodoo in Alabama, in particular, was recorded by one of the state's most notorious chroniclers, Carl Carmer, a New Yorker who came to Tuscaloosa to teach at the University of Alabama but ended up writing a kind of Deep South tell-all-and-invent-some. Carmer's *Stars Fell on Alabama* offered an unconventional but romantic explanation for why Alabamians were drawn to voodoo and susceptible to other superstitions. According to him, the entire state had fallen under the spell of sorcery during an unusually heavy meteor shower that dazzled the southeastern United States in 1833, and some counties remained more prone to it than others—in particular an area he called "Conjure Country." "I got troubles," Carmer told a black woman who lived there, Ida Carter, "and the white folks up around Birmingham say you can help me." She did, apparently: for a dollar and a quarter, Carter told him how to ward off the woman who was causing him problems; for another dollar and a half, she taught him how to cure his back pain.

Among Carmer's more astute observations was that even those who claimed not to believe in voodoo at all were not immune to being scared of it or above resorting to it. Think of Mark Twain and the dozens of cures, tricks, and old wives' tales earnestly invoked by Tom Sawyer and Huck Finn. Like their literary equivalents, southerners were steeped in a culture that gave them something to do when the world was alarming or incomprehensible. In that, of course, they were not alone; like banshees in Ireland or fairy glens in Scotland or the ghosts and goblins of the Tohoku region of Japan, the influence of voodoo culture in the South pervaded its landscapes and enchanted its people, regardless of race, from cradle to grave.

WHETHER OR NOT THE REVEREND WILLIE MAXWELL WAS ACTU-ally a voodoo priest, he lived in a community willing to believe that he was. Plenty of good Christians in Coosa County shook out their pillows at night and scrubbed their steps in the morning to fend off spirits and spells, warned their children that the hoodoo man would get them if they stayed out too late, and told their spouses that they would lay a trick on them if they did not stop drinking or lying or lying about drinking. "Coincidence" just wasn't a word that rolled off tongues in Alabama as easily as "conjuring," so when Willie Maxwell was acquitted of murdering his first wife and remarried the young widow of his conveniently deceased neighbor, a lot of people were convinced that he had used voodoo to fix the jury, put death on his neighbor's trail, and charm a younger woman. Maybe Maxwell had burned a court-case candle or used law-stay-away oil; perhaps he had nailed a photograph of Abram Anderson to the north-facing side of a tree and added another nail every morning for nine mornings until the man weakened and died; as for Dorcas Anderson, well, he might have sprinkled wishing oil on a sample of her handwriting, worn it for nine days by his heart, and then buried it under his front steps.

However unlikely such theories might seem, they were more comforting than the alternative. For many of the Reverend's neighbors, it was better to believe that, in the face of conjuring, there was nothing that law enforcement and the judicial system could do than to believe that, in the face of terrible crimes, they had not done enough. Supernatural explanations flourish where law and order fails, which is why, as time passed and more people died, the stories about the Reverend grew stronger, stranger, and, if possible, more sinister.

The most widespread one began, like a fairy tale, with seven sisters and seven brothers. Willie Maxwell, people said, was the seventh son of a seventh son, a numerological curiosity that meant that he had been born with power over life and death. To augment this natural gift, he supposedly went down to New Orleans to study voodoo with the Seven Sisters, a fearsome septet well known throughout the South. "I went to New Orleans, Louisiana," one old blues song began, "just on account of something I heard. The Seven Sisters told me everything I wanted to know, and they wouldn't let me speak a word." After the sisters help the singer, someone recognizes his new powers and tells him, "Go, Devil, and destroy the world."

Although their history and even their existence are disputed, stories about the Sisters have circulated since the 1920s. They were said to be clairvoyant, ageless, and available to sell their blessings, curses, candles, and potions to anyone who came calling at their seven identical dwellings on Coliseum Street in the Garden District. Out-of-state license plates were always pulling up there, and people came and went at all hours of the day and night. Some of the visitors were just customers, but others were disciples—including, supposedly, one lean, elegant, well-dressed man from Coosa County.

Never mind that the Reverend Willie Maxwell actually had just four brothers, plus four numerologically inconvenient sisters: the rumors about him grew taller than loblolly pines. He hung white chickens upside down from the pecan trees outside his house to keep away unwanted spirits, and painted blood on his doorsteps to keep away the authorities. He carried envelopes filled with deadly powders. He had a whole room at home just for voodoo, lined with jars labeled "Love," "Hate," "Friendship," and "Death." If he got sick, he drank someone else's blood to feel better. Drive by his front door, and the headlights of your car would go dark. Say a cross word against him, and he would lay a trick on you. Look him in the eye, and he would curse you forever. He could move faster than was humanly possible, traveling the 150 miles from Birmingham to Atlanta in twenty minutes. When he needed to vanish quicker than that, he could turn into a black cat.

Like many rumors, these might have contained a grain of truth. Reporters whom Willie Maxwell later invited inside his house found no evidence of voodoo there, but then, given the lengths to which Zora Neale Hurston had to go to see voodoo in action, they likely wouldn't have found any whether he was a practitioner or not. As for the Seven Sisters, it is perfectly possible that Maxwell met them, in a manner of speaking, but extremely unlikely that he did so in Louisiana. Like Marie Laveau—the most famous voodooiene in America, who was said to have worked her dark magic near the Bayou St. John for so long that the Marquis de Lafayette kissed her when he came through New Orleans after the American Revolution and soldiers returning from World War I passed her in the streets—the Seven Sisters obeyed no chronological or geographic boundaries. People all over the South claimed to be one of them or to have been trained by all of them, and many individual women went by the name "Seven Sisters." One of these was the conjurer Carl Carmer interviewed, otherwise known as Ida Carter, who lived not far from the Reverend Maxwell near the Georgia line. If Maxwell studied voodoo with anyone, it probably was not with the septet and it probably was not all the way down in New Orleans.

Up in Nixburg, though, people were less inclined to fret about where the Reverend Maxwell had learned his magic than about how he used it. Virtually everyone was convinced that he had killed his wife, and most people thought he'd had a hand in the death of his neighbor, too—before, during, or after successfully wooing Abram Anderson's wife, a woman half the Reverend's age. The only reason she would have lied for him in court, they thought, was that she had quite literally succumbed to his charms. Because the authorities could not get a homicide conviction, the toxicologists could not detect any poisons, and no one was in a position to say why Dorcas fell in love, it was easy for people around Lake Martin to believe that the Reverend Maxwell had mastered the three chief domains of voodoo: justice, death, and love.

As another year of flowers faded on the grave of Mary Lou Maxwell and the grass began to cover the fresher one of Abram Anderson, the people of Coosa County kept wondering and worrying—not just about what Willie Maxwell had done, but about whether he was done doing it. Unlike those around him, though, the Reverend's mind was not on otherworldly matters but on worldly ones. With both of their spouses dead, the widower Maxwell and the widow Anderson said their vows on November 21, 1971. The day after that, the Reverend's insurance man came by.

# 5

# Just Plain Scared

PERHAPS IT WAS THE ACT OF A CONSCIENTIOUS HUSBAND, tending to all the logistics of forming a new family; perhaps it was a colder calculation. Whatever the motive, the facts were this: if anything happened to Mrs. Dorcas Anderson Maxwell, starting on November 22, 1971, Independent Life and Accident would owe the Reverend Maxwell one thousand dollars on Policy No. 71-0890563D, another thousand on Policy No. 71-0890563A, another thousand on Policy No. 71-0890563C, and two thousand dollars on Policy No. 71-0890563B. Within two months, Bankers Life and Casualty would be on the hook for another twenty thousand dollars in the event of Mrs. Maxwell's death, and the Old American Insurance Company for twenty-five thousand more.

It was a lot of insurance for what was, by all appearances, a modest life. After the marriage, the Reverend moved next door, into the house that the second Mrs. Maxwell had shared with her late husband. Despite their eighteen-year age difference, the newlyweds seemed mostly happy. He thought that she drove too fast, and she did not like how he refused to go to dances or parties; it was one thing to live next door to a preacher, she learned, and another to be married to him. But he helped look after her two boys and went through the legal process of adopting them. Together, the new Mr. and Mrs. Maxwell also created a survivorship estate so that if either died, the other would inherit their property. They filed the paperwork with the

Coosa County Probate Court, paying the registration fee to Judge Mac Thomas, Maxwell's old friend from his sharecropping days.

One week later, the Reverend found himself right back in the same courthouse in Rockford, for a very different reason: to bail out his older brother, John Columbus Maxwell, who had been arrested by the county sheriff for driving while intoxicated. J.C., as he was called, was fifty-two years old, worked in a pipe shop, and, according to his brother, was something of a lush, albeit a polite one. "He was a nice guy," the Reverend said. "He was even nice when he was drinking." The Reverend paid the three-hundred-dollar bond and agreed to make sure that his brother appeared in court on February 7, 1972.

He did not. The day before his court date, John Columbus was found dead on the side of the road near Nixburg. Someone who refused to identify himself had called the Alexander City Police Department to say that a pedestrian had been struck by a car where Highway 22 meets Highway 9. But when the authorities found a body at that crossroads, it did not seem to have been hit by an automobile. There were no visible injuries, but the body had been out in the cold all night, and it reeked strongly of alcohol. The county coroner, a man named Jimmy Bailey who was an electrician by training, could not tell the cause of death right away, but knowing that J. C. Maxwell was related to W. M. Maxwell and knowing the rumors about the Reverend, Bailey sent a sample of his blood to the Department of Toxicology and Criminal Investigation.

An analyst with the crime crew found that the deceased's blood contained .41 percent ethyl alcohol, in the life-threatening range—high enough that it could cause even a 165-pound habitual drinker to experience loss of consciousness, alcohol poisoning, and death. The police did not notify John Columbus's wife and children of this finding, because John Columbus did not have a wife or children. But he did have life insurance, and the beneficiary on the policies was the Reverend Willie Maxwell.

According to his death certificate, John Columbus died of a heart attack, caused by the overconsumption of alcohol; according to nearly the whole of Nixburg, John Columbus died of being a Maxwell.

Whatever his previous drinking habits had been, no one believed that he had gotten all of that alcohol into his bloodstream by himself. Some thought it had been forced down his throat; others thought it was a cover for some sort of toxin in his blood. Maxwell, who had now lost one wife, one inconvenient neighbor, and one brother in less than two years, demurred. "They said someone had to have held a gun to his head to make him drink that much whiskey," the Reverend said dismissively, "but I knew my brother, and he did it to himself."

The residents of Nixburg, skeptical as they were, were not nearly as skeptical as the insurance companies that still counted the Reverend Willie Maxwell among their clients. In two years, Maxwell had collected almost a hundred thousand dollars in life insurance, well over half a million dollars in today's money, and the companies who had paid him were starting to lose patience with the speed at which he was cashing in his policies. Some of them asked the law firms that had represented them in the matter of the first Mrs. Maxwell to take another look at the Reverend, and soon insurance lawyers all over the country were reviewing handwriting samples, comparing application addresses, sending investigators to interview witnesses, and requesting information from the crime lab at Auburn.

One of the first companies to sever its ties with the Reverend was Central Security Life Insurance Company, headquartered in Texas. In addition to refusing to issue Maxwell any more policies, the company's lawyers required him to sign a release indicating that in exchange for $2,812.55, the present value, they were canceling the ten active policies he had with their company. He also had to sign a witnessed agreement that "neither he nor any members of his family including but not limited to Jimmy Maxwell, James Hicks, Dorcas Maxwell, Herman Maxwell, Flora Hicks, Henry Maxwell, Adrian Anderson, Abram Anderson, Ada Maxwell, Mae Ella Maxwell, and Samantha Maxwell will apply for or in any way become an insured or a beneficiary."

Around the same time, Pioneer, an insurance company out of Illinois, refused to issue a policy on the Reverend's mother, after learning that the physician listed on the application form had no record of an Ada Maxwell. Pioneer got no reply when it sent a request for a current health assessment to the correspondence address listed on the policy: Box 273A on Route 1 of Alexander City, the same one that appeared on every policy for which the Reverend Maxwell was the beneficiary.

WHETHER DORCAS MAXWELL EVER CHECKED THE MAIL AT THAT address or read any of the many life insurance notices that arrived there is not clear. By the time the insurance companies were taking a closer look at her husband, she was busy with other things; six months after marrying Maxwell, Dorcas gave birth to a third son. That was in May 1972, the same month that Alabama governor George Wallace was shot and paralyzed from the waist down by a would-be assassin. That summer, a reporter for the Associated Press broke the news that for the past forty years the federal government had knowingly deceived hundreds of impoverished black sharecroppers participating in the Tuskegee Syphilis Study, taking notes and withholding treatment as many of them sickened and died. The Vietnam War was winding down and Watergate was heating up. In the middle of September, *The Waltons* began its ten-year television run, and one week later Muhammad Ali hit Floyd Patterson so hard he cut open his eye and ended his career.

On that same night, September 20, 1972, almost eight months after Maxwell's brother died, three men, Jerry Fuller, Ronnie Watts, and Stanley Ingram, went for a drive down Highway 9 in Nixburg. Sometime between ten and eleven, they came upon a car idling by the side of the road, its headlights cutting two long tunnels in the fog. When they got out of their truck to look, they saw a woman wedged awkwardly on the floor of the front seat, motionless. They turned around, raced back up the road to Dunlap's Grocery, and called the police from the telephone there. Around twenty minutes after eleven, the emergency dispatcher in Alexander City called State Trooper L. A. Wright, who lived nearby in Goodwater. Wright got dressed, jumped in his car, and found the wreck fifteen minutes later. The car had come to a stop some thirty feet from the road and perpendicular to it, near a stand of saplings. Its right front corner was lightly crumpled and the lower half of the windshield was cracked, but the extent of the damage suggested nothing worse than a fender bender. Inside, laid out across the floor of the front seat, facedown—her head on the passenger side, her feet on the driver's side—was Dorcas Anderson Maxwell.

As the Reverend would later tell it, what had happened that night was this: After his wife had made supper for her family and gotten her three children to bed, she left Nixburg to see her mother in Alexander City. Her mother had gone fishing earlier, and Dorcas wanted to swing by to pick up some of the catch. "I'm going to get some fish," the Reverend recalled his wife saying as she left home. She would be right back, she said; her mother lived only eleven miles away. Dorcas left around nine o'clock in the evening, while Maxwell stayed with their seven-year-old, six-year-old, and four-month-old sons.

When an hour passed and his wife had not returned, the Reverend called his mother-in-law, who said she had not seen her daughter all day or heard from her since that morning. Wrapping up the baby and waking up the two older boys, he set out, he said, to look for Dorcas. Instead of retracing the route she would have taken, though, he drove in the opposite direction to talk with some neighbors, Clifford and Anita Coggins. The couple did not have a telephone, and Maxwell wanted to ask if his wife had gone over to their place instead of going to see her mother. His wife was not there, but the Reverend stayed and talked with Mr. and Mrs. Coggins for a while, and then got back in the car and headed back the way he came.

By then, Fuller, Watts, and Ingram had already found the car, only a quarter of a mile from the Reverend's home, and Trooper Wright had already found Dorcas Maxwell inside. Unlike the first Mrs. Maxwell, she had very little in the way of visible injuries, but her dead body had already begun to stiffen. Wright radioed back to dispatch and asked his supervisor, Sergeant William Gray, to come to the scene. As soon as Gray got there and saw what had happened and to whom, he turned right around and went back to Dunlap's Grocery to call for just about all the backup he could think of: the sheriff at Rockford, the investigators from Opelika, and the medical examiner and toxicologist at Auburn.

By the time the last law enforcement officer approached the scene, he could see it from a mile away: the lights from all the cruisers made a dome of blue in the dense September fog. Everyone there knew exactly whose wife had been found and that his first wife had been murdered and left in a car at an almost identical scene. Maxwell had been acquitted in that first homicide, and this time the authorities were determined to get a conviction. An officer from the Alexander City Police Department photographed the exterior and the interior of the car, the body inside it, the stretch of highway behind it, and the shoulder around it.

Before dawn that September day, two things had happened: Dorcas Anderson Maxwell's body had been moved to Armour Funeral Home in Alexander City for an autopsy, and the Reverend had called his lawyer, Tom Radney. The autopsy was more notable for what the coroner did not find than for what he did. There were leaves stuck in Dorcas's brown leather sandals, and she had a few small abrasions on her shoulders and elbows, plus a larger cut above her right eye. But tests of her organs, tissues, and fluids revealed nothing. Her blood contained no alcohol, no glycols, no carbon monoxide, no cyanide, no metallic poisons, no acidic poisons, no salicylates, no phenols, and no barbiturates. Her liver contained no strychnine, no narcotics, and no amphetamines. Her stomach contained no drugs and no known poisons. She did have a fractured hyoid, the bone that supports the tongue, which is sometimes a sign of strangulation, but because that bone can also be damaged during autopsies, the authorities rejected it as a cause of death. In the end, the crime doctor, Dr. Rehling, could do nothing but declare that Dorcas Maxwell had died from natural causes. Despite no previous history of asthma, bronchitis, or pneumonia, and even though she had suffered no illnesses whatsoever for the entire year before her death aside from a minor cold, he concluded that the twenty-nine-year-old had succumbed to acute respiratory distress.

There were no witnesses to the death of Dorcas Maxwell, but if no one could say exactly what happened, no one could stop talking about it either. In just two years, the Reverend had lost his first wife, his neighbor, his older brother, and now his new wife, too. The first marriage had lasted two decades, but the second hadn't even lasted a year. Between the increasing pace of the deaths and the loss of a second Mrs. Maxwell under similar circumstances to the first, the Reverend's already bad reputation grew starkly worse. "People really began to fear him," a friend of Dorcas's said of the Reverend Maxwell after his second wife's death. "White and black were afraid of him."

Maxwell still peppered his speech with scripture and preached over in Pike County, but closer to home most people saw him as a man less sinned against than sinning. Rumors about him grew even more insidious, and not all of them were about voodoo. "They just didn't know who all he had insurance on," said a Coosa County resident. "They didn't know who might be next." The wife of one of the funeral home directors in Alexander City put it plainly: "Most people were just plain scared to death of that man." While the Reverend had previously been thought handsome, now women called him "rough-looking" and whispered a warning to one another: "Don't let Will look in your eyes."

All around Lake Martin, neighbors played games of terrified telephone, repeating what someone had heard the Reverend say, relaying what some other someone had seen him do. It did not help to lock your doors at night, because he knew spells for opening them, and failing that, he had ways of harming you through walls. An unsolved crime often spreads hysteria, but the people of Nixburg did not think the crimes that plagued their community were unsolved. They knew who had committed them; they just did not know how, or how to stop him. They did know, though, that the only thing scarier than an unknown murderer is a known one.

IF THE COMMUNITY WAS FRIGHTENED AND THE POLICE WERE frustrated, the insurance companies were furious. Here again was the preacher from Coosa County, come to collect tens of thousands of dollars in life insurance on a family member. Two companies, Southern Farm Bureau and Booker T. Washington Insurance, had no choice but to pay up without protest, because their three policies—for ten thousand, one thousand, and five hundred dollars—had been taken out by Dorcas and her first husband, Abram. Maxwell was simply the current beneficiary. The Andersons had also taken out mortgage insurance, which covered the thirteen thousand dollars still owed on their house, which now passed to the Reverend through the survivorship estate.

The other companies, however, were not going to make good on their policies without a fight. It is impossible to know exactly how many of those policies Maxwell held on Dorcas at the time of her death—or, for that matter, how many in total he ever held on anyone—because those that were not litigated left no trace. But of the policies that eventually became the subject of court battles, four had become effective the day after Maxwell married Dorcas in November 1971, a fifth had kicked in two days after that, a sixth in January 1972, a seventh that March, and the remainder by late spring of that year. All told, the Reverend had at least seventeen separate insurance policies on Dorcas, for which he had paid ten dollars a week in premiums. Now he was owed a small fortune in return.

Imperial responded by hiring the Birmingham law firm of Lange, Simpson, Robinson & Somerville. Bankers Life hired a firm out of Opelika, as did Beneficial Standard and Old American. Independent went with a firm in Tuskegee. Allstate found one in Montgomery. Pretty soon, Tom Radney was fighting what must have felt like every law firm in the state, and if he had worried about running out of juries after the death of Mary Lou Maxwell, he was draining the pool dry now. A year after Dorcas's death, it seemed there was hardly a man or woman of voting age in the tri-county area who had not heard the Reverend plead his case against one insurance company or another. Radney brought multiple suits in the circuit courts of Tallapoosa, Clay, and Macon Counties, and in the district court for the Middle District of Alabama, and he followed one lawsuit all the way through the appellate process to the Alabama Court of Civil Appeals.

These cases turned on a series of complicated technicalities around cause of death—namely whether the second Mrs. Maxwell had died from the car accident alone, from a preexisting condition alone, or from a preexisting condition aggravated by the car accident. As soon as the Reverend had called him on the night that Dorcas died, Radney knew that he would be handling another spate of criminal cases or civil suits or both, and he had immediately taken an unusual precaution: by the following morning, he had paid a thousand dollars for a private coroner to follow up the state's autopsy with one conducted on behalf of his client.

The two coroners wound up agreeing on the basics—that Dorcas had died of acute respiratory failure—but quibbled on the finer details, in ways that mattered once litigation began. In depositions and examinations that went on for hours, the dueling coroners were grilled on the minutiae of bronchial walls, interstitial pneumonitis, and mucus plugs. The insurance companies seized on some of these findings to argue that Dorcas would not have died without her underlying respiratory problems, which had not been disclosed at the time the insurance was purchased, and therefore invalidated the policies. Radney seized on other findings to argue that if it had not been for the accident, the underlying respiratory condition would never have killed Dorcas; thus her death was accidental, and the policy was valid.

To everyone involved, it must have felt like they were fighting over the relative size of the lice that lived on the elephant in the room. None of the witnesses were allowed to mention it and the lawyers were forbidden from litigating it, but countless people from the county coroner on down felt certain that Dorcas Anderson had been murdered. Perhaps the hyoid bone had been a clue after all, and she had been strangled, like the first Mrs. Maxwell, or perhaps she had been poisoned, by the same undetectable method that many thought the Reverend had used on Abram Anderson and John Columbus Maxwell. Decades later, one of the coroners involved could still rattle off poisons for which they had no tests back then—some of them easily obtained, like life insurance, through the mail. But none of those suspicions could be entered into evidence.

In the end, the only life insurance company to persist was Independent. Although the four policies it held were among the smallest the Reverend had taken out on Dorcas, the company's lawyer, Harry Raymon, would not stop fighting payment. Tom Radney responded by bringing in help, in the form of a colleague in Tuskegee by the name of Fred Gray. Gray was not an insurance specialist; he was one of the most prominent civil rights attorneys in the nation. He had gotten his law degree from Case Western Reserve University, in

Ohio, before any Alabama law school would admit African American students, then returned home to use it in the fight for racial justice. Gray represented Rosa Parks after she refused to surrender her seat on a segregated bus, and then represented the Montgomery Improvement Association during the resulting boycott. He won an acquittal from an all-white jury for Martin Luther King Jr. after he was charged with tax evasion, took on Governor Wallace when he tried to block the march from Selma to Montgomery, and got a ten-million-dollar settlement from the federal government on behalf of the surviving victims of the Tuskegee experiment. In addition to his legal practice, Fred Gray served in the Alabama House of Representatives, one of the first black legislators since Reconstruction.

It was through his legislative work that Gray had come to know Tom Radney, but taking on the Maxwell case was more than doing a favor for a friend; it was an opportunity to mount a legal challenge to another form of discrimination. Racial bias was ubiquitous in the insurance industry. African American policyholders were routinely required to pay more money for less valuable coverage, refused consolidation offers for discounts on multiple policies, forced to pay premiums exceeding the value of the payout, and denied benefits based on capricious claims of lapsed coverage. Some companies maintained dual rates for white and black clients, based on separate mortality tables that were used to justify charging nonwhites more than whites for the same policies; others maintained dual plans, using one mortality table but offering two levels of insurance, and paying agents the full commission only when minority clients bought substandard policies. Some companies simply refused to insure black lives at all.

Black families were also disproportionately targeted for the predatory policies known as burial insurance. These small policies, enough to cover funeral expenses, were first marketed to factory workers in the United Kingdom, where they were known as industrial insurance; they became popular in the United States after 1875 and appealed to those who could not afford quarterly or annual life insurance payments but could scrape together a few pennies or nickels once a week to spare their families the financial burden of burial when they died. Such policies were sold in droves to emancipated slaves, and later to their children and grandchildren and great-grandchildren, by insurance agents who went door-to-door every week to collect the tiny but cumulatively lucrative premiums. One of those agents was the father of the novelist Philip Roth, who passed "the eerie evenings collecting pennies from the poorest of Newark's poor," as the younger Roth put it in his memoir *Patrimony*. Roth's father recalled how some black families were "still paying premiums twenty, thirty years after the death of the insured." When his son asked why they kept paying, the older Roth said, "They never said anything to the agent. Somebody died and they never mentioned it. The insurance man came round and they paid him."

That kind of predation and fraud was common. Insurance companies around the country profited off African American customers through exploitative sales, underwriting, and administrative techniques, and such practices were particularly prevalent in the South. Civil rights lawyers like Fred Gray knew that the discriminatory actions of insurance companies not only depleted blacks of their current wealth but deprived future generations of the financial benefits burial insurance and life insurance provided for whites: a safety net, a leg up, an inheritance. Decades later, class-action lawsuits by living clients and surviving beneficiaries would reveal the appalling extent of the abuse: half a billion dollars in restitution and legal fines were wrenched from almost one hundred companies in the redress of more than fourteen million biased policies.

At the time that Independent Life and Accident was taking its stand against the Reverend, however, all of that was still in the future. The company, indifferent to racial injustice in the industry, tried to make the case that Dorcas Anderson Maxwell's death had not been natural—and, failing that, had certainly not been caused by a car accident—and therefore should not be covered. Radney and Gray, meanwhile, knew that their legal case depended on proving that her death was covered by an accidental death policy, but also that their appeal to the jurors would be aided by making a broader argument about discrimination and predation in the insurance industry. "That insurance man came and knocked on the door every time and got the money and took the money home and sent it to the insurance company," Gray said in his closing statement, "and then when the time came to pay off, they said, 'Oh, no, we're not going to pay it.' That's what these big companies do. They want your money, but any time they can weasel out of it, they weasel out of paying."

Never mind that their client was possibly the least likely poster boy for civil rights in the entire African American population of Alabama. Never mind that unlike the policyholders described by Philip Roth's father, there was zero chance that Maxwell would ever pay a dime of a dead person's premiums, or fail to collect on a policy. The strategy used by Tom Radney and Fred Gray worked—not only in Macon County, where a jury awarded the Reverend Maxwell his full five-thousand-dollar payout on April 26, 1973, but again in Montgomery, where the Alabama Court of Civil Appeals upheld that decision over a year later.

That was the last of the half a dozen lawsuits over insurance payouts on policies in the name of Dorcas Anderson Maxwell. Of the $131,000 in insurance that the Reverend was known to have held on his second wife at the time of her death, Tom Radney managed to recover nearly $80,000 of it. For the Reverend Willie Maxwell, becoming a widower was proving to be a lucrative business.

# 6

# No Exception to the Rule

WATER, LIKE VIOLENCE, IS DIFFICULT TO CONTAIN. NO sooner had the Alabama Power Company dammed the Tallapoosa than the river began seeking its revenge, in a series of floods that brimmed Lake Martin over its boundaries and droughts that drained it dry. Sometimes the towns submerged beneath it seemed to be avenging themselves, too; late at night, boaters on the lake and people along its shoreline claimed to hear the tolling of the church bells long since drowned.

Other, more deeply buried histories haunt the waters, too. On March 27, 1814, the warriors of the Creek nation, having lost most of their land by force and the rest by treaty, took their last stand just north of Lake Martin, at a spot where the Tallapoosa River doubles back on itself in a sharp oxbow known as Horseshoe Bend. It was there that future president Andrew Jackson and his troops slaughtered 557 Creeks, leaving hundreds more to die while trying to escape across the river, and taking the survivors prisoner; later, he forced those survivors across the Mississippi on the Trail of Tears. Sunk beneath Lake Martin are Creek burial grounds, and on the pocket of land inside Horseshoe Bend, where the weeds grow wild and the river and its bloody history are always just behind you, the sound of a turtle slipping off a rock into the water can make a grown man jump.

Ghost bells, war cries, the clanging of slave chains: if ever a land came by its haunting honestly, it is eastern Alabama. In the long empty miles between towns there, the highways rise and fall over hills that keep most things out of view and make every sight a sudden one. Where the pavement ends, the roads turn to dirt as red as rust or blood. Pines and oak trees line them, tattered moss hanging from their branches like wraiths. At night, the fog is so thick that anything can disappear into it or come walking out of it.

The Reverend Maxwell claimed that he was afraid of what was out there, too. All his life, he insisted that he was innocent—of his first wife's murder, of his neighbor's death, of his brother's death, of his second wife's death, of any crime whatsoever, of the practice of voodoo. All claims to the contrary, he said, amounted to vicious gossip spread at the expense of a righteous man widowed twice in only two years. The fact that he had insurance on all those who died did not suggest a motive; it showed only that he was a scrupulous spouse and sibling. While everyone in town whispered about him and hid their eyes when he passed, he maintained that the real wickedness in their midst—his enemy, whoever that was—was going unchallenged. When a reporter from *The Montgomery Advertiser* asked him about the strange way that death seemed to stalk his relatives, the Reverend said, "I have prayed and thought about it a lot and several thoughts have crossed my mind."

His first wife, he claimed, had been murdered in his stead, though he did not know by whom: "I think they were waiting for me and when they saw the car, they thought it was me but when they stopped her, they found it wasn't me and they decided to take her instead." Why he thought that shadowy "they" might want to kill him, he did not bother to explain. As for the other deaths, he felt he was being tested by some terrible force, perhaps human, perhaps not: "some enemy or another sticking around to hinder me, slipping around somewhere I haven't seen him, but I'm asking the Lord to see and he will see." The Reverend did not yet know who or what was tormenting him by taking the lives of those he loved, but he said, "If I stick close to the Lord, I'll see."

Yet the Reverend could no longer stay as close to the Lord as he once had, because none of his churches wanted him preaching anymore. Against his will, he swapped the pulpit for the pew and began worshipping at Peace and Goodwill Baptist Church, in Cottage Grove, not far from where he lived in Nixburg, and where he had buried his two wives. The other parishioners might have disapproved, but Maxwell kept his head high, kept wearing his fancy suits, kept speaking in his strangely formal fashion, and not that much time passed before he found himself back at the altar again, although in a different way. Three years after the death of the first Mrs. Maxwell and two years after the death of the second Mrs. Maxwell, the Reverend took another wife.

NO ONE EVER WONDERED WHY MARY LOU WOULD HAVE WANTED to wed Willie Maxwell, that handsome, hardworking young man newly home from serving his country. Plenty of people wondered why Dorcas Anderson would have agreed to marry him, though given the timing of her first husband's death, some of them had their theories. But what kind of woman would agree to become the third Mrs. Willie Maxwell?

The answer, as it turned out, was obvious. Depending on your perspective, the woman who married Maxwell in November 1974 had either less reason to fear him than anyone else or considerably more, but in either case she certainly knew what she was getting into. The third Mrs. Maxwell was Ophelia Burns: the woman who had been indicted but never tried for the murder of the first Mrs. Maxwell.

"He could not help it that people liked to spread rumors about him," Ophelia Maxwell said of her new husband. Somewhat oddly, though, she herself was mostly spared such rumors. Even though there was talk of the Reverend's having an accomplice who had ferried him like Charon to and from the scenes where his relatives had been found dead, and even though countless law enforcement officers, witnesses, and grand jury members had known at one point about the indictment brought against Ophelia in the death of Mary Lou, by 1974 her alleged involvement had somehow faded from the town's collective memory, overshadowed by the menace of the Reverend. If she herself knew anything about Maxwell's other crimes, she never said a word; like the Reverend, she always maintained his innocence. "Just because he was accused of one thing," Ophelia said, "I don't think it's right to think he's involved in everything."

Between them, Willie and Ophelia had a large, complicated family. She, too, had been married before, but divorced her husband after getting caught running around with the Reverend. They had some children from their earlier marriages and others that were adopted by varying degrees of formality. The Reverend was raising his youngest son, the one he'd had with Dorcas, but the two older boys he'd adopted after marrying her were being raised by their grandparents over in Dadeville, and the daughter he'd legitimated was living with her mother in Alexander City. Ophelia had older children who no longer lived with her, but she was raising a child named Shirley Ann Ellington, whom she had taken in from a relative during her first marriage but never officially adopted.

Heading up a large household but unable to preach, the Reverend threw himself into pulpwooding. He bought some more land along Highway 9 and leased some of his mother's property to one of the timber companies, a profit-sharing outfit called Bama Wood. One of its managers, Frank Colquitt, later described the Reverend as among the best workers he'd ever had—good enough that he was worth the time it took to quash the fears of nervous customers who would have preferred having almost any other pulpwooder on their property. Colquitt soon learned that the best bet was to take the bull by the horns: he would bring the Reverend by a client's home, introduce him, and then "tell 'em a short version of what he'd been accused of—that he was a preacher, voodoo, and all of that—and they'd say, all of them would say, 'He seems like a nice fellow to me.'" That strategy would not have worked as well among African Americans, but not many African Americans in Coosa County owned enough acreage to lease their land to a timber company; the whites who did, Colquitt said, mostly found Maxwell to be a polite object of curiosity, a macabre sort of entertainment, and something to brag about to their friends. If asked how he himself could feel safe around his employee, Colquitt had a joke at the ready: "I always said I wasn't worried because *I* had insurance on *him*."

Plenty of others remained scared of Maxwell, though, including members of his pulpwooding crew, who quit out of nervousness with some frequency. One of these was a nephew of the Reverend's, a young man by the name of James Hicks, whose mother was Mae Ella Maxwell, Willie's older sister by two years. Hicks was twenty-two years old, five feet eight inches tall, and barely more than 120 pounds, with the slender frame and wispy facial hair of a boy only barely a man. But he was grown enough to get married, and after he stopped working for his uncle, he got a job at one of the mills in Alexander City, then moved with his wife to Hissop, a town not far from Maxwell's place in Nixburg. On February 14, 1976, Hicks went missing. Two days later, in the small hours of the morning, a woman phoned Otis Armour, one of the funeral directors in Alexander City, and told him to send a car to Highway 9. She refused to give her name, but when she called back a second time, Armour set off to see what was going on. By then, though, James Hicks had already been found dead in a car, ten miles south of Goodwater, on the shoulder of Route 9—the same highway where the second Mrs. Maxwell had been found and where the Reverend was still living, now with his new wife, Ophelia.

The lawmen who showed up on the scene must have felt a strange and terrible déjà vu. The 1968 Pontiac Firebird in which Hicks was found looked as if it had been parked, not wrecked. A patch of pines by the car was undisturbed. Inside the vehicle, Hicks's body was lifeless but showed no signs of injury. Jimmy Bailey, still the county coroner and by this time extremely frustrated by all the deaths accumulating around the Reverend Maxwell, immediately contacted District Attorney Harold Walden, who ordered an investigation.

That Monday, back at the Armour Funeral Home, one of the state medical examiners came from the crime lab to autopsy the body. It was the middle of February, so in addition to his red short-sleeve shirt, James Hicks had on a denim jacket and jeans. He was still wearing his class ring from Coosa County High School. He had a few small cuts on his legs and arms, across his chest, and on the inside of his lower lip. He had some caffeine and a little alcohol in his system, but no drugs of any other kind. As the medical examiner ultimately indicated on the autopsy report, there was nothing "which would adequately account for the death of this subject."

As startling as that finding or lack of finding was, it would not have surprised Willie Maxwell. "There will be no evidence," the Reverend assured Tom Radney when he went into his lawyer's office to discuss the death of yet another one of his relatives. Like so much of Maxwell's speech, that locution was a strange one: far from being a protestation of innocence, it all but suggested direct knowledge of the crime.

However peculiar that turn of phrase might've been, it was correct. To the extent that anything ever turned up that could have been considered evidence in the death of James Hicks, it was found not on his body or at the scene but later, among his effects. When the Alabama Bureau of Investigation went through Hicks's belongings, they discovered an insurance policy that had been written in the Reverend's own handwriting. It was circumstantial, and it brought the state no closer to a conviction or even an arrest, but it did capture the attention of two ABI agents. James Abbett was new to the office but familiar with the failures of the earlier Maxwell investigations. He and his partner, Herman Chapman—"The Bear Tracker"—were eager to make sure that this one ended differently.

When Abbett interviewed James Hicks's widow, she told the investigator right away that she was sure the Reverend Maxwell had killed her husband. A week or so before he went missing, Mary Dean Riley Hicks said, she and James were in the car together, sometime after nine at night, when the Reverend Maxwell drove up behind them and got them to pull over. Her husband told her to wait in the car while he went to see about his uncle.

When Hicks came back to the car, he was vague about what his uncle had wanted, but Mrs. Hicks learned afterward that Ophelia Maxwell had been calling around to various relatives trying to get James's Social Security number. "They must have wanted it to put on his insurance policy," Mrs. Hicks told Abbett. " 'Cause so many people have been killed." And not just any people: "Will Maxwell always have insurance on them." She said that her father had even heard a woman bragging about having thirty-eight thousand dollars' worth of insurance on James.

Mary Hicks's certainty made Abbett want to keep investigating. Pretty sure he already knew the motive, he went looking for the means. It took him two months, but finally he turned up something damning. On April 14, Abbett interviewed a local man named Aaron Burton, who swore under oath that the Reverend had run into him at Smith's Grocery two weeks before James Hicks was found dead and called him over to his brown Continental—where, Burton said, he "asked me how dirty I was." When Burton replied that he was as dirty as Maxwell needed him to be, the two arranged to meet a few hours later. Only then did Maxwell make Burton agree to take to his grave what they were about to discuss.

What the Reverend wanted to know was if Aaron Burton would help him murder two of his nephews. "The reason for killing them," Burton said, "was that the two owed him a lot of money." The Reverend was serious enough about his plan to negotiate with Burton for a fee, and they settled on four thousand dollars each for the murder of James Hicks and his brother Jimmy Maxwell.

They talked for almost an hour and then met again later that week, when the Reverend drove Burton down Highway 9 to show him the spot where he thought the murders should take place. The Reverend parked his Continental on a hill near Elam Church and suggested to Burton that once Hicks arrived there, they could overpower him. "Will told me that all I had to do was hide in the woods, and when James Hicks came up that he would be talking and for me to come up behind him and touch James in the back and that he would do the rest. Will told me that he had two pair of gloves for us to wear to keep the fingerprints off."

It was when Maxwell pulled a pair of white and blue work gloves out from under the seat of the Continental that Burton lost his nerve and told the Reverend that he'd changed his mind and didn't want to be involved. That didn't stop Maxwell from showing Burton another ridge on Highway 9, on the drive home from the church, where he thought they could nudge his nephew's car off the road to make the murder look like an automobile accident. "He told me that he would use his car to push James's car off into the hole. I told Will the rubber bumpers on his Continental was too low, and Will said he would get his Ford Torino."

When Burton again refused to take any part in the murders, Maxwell offered him some money to keep quiet. Burton told him no money was necessary, but after James Hicks's body was found the next week, the Reverend went to visit Burton's father and brother to warn them both that Aaron better keep his mouth shut. Burton also told Agent Abbett that the ridge on Highway 9 where the Reverend had stopped was near the home of a family named Edwards and suggested that the ABI talk with Mrs. Edwards's son about the Reverend Willie Maxwell, too.

The next day, Agent Abbett interviewed Calvin Edwards, who had once worked on Maxwell's pulpwooding crew. If he had not just interviewed Aaron Burton, Abbett might never have believed the story that Edwards had to tell. Edwards swore that he too had been approached to help murder two of the Reverend's nephews. "Reverend Maxwell came to my house, and asked me how dirty I was," Calvin Edwards recalled. "I asked Maxwell what he was talking about, and Maxwell told me that he needed two knocked off."

Edwards claimed the conversation had taken place in February 1975, almost a year before James Hicks was found dead and a month or so after Maxwell had bailed Edwards out of the Coosa County Jail in Rockford, put him to work on his pulpwooding crew, and started asking him about his willingness to break the law again. According to Edwards, Maxwell had complained about how his nephews owed him money, and promised that within four months of their murders he would have enough insurance money to pay an accomplice four thousand dollars for each of them.

As Abbett listened, Edwards described exactly how the Reverend planned to kill his nephews. "Maxwell told me he had some pill to go in some whiskey that would make them dizzy, and wanted me to get them drunk and call him and then meet him." Once the young men were drunk, all Edwards had to do was take them to a church near Tallassee. The Reverend would be there waiting, and he promised

Edwards that he would be the one to "smother them and then run their car off a cliff above Elam Church."

Agent Abbett found both Edwards and Burton credible, but neither of their statements became public. Although the evidence that Abbett uncovered made the Reverend the prime suspect, neither he nor anyone else could be charged for a death by natural causes: there could be no murderer because, at least according to the coroners, James Hicks had not been murdered. Once again, what the authorities suspected was a country mile from what they could prove. For people around Lake Martin, to say nothing of those close to James Hicks, it was almost as difficult to accept that no cause of death would ever be determined as it was to realize that no charges would ever be filed: but it was not, and they never were.

As a result, there was nothing Agent Abbett or anyone else could do when claims on James Hicks were submitted to Beneficial National Life Insurance Company, Vulcan Life Insurance Company, John Hancock Insurance Company, and World Wide Insurance Company, and nothing they could do when Tom Radney accepted those claim checks on behalf of his client the Reverend Willie Maxwell. As with every one of his deceased relatives, the Reverend was not convicted of any crime, and as with every death since that of his first wife, he faced no charges. He cashed his checks and went about his business while those who believed the voodoo rumors, plus plenty of those who did not, fumed about what the object of their fear and hatred boasted about: that the law would never be able to touch the Reverend Willie Maxwell.

Meanwhile, the long, slow year carried on until America celebrated its bicentennial. Later that July, a man shot two teenage girls in the Bronx; one of them died, the other survived. It was the first of a series of attacks involving a .44-caliber revolver, and by January 1977, when another victim died, the authorities had created a task force to find the shooter. In March, a college student was murdered on her way home from class; in April, a couple was murdered in a parked car. That time, the killer left a letter and signed it Son of Sam. More letters and more murders followed. Soon, afraid of becoming the next victim, women began changing the way they wore their hair and lovers stopped parking. Police, reporters, and citizens alike puzzled over the clues in the killer's messages, and New York was aflame with fear.

One headline at a time, the rest of the country learned of the violence there, too, including down in Alabama, where even *The Alexander City Outlook* covered the Son of Sam. A few years before, an FBI agent had used the term "serial homicide" in a lecture, but now the nation became gripped by the idea of a serial killer: someone who murders multiple people over an extended period of time, sometimes out of rage, sometimes for revenge, sometimes for psychological gratification, and sometimes just for money. The killings in New York caused a sensation around the United States, dredging up memories of the Manson murders and the Zodiac killer and setting the tone that would dominate the coverage of future serial killers.

THE SUMMER OF SAM WAS A TRYING ONE FOR THE MAXWELLS, at first because of the teenage surliness of their adopted daughter, Shirley Ann. At sixteen, she was considerably more difficult than she had been in her single-digit years, and Ophelia, in particular, was worried about her. Shell, as her friends and siblings called her, had already run away from home a few times and just "wasn't Shirley" anymore, Ophelia lamented. "She was just a different person. She was just looking forward to going places. She didn't help in the house." Like many teenagers, Shirley was rebellious, and like many of them, Ophelia recalled, "she believed she could make it without any help. She was happy as long as she had things her own way."

Ophelia thought a summer job might settle her daughter down, and right after the end of her sophomore year Shirley Ann found work waitressing at a fast-food restaurant in Alex City. She did not yet have a license, so she had to be driven to the Hardee's and everywhere else. Two weeks later, on the second Saturday of June, Ophelia drove Shell to visit one of the girl's sisters in Perryville, then stopped on the way back for ice cream. They got home around seven, but Shirley, unappeased by the day's itinerary, complained about wanting to go back out again. Ophelia told her they were almost out of gas and tried to delay any argument by telling the girl to wait to talk with the Reverend once he got home from scouting timber sites.

Instead, according to Ophelia, Shell took off in the car. Ophelia did not see where she went but figured it was back to Perryville. She was furious, but rather than chase after her, she decided to wait for the girl's sister to call; when she did not, and Shirley failed to come home, Ophelia called the police, and when the Reverend returned, they set off together to look for her. As night settled in and they still had not seen or heard any sign of their daughter, they stopped by the Alexander City Police Station, where they were informed that the girl was no longer missing.

The Maxwells were directed to a patch of Highway 9 a mile or so from their house, beside an old cemetery with sagging fences and moss-covered headstones, where, a little while earlier, a man had found the Reverend's 1974 Ford Torino. When the Maxwells got to the scene, only Ophelia was allowed near it. "They wouldn't let me get out of my car," the Reverend said. "They said it didn't concern me. That stirred me up." From a distance, it looked as if the front tire on the driver's side had gone flat, so Shirley had jacked up the Ford, loosened the lug nuts with a tire iron, and wrestled the wheel from its axle, only to have the rim slip from under the jack, and drop the full weight of the car on her slender frame.

It looked that way because it was meant to look that way. But the tire that Shirley Ann was supposed to have been changing was not actually flat. Her hands were clean, not covered with grease and dirt. The lug nuts from the Torino were not beside her body but pinned underneath it. By Sunday morning, when no telephones were needed because people could whisper to each other across the pews, people in Coosa County were breathing more gossip than air. Who ever heard of a sixteen-year-old girl changing a tire when she could have walked the mile home to avoid doing it? What was the Reverend doing cruising timber so late in the day and on a weekend? How come Maxwell's relatives were always found dead by the sides of these roads? Why were there never any witnesses to say what had happened to them? Why had the police not done something sooner? Who could kill a child at all, much less a child of his own? When would someone put a stop to all this? All of that long week between Shirley Ann's death and her funeral, the rumors and anger grew, and so did the Reverend Willie Maxwell's paranoia. "I know they're talking about me," the Reverend said. "I feel they're at me, and it's not true."

ON SATURDAY, JUNE 18, 1977, THE DAY BEFORE FATHER'S DAY, the Reverend and his wife walked into a funeral home in Alexander City and took a seat near the front of the chapel. It already felt like full summer, and the oak trees on the front lawn did not provide much shade. With only one story in the House of Hutchinson Funeral Home, there was nowhere for the heat to rise. Ceiling fans shuffled air around the room, but it was so hot that many of the three hundred mourners took a paper fan from an usher as they made their way to the pews. Up in front of them all, past the first row, Shirley Ann Ellington's body rested in an open casket. Once everyone had settled into their seats and the audible grief in the room had hushed, a pastor from the nearby Great Bethel Baptist Church, the Reverend E. B. Burpo Jr., led the memorial service. The eulogy he offered for Shirley Ann lifted high her warmth and energy while reminding everyone in the room that neither those qualities nor any others could protect anyone from death. Young or old, attended or alone, innocent or otherwise: sooner or later, everyone would meet the same fate. "All of us must go the way of all men," the Reverend Burpo lamented. "There is no exception to the rule."

A collective "amen" ended the liturgy, and after the service all of the mourners came forward to say their good-byes to Shirley. Ophelia Maxwell was so overwhelmed after looking in the casket that she had to sit down again, so her husband led her back to the third pew, where she rested her head against his shoulder while he held a white handkerchief. People lingered together at the front of the chapel while the last few rows of mourners filed up from their seats, including one of the teenager's sisters, Louvinia Lee. "She didn't look the same, and that's when I started crying," Lee recalled about what it was like to see her younger sister's body. "I was looking at Mr. Maxwell, and it seemed like he didn't have nothing to worry about. There were no tears or nothing in his eyes, and that's when I said what I said." What she said, pointing her finger at the Reverend and raising her voice so high that everyone gathered that day could hear it, was this: "You killed my sister and now you gonna pay for it!"

Before anyone in the chapel could react, a man in a green suit pulled a pistol from inside his pocket and fired three rounds into the Reverend Maxwell's head. The shots came from closer than close range. The man with the gun was in the pew in front of his target; had he been any nearer, he would have brushed Maxwell's mustache with the dovetailed sight of his Beretta. The Reverend tried raising his handkerchief to wipe the blood from his face but died before the white cotton touched his skin.

The sound of the pistol sent the hundreds of mourners in the funeral home stampeding through doors and diving out windows. "They tore my chapel up," recalled its owner, Fred Hutchinson—the same Fred Hutchinson who, twenty years earlier, had himself been convicted of murder and insurance fraud in the arson death of an elderly man he buried with suspicious rapidity. Released early from prison, he had resumed his old career, but the shooting left his funeral home in shambles. "There was pictures busted, and ladies pocket books, and glasses, and umbrellas scattered all over the floor."

Surveying the chaos was a cub reporter from the local newspaper, Jim Earnhardt. Only a few years out of high school, Earnhardt had drawn the short straw and lost his Saturday to the assignment of covering Shirley's funeral. He had left when everyone began paying their respects and was just outside the chapel, starting to draft the story in his head, when he heard the first shot. When everyone else was racing out of the chapel, he turned and raced back in. "There's been a shooting," he heard someone say. "Will's been shot!" someone else exclaimed.

Earnhardt left House of Hutchinson long enough to call his editor from a telephone next door, then returned to the scene to interview witnesses. "I thought someone was flashing their camera, because it was to the side of me," Millie Sistrunk, the organist, told him. Johnnie Ruth Minniefield, one of the mourners, said she heard two shots, but another woman, Myrtrice Sutton, had not even been able to count them: "I was so scared. I just tried to get out."

Not long after, before the medical examiner had removed the body from the pew, Earnhardt's editor, Alvin Benn, arrived with a camera. He took photographs of everything, including one they knew they would never be able to run: the Reverend Willie Maxwell, still looking startlingly young and handsome, his head rolled back, his dark eyes open, staring blankly up toward the ceiling of the funeral home. In the coming weeks, Benn and Earnhardt would fill the front page of *The Alexander City Outlook* with articles and interviews about the life and death of the Reverend Maxwell: the three marriages, the five family members who had succumbed to strange deaths, the zero convictions, and the one man who had finally put an end to it that day in the chapel.

The police arrived at House of Hutchinson almost immediately after the murder, from a station only a few blocks away. But by the time they pushed through the confused crowds of witnesses and bystanders, the shooter had already surrendered himself to the two black officers who had been assigned to traffic duty for the funeral. He confessed in the police car on the way to the station. Whether he was a hero or a cold-blooded murderer depended on whom you asked, but one thing was clear: the man who shot the Reverend was going to need a good lawyer. And, as it turned out, the best lawyer in town needed a new client.

# PART TWO

# The Lawyer

# 7

# Who's in the Stew?

T OM RADNEY WANTED THEM TO LOOK LIKE THE KENNEDYS. Dashing parents, darling children: a Dixie Camelot. His wife, Madolyn, had bought the dresses weeks before, but once she got them home, she wouldn't let the girls so much as try them on until that morning. She didn't want their outfits stretched or stained, and not even the best-behaved six-year-old, four-year-old, and two-year-old could promise that. The photographer Tom had hired was meeting them in Montgomery in front of the statehouse, a block away from the First White House of the Confederacy and at the same intersection where, four years before, Martin Luther King Jr. had reassured the twenty-five thousand civil rights protesters who had just arrived on foot from Selma that they weren't going to turn back now.

Whatever the photographer wanted, the Radney family did. Wherever he beckoned with his waving fingers, they walked; whenever he held up his hand like a stop sign, they stood and smiled. Little Hollis got tired and had to be carried, but Ellen and Fran were excited. They understood that the photographs were important, and as best as such young children could, they understood why: their daddy was running for lieutenant governor. Before he became famous, or infamous, as the Reverend Willie Maxwell's lawyer, Tom Radney was already well known in Alabama for taking on another nearly impossible cause: liberal politics in the Deep South.

His first political campaign had come seven years earlier, in 1962, when, in a preview of what his life would be like as a Southern liberal, he managed to lose a race he had indisputably won. On the first day of May, Tom had defeated a poultry farmer from Alexander City and a lumberman from Daviston for a seat in the Alabama House of Representatives. Afterward, he and his campaign manager went down to celebrate on the Gulf Coast of Florida, which is where Radney was when he learned that the legislative seat he was supposed to occupy had been reapportioned out of existence.

Apportionment had barely changed in Alabama since 1901, the year that the state had ratified a new constitution, but while Tom was celebrating, a federal court found that demographics had shifted substantially and ordered the state to redistrict. The court did not change the total number of seats in the legislature, but it did require them to be distributed differently across counties. The redrawn map gave additional seats to some counties by taking them away from others—including Tallapoosa, where the seat Tom had won disappeared. That left him facing a special election for the one seat into which his had been consolidated. On the last Tuesday of August, when the returns came in, Tom Radney lost.

Four years later, though, that same legal mandate proved pivotal to Tom's political career. In 1966, Radney ran to represent Alabama's Sixteenth District in the state senate. Before reapportionment, that district had consisted of two counties, Elmore and Tallapoosa, where the local political machine had cooked up an arrangement called senatorial rotation; they alternated running residents of one county with residents of the other, passing the seat back and forth with every election. But reapportionment added Macon County, home to the Tuskegee Institute, to the Sixteenth District, thereby killing that long-standing practice and changing the landscape for candidates in another way as well. Between 1964 and 1966, four thousand names had been added to the rolls of Macon County, mostly thanks to the Voting Rights Act, bringing its total number of registered voters to more than eleven thousand. Almost seven thousand of those voters were African American, meaning that for the first time a candidate for the Sixteenth District had to campaign in a county that was majority black.

That didn't bother Tom, and early in January, in front of hundreds of friends, he announced that he was running for the seat. The platform was hazy, but the candidate was dreamy: born and raised in a small Alabama town, the young lawyer was a Methodist, a Mason, a Shriner, and an Elk; a member of the American Legion, the Chamber of Commerce, and the Kiwanis Club; an Auburn Tiger from his college days and part of the Crimson Tide since law school; a Sunday school teacher and an army vet.

Tom's opponent in the primary was a man from Elmore County named H. H. "Runt" O'Daniel. Runt had almost more years in business than Tom had in life, and the farmer turned car dealer had a lot of customers who could be counted on to vote for him. But Runt was nowhere near as eager as Tom to campaign in Macon County. Instead, he planned to target the Sixteenth District's segregationist vote, and he had the help of a powerful ally: Governor George Corley Wallace Jr.

It's easy to forget these days, but George Wallace was a Democrat; the tectonic plates of the parties hadn't yet shifted on race, and the GOP was still reviled in the South as the party of Lincoln, so segregationists and integrationists alike ran as Democrats. But the long career of George Wallace began years before and moral light-years away from his infamous promise of "segregation now, segregation tomorrow, and segregation forever." The grandson of a probate judge, Wallace had risen up the ranks of a legal career to become an assistant attorney general and then a judge for the state's Third Judicial Circuit. Along the way, he earned the admiration of black lawyers, who saw him as one of Alabama's more liberal judges and one of the few who addressed both whites and blacks in his courtroom as "mister." When he first ran for governor, in 1958, he had the endorsement of the National Association for the Advancement of Colored People, while his opponent was backed by the Ku Klux Klan. Wallace's defeat, by a margin of more than thirty thousand votes, left him livid. "You know why I lost that governor's race?" he confided to a campaign aide afterward: "I was outniggered." It was a vicious assessment, and it spawned an equally vicious political philosophy: "I'll tell you here and now, I will never be outniggered again."

So began the inauspicious age of Wallace in Alabama politics. These were dark, demersal years, when white voters were pandered to by politicians at every level of government, promised power they'd never had at the expense of African Americans they were assured never would. It was Wallace, by then governor, who stood in a doorway at the University of Alabama in June 1963 to prevent two black students from enrolling, and it was Wallace who three months later ordered state troopers to prevent black kids half their age from integrating the public schools in Birmingham. He could find the race card in any deck and played it against everyone who dissented from his white-supremacist brand of populism. Anyone who criticized him, he said, was a "low-down, carpet-baggin', scallywaggin', race-mixin' liar."

In his rhetoric, Wallace was a law-and-order man, but in real life he liked making his own rules. Despite his tremendous popularity, he was unable to run for reelection in 1966, because Alabama forbade governors to serve consecutive terms. After the legislature refused to amend the state constitution to make him eligible, Wallace ran a proxy candidate instead: his wife, Lurleen. At campaign events, Lurleen would talk for a few minutes; then Wallace would take the stage and rant and rage for over an hour. He went around the state promoting not only his wife but also a whole slate of mini-Wallaces, including the Sixteenth District candidate Runt O'Daniel.

ALABAMA HAD LONG BEEN A ONE-PARTY STATE; BY THE MID-1960s that party was Wallace. Tom Radney, however, was not a member. Born on June 18, 1932, in the tiny town of Wadley, just across the Tallapoosa County line, Radney was the sixth child of Nancy Beatrice Simpson and James Monroe Radney, known as Beatrice and Jim. His birth certificate reads "John Tomas," and all his life, the missing *h* would appear and vanish and reappear at the whim of reporters, pundits, calligraphers, and copy editors.

Although he would eventually be known in Alexander City and around Alabama as Big Tom, he was the baby of the Radney family, and his mother treated him accordingly. Tom later claimed that his father never once said he loved him, but Beatrice favored her young-est son fiercely. After her husband left for work in the morning, running a branch of his father-in-law's mercantile business and managing his plantation, she would fetch Tom from his bed and bring him to theirs, where it was warmer, and if the dinner table did not have something on it he liked, she would wait until the rest of the family was asleep, then cook him whatever he pleased. If their mother could have chewed his food for him, an older sister once recalled, she would have.

Yet all that spoiling made Tom sweet, not rotten. Beatrice would send her son to deliver milk or jam to other families, telling him that while they were lucky today, they might not be tomorrow, in which case they would want people to remember their kindness. Those lessons in human decency, which Tom learned from his mother by example, he learned from his father by contrast. The property Jim Radney managed included an area called "the Quarters," which was farmed and occupied by twenty-nine sharecropping families, akin to the arrangement that the Maxwells had in Coosa County. One of the families at the Quarters had a son only a year older than Tom, and as children the two became close friends. But when the boy's father lost his right arm to a cotton gin, Jim refused to help the family, then forced them off the Quarters. The shame of that experience skipped the father but struck the son and stayed with Tom all his life.

Tom was bothered, too, by a revival he attended one summer at a church in Wadley, the white version of the sort the Reverend Maxwell used to lead. He had gone with two friends, and all three boys watched wide-eyed as pictures were passed around of burning flames—like the ones waiting for them in Hell, the preacher said, if they committed any of the sins he shouted at them. The boys raced for the door, and later Tom swore he'd never worship anywhere that preached God's judgment without God's love. He found a spiritual home in the Methodist Church, and for the rest of his life he said it was his faith that led him to believe in the equality of the races and the dignity of all people.

It was this belief that helped animate Tom's bid for the state senate in 1966, and his campaign strategy, too. From his perspective, the

African American citizens in Macon County were just as deserving of his time and attention as white citizens elsewhere in the district. Voters were voters, he thought, and he was out to win votes. Tom's opponent, meanwhile, had resigned himself to losing Macon County but had a plan to steal Tom's home county out from under him. Runt knew that Tom might well win the primary outright by getting more than 50 percent of the vote, but if he could force his opponent into a runoff, then he could use Tom's African American supporters against him. To do that, he needed to split the voting population into smaller slices, which is why two months before the primary a spoiler made himself known: a mustachioed country singer named Gene "Mutt" Lanier put on his cowboy hat and announced that he was running for the senate. Radney couldn't do anything about Mutt, and he couldn't prove that Runt was behind the last-ditch candidacy, but he saw right through their plan. Between them, Runt and Mutt would get more than enough votes to keep Tom from winning outright in the primary and then, as he put it, "tie the Negro vote around my neck in the runoff."

Mutt, Runt, and Tom all appeared on the ballot during the first week of May. Radney got the most votes, but was still about five hundred short of the majority he needed to avoid a runoff. Tallapoosa County went for its hometown boy, as did Elmore County, but, in the words of *The Tuskegee News*, "Negro support went bloc-fashion," and it went for Tom Radney. That was all the information Runt needed to, in the parlance of the time, "seg" his way to victory, and he took his racist strategy straight to the printers and the radio stations. The runoff wasn't until the end of that month, and all Runt wanted white voters to hear until then was how much he had in common with the Wallaces and how much Radney had in common with the district's African American population. Leaflets went around encouraging hesitant supporters to call and verify that Wallace wanted Runt to win; when voters dialed the printed telephone number, they were put through to Wallace's state finance director, who could stump for Runt and take a donation at the same time. "You can easily see who stands for whom," Runt said of his young liberal opponent, then promised to fight with "Mrs. George C. Wallace's Administration against the Left Wing Liberals in Washington" on behalf of "our State's rights and Southern way of life."

"State's rights and Southern way of life" was a barely coded appeal to white supremacy, but it had nothing on the most pernicious piece of campaign literature that Runt produced in his fight against Tom Radney. That was a folded brochure, the front of which featured a cartoon man, black as tar, barefoot and naked but for a tiki skirt, clenching a white bone between his lips, stirring a simmering cauldron. Above him, written in blood-dripping red ink, was the question "WHO'S IN THE STEW . . ." Opening the brochure, voters were warned, "MAKE SURE IT'S NOT YOU!" Below that, Runt printed the results of the primary, making plain as day that Radney was the favored candidate among African Americans.

The advertisement was execrable but efficacious, and at first Tom couldn't figure out what to do about it. He knew that Runt had sent the brochure to white voters in two counties, and he couldn't stop staring at it, furious and stymied. He was in the middle of turning it over and over, in his mind as well as his hands, when he noticed the tiny union mark on the back cover. He called up the printer, learned that they still had the proofs of the brochure, paid them to run off another fifteen hundred copies, and then distributed them himself to black voters in Macon County. He also took copies around to his white country-club friends. None of them were liberals, but many of them were dismayed by such offensive politicking in Tallapoosa County. Alexander City was a town on the rise, flush with money from the cotton mills, and its leaders were trying to attract business from around the country. The clean, crew-cut Radney was a poster boy for the New South, and soon enough the Chamber of Commerce types were in the stew with him, too.

The bedrock of Radney's campaign was his wife, Madolyn Boyd Anderson, who was both Eleanor to his FDR and Jackie to his JFK. She was raised in Montgomery, and her parents still lived there; the Andersons had already promised their son-in-law a room in their home if he needed it during legislative sessions. When Madolyn and Tom met, she was teaching first grade and cared deeply about public education. Tom, who had gotten both a bachelor's and a master's degree in education from Auburn, impressed her with how seriously he had thought about the field and how passionately he believed that public schools promoted equality and social mobility. Madolyn sized Tom up quickly and knew what she was getting: a man made up of equal parts idealism and ambition, a politician with one eye on Montgomery and the other on Washington. They got married in the First United Methodist Church on September 8, 1962, and moved into a little apartment in downtown Alex City. After they'd saved enough money to buy some land on nearby Ridgeway Drive, her father, an engineer, supervised the construction of a home for them there. It was as modern as they were, and they would share it for the rest of Tom's life.

When Tom first began campaigning, Madolyn went with him to most of his events, driving so that he could finish writing speeches in the car and entertaining the press once they arrived. But it was Tom who entertained the voters. His politics inspired those who shared them, and his enthusiasm, sincerity, and optimism won over even some of those who did not. A few days before the election, Tom published an open letter in a local newspaper asking the people of the Sixteenth District to vote for him. In exchange, he promised them "hard work, clean representation, and a voice you will be proud of in the Senate."

When the runoff returns came in, Tom's lead in his home county had fallen by more than five hundred votes, and in Elmore County, Runt had picked up another fifteen hundred supporters. But Tom Radney won Macon County by almost two thousand votes, enough to hand him the runoff—and with it, the senate seat. The Voting Rights Act of 1965 had not yet caused white Alabamians to abandon the Democratic Party en masse, so at the time—and for just about the last time—winning the Democratic primary in the state effectively meant winning the general election, just as winning a Republican primary in Alabama often does today. Come November, he easily defeated the sixty-year-old farmer who ran against him.

The following session, Tom Radney was sworn in as state senator. He was thirty-four and, as Madolyn had known since their first date, ambitious enough to already imagine running for an office he wasn't yet old enough to hold. But he would never make it to Washington. Instead, in the years between when he was elected to the state legislature and when he and his family went to Montgomery to shoot those picture-perfect photographs for his lieutenant governor campaign, Tom Radney was nearly run out of politics entirely.

# 8

# Roses Are Red

IF IT WAS TOUGH TO RUN AS A LIBERAL IN ALABAMA, IT WAS almost impossible to govern as one. Tom Radney's colleagues in the legislature had no choice but to let him in the chamber, but they had no intention of letting any of his bills out of it. One year into his term, Tom confessed to a church group in Auburn that he felt as if he "had to spend more time fighting bad legislation than passing good legislation."

That bad legislation included a serious, if inexplicable, effort to remove Alabama from the United Nations, which made it through the house but not the senate; a bill that would have allowed the legislature to approve or reject speakers at state schools, which Tom managed to quash, partly through a public debate at Auburn University, where he mounted a passionate defense of academic freedom; and a Wallace-backed effort to defund the Tuskegee Institute, a recipient of state funding since 1881, which Tom derailed by threatening a one-man filibuster. The good legislation, proposed by Radney and resoundingly voted down, or denied a vote, included lowering the voting age in Alabama to eighteen (on the grounds that anyone old enough to die for their country in Vietnam was old enough to vote for its leadership), revising election laws around absentee voting, and removing a line item in the University of Alabama budget for the purchase of Confederate flags.

Tom Radney had gotten his idea of good from his mother and from the church, but he'd gotten his idea of good legislation from President

Kennedy. In 1960, Tom had gone to the Democratic National Convention intending to nominate Adlai Stevenson. Then he met JFK at a cocktail party and switched his vote on the spot. "It's sort of a silly way to say it," he recounted years later, "but he made you feel that he was talking to you. Those eyes were penetrating."

It was an apt description of what was, in essence, the beginning of a political love affair. Over the years, Tom's admiration for the Kennedys led him to work for their campaigns, bring them on retreats to Lake Martin, and frame their business cards. He had been devastated when JFK was shot and came home from work that day to cry. But he never gave up on Kennedy's vision of what a government could do for its citizens, and when the time came to take his wife, Madolyn, to Chicago for another nominating convention, he had another Kennedy on his mind.

The 1968 Democratic National Convention was an unusually turbulent one, in unusually turbulent times. Martin Luther King Jr. had been assassinated four months before, and Robert Kennedy two months after that. There were violent clashes between Vietnam War protesters and the Chicago police outside the convention center, and very nearly as much tumult inside it. President Lyndon Johnson had announced that he would not seek reelection, so Vice President Hubert Humphrey and Senator Eugene McCarthy were fighting for his job. Robert Kennedy had also been a presidential hopeful, and his assassination that June had left hundreds of delegates uncommitted. On top of that, several southern states had sent competing slates of delegates—some segregated, some integrated. Four years earlier, nearly the entire Alabama delegation had walked out of the convention to protest the seating of integrated delegates from Mississippi; this time, three separate slates of Alabama delegates had shown up, and it took the credentialing committee to sort them out.

When it did, Tom Radney was among those seated. He promptly pinned a "Draft Ted" button on his blazer and went looking for a camera. "Edward Kennedy has shown a great enthusiasm for the South and its problems," Radney declared, "and he will be a popular candidate in the South. I cannot support any other announced candidate." It was a startling enough declaration to get him interviewed from the floor of the convention by CBS News, which is when his problems started. "Walter," a fresh-faced Dan Rather said to anchorman Walter Cronkite, "you automatically assume that everyone from Alabama is a Wallace man. Not true. There is, in the Alabama delegation, at least one strong supporter of Senator Edward Kennedy. Tom Radney from Alexander City, Alabama, is that man."

Looking and sounding as comfortable on national television as Cronkite himself, Tom described Ted Kennedy as "the most formidable Democratic candidate we have" and, somewhere between his smiles and his shucks, predicted that Senator Kennedy would "sweep the South." After he was done talking with CBS, Tom gave interview after interview, offering himself as an ambassador of the New South for anyone who would listen.

The Old South immediately went up in arms. That year, George Wallace was running for president as an independent candidate, to the delight of many both in his home state and farther afield. (He would ultimately win Alabama, Georgia, Mississippi, Louisiana, and Arkansas, plus a faithless elector from North Carolina, for a total of forty-six electoral votes, the most won by a third-party candidate since former president Theodore Roosevelt ran as a Progressive.) But even if Wallace hadn't been running, almost nobody watching the convention back home in Alabama wanted another Kennedy in the White House, and they let their state senator know exactly how they felt about him grandstanding on television at their expense. Almost instantly, telegrams began arriving for Tom at the convention hall, and messages started piling up for him back at his hotel. They were nearly all anonymous, and all vicious. One of them, a telegram sent from Birmingham and signed only "Concerned Citizens of Alabama," read, "Roses are red, Violets are blue. Two Kennedys are dead and so are you."

Tom had been mocked for his politics in the past, and made to feel like a traitor to his state and his race, but he had never really been threatened, and never before had he been made to feel afraid. Madolyn was immediately distraught, especially for their children, who were back home in Alexander City. Her parents were staying in the house on Ridgeway Drive with the girls, who were five, three, and ten months at the time, when the phone started ringing there, too. Tom asked the Alexander City Police to send a car to protect his family while he and Madolyn figured out what to do. In the end, they left Chicago early, but not immediately; Tom didn't want to leave before doing his duty as a delegate, and even though Kennedy refused to be drafted, Tom voted for him anyway.

The Radneys returned to Alex City and the convention ended soon afterward, but the threats did not. They came mostly by phone now, and they came morning, noon, and night, and the anonymous voices behind them didn't bother to make sure it was Tom on the other end of the line. They threatened his wife. They threatened his daughters. They threatened him. "I'd pick up the phone at 3 a.m.," he said, "and a voice would tell me that when I cranked up my car that morning I'd be blown to bits." After a day or two, Tom stopped counting how many calls he had gotten. He tried to remain sanguine, but he was shaken. He said he knew his actions in Chicago wouldn't be popular; "however, I do not believe that the hope of popularity should be the criteria by which a public official expresses his convictions. I did what I thought was right and I have no apologies." He respected the opinions of those who disagreed with him, he said; he just wished they would extend the same respect to him.

Whoever the anonymous callers were, they did not, and soon they weren't just calling. Someone stole the American flag from the pole in the Radney family's yard, and their nameplate out front was smashed. They had a cabin down on Lake Martin, and one day Tom drove the girls down there in his black Simca, a tiny French car that was fast and fun. They took their boat out round the slough a few times, and the girls went for a swim. Then they headed back to their car, but when they got to the top of the hill where they'd parked, there was no Simca.

Tom distracted his daughters by telling them to look for blackberries so that they could make a cobbler, and as the girls gathered berries, he herded them up toward the highway where he thought he might be able to flag someone down for a ride. At the bend where the dirt road to the cabin met the blacktop, they found the Simca, in the middle of the road, upside down. He told them the wind must have blown it over and laughed with them, then tried to do the same thing when he discovered later that their cabin had been vandalized, and then again when their boat sank because someone had punched a hole in the hull.

Tom's daughters were placable; his wife was not. While he tried making light of everything that was happening, Madolyn grew more worried and insisted on bringing the girls into their bedroom at night. She had them sleep on the floor, below the windows, where she hoped they'd be safe from anything that might come crashing through the glass. "George Wallace has planted a seed of fear around here and it's frightening," she told *The Washington Post,* which, together with *The New York Times* and many other newspapers, covered the harassment of the Radney family after the convention. "My husband is being condemned simply because he disagrees with those in power here, because he refuses to be a rubber stamp."

She was right, of course, about Wallace and the vitriol he had stirred in so many Alabamians. As the Radneys knew, a tragic roster of activists and innocents had died for the crime of being black or supporting blacks in their state. There was Willie Edwards Jr., the truck driver forced off a bridge to his death by four Klansmen in Montgomery. There was William Lewis Moore, the man from Baltimore shot and killed in Attalla while trying to walk a letter denouncing segregation 385 miles to the governor of Mississippi. There were four young girls, Addie Mae Collins, Denise McNair, Carole Robertson, and Cynthia Wesley, killed by the bombing of the Sixteenth Street Baptist Church in Birmingham. There was thirteen-year-old Virgil Lamar Ware, shot to death on the handlebars of his brother's bicycle in the same city. There was Jimmie Lee Jackson, beaten and shot by state troopers in Marion while he tried to protect his mother and grandfather during a protest. There was the Reverend James Reeb, the Unitarian minister beaten to death in Selma. There was Viola Gregg Liuzzo, shot by Klansmen while trying to ferry marchers between Selma and Montgomery. There was Willie Brewster, shot to death while walking home in Anniston. There was Jonathan Myrick Daniels, a seminarian registering black voters who was arrested for participating in a protest and then shot by a deputy sheriff in Hayneville. There was Samuel

Leamon Younge Jr., murdered by a gas station owner after arguing about segregated restrooms.

Alabama had seen the martyrdom of so many, and the attempted martyrdom of so many more, often for a lot less than what Tom stood accused of doing. As the threats worsened, Tom started to worry as much as his wife about his family's safety. "At night," he said, "I'd take out my gun, look under the bed, search the closets and then lock the bedroom door." He was horrified when his oldest daughter answered the telephone to hear someone shouting, and when she started having nightmares, he decided he was done. "I saw what it was doing to Madolyn and the children—what it was doing to us as a family, living in fear all the time," he said. "I decided the price was too high." To protect his family, Tom announced that he would leave politics after his term was up. "My wife and I have prayerfully decided upon the future course of our lives," Tom told *The Montgomery Advertiser*. "My three daughters are too precious to me to allow their safety to be in doubt."

HOPING THAT PEOPLE WOULD STOP THREATENING HIM, TOM began spreading the word that he was no longer a threat. "I only wish I could express myself in Alabama without fear of my life," he told one reporter, but because he couldn't, he was emphatic about his decision "never again to be a candidate for any public office." The safety of his family, Radney insisted, was more important than his political career.

After the news reports came the editorials, in all sorts of newspapers, decrying the lack of civility in politics, lamenting the cost of dissent in Wallaceland, and praising Radney's courage. *The Birmingham News,* which Tom had delivered as a young paperboy in Wadley, called for "freedom from abuse," praised Tom's "openly expressed position," and said he deserved respect whether or not his politics "matched the prevailing temper of political thought in this state." The *Alabama Journal* wrote that his "decision to leave politics could only result in Alabama's further isolation in the political spectrum." "Radney can hardly be faulted for such a decision," declared another newspaper down in Louisiana, "but the same cannot be said for an apathetic Alabama citizenry that casually shrugs off the loss of precisely the kind of man needed to guide the state's politics out of the dark ages into the light."

These public expressions of support were accompanied by private ones—not always for Tom's politics, but always for him. Nearly two hundred telegrams piled up at his law office, and almost a hundred letters arrived at the family home. Some were brief notes bearing a simple message: "I was proud of you." Others were longer handwritten cards, saying that Tom was entitled to his opinions, even though "your views are not mine." Some came on typed letterhead, reassuring Tom—"There are a lot of people who feel as you do"—or imploring him: "We so hope that these evil days will someday pass and you will be able to return to public life to make the wonderful contributions which only you can."

The letters came from cities and towns around Alabama. They came from Massachusetts and New York, from students at Kent State University and reporters in Illinois. They came from Missouri and Michigan and a woman in Pennsylvania who wanted Tom to move and run for office there. They came from Iowa, Oklahoma, Kentucky, Georgia, Florida, Virginia, Texas, Arkansas, and the Office of the Vice President of the United States of America. They came from a student in Texas who closed his handwritten letter by saying, "I am a Negro and am able to understand the type of fear that you now experience," and from one of Tom's own constituents, a former leader in the NAACP who described his own history with harassment: "So bad were the telephone calls and threats that for nearly twenty years, I was forced to have an unlisted telephone. In my files here at Tuskegee, I have nearly a hundred copies of anonymous letters filled with filth and threats."

At the end of September, a few weeks into this avalanche of support, Tom called in to a national radio program produced by the Methodist Church. He was interviewed along with former congressman Lawrence Brooks Hays of Arkansas, who had lost his seat in the U.S. House of Representatives after declining to fight the integration by President Eisenhower of Central High School in Little Rock.

When the two men talked about "the race question" in their home states, the one from Alabama seemed more humbled than hopeful. Although the national convention had been only a month before, Tom sounded infinitely aged. He didn't say anything about men like Kennedy sweeping the South, or men like himself moving into the Governor's Mansion on South Perry Street. Instead, the state senator from Alabama told *Night Call*'s host, Del Shields, about going around to college campuses, telling the students that "there's been some people that I picked up from that left off" and asking them to "pick up where Tom Radney left off."

Having left off, Tom Radney was finally left alone. As the summer of 1968 slowly cooled, so did everything else; the abuse stopped, the threats ended, his whole family exhaled. When Tom answered what turned out to be the last of all the anonymous telephone calls, he heard someone laughing into the line: "Well, we wanted to get you out—and we did."

# The Fight for Good

YOU CAN'T KEEP A YELLOW DOG DOWN. TOM THREW AWAY ALL of the threats, but he saved every single card, letter, and telegram encouraging him to stay in public service. He read them over and over again. He also read biographies of famous men both good and evil, immersing himself in the lives of Jesus, Jefferson, and Hitler. He learned the Tennyson poem that Harry Truman kept in his wallet ("There the common sense of most shall hold a fretful realm in awe, / And the kindly earth shall slumber, lapt in universal law"), and he memorized the last words of Stonewall Jackson and quotations from the speeches of Jefferson Davis. That fall, he wrote an essay about turmoil on college campuses; the next spring, he wrote a guest editorial for the University of Alabama at Huntsville, placing the chaos of the 1960s in the context of other crisis periods in world history. He was reading widely, thinking about the past, and praying about the future. Late in the spring of 1969, after passing a season and a half that way, he began pointing out to Madolyn that the next year's race for lieutenant governor was wide open.

Lurleen Wallace had died in office, leaving Albert Brewer, her lieutenant governor, in charge. Brewer had already announced that he would try to keep the seat by running for governor in the next election, but George Wallace, having taken his mandatory term off, was planning to run again, too. The race was one of the nastiest in Alabama's history. Brewer was buoyed by secret infusions of cash from

Richard Nixon's Committee to Re-elect the President, which was trying to keep Wallace from regaining a platform from which to launch
another presidential campaign. Wallace, meanwhile, was lobbing the
kinds of attacks that were cheap in both senses: for a pittance and a
huge payoff, he spread rumors that Brewer was gay, that his wife was a
drunk, and that his daughter slept with black men. But Brewer wasn't
backing down, and he wouldn't settle for lieutenant governor, so the
number two spot was there for the taking.

For weeks, Tom pestered his wife about the race. At first, he talked
her ear off about why it would be perfectly safe to run this time;
then he started counting off all the reasons he thought he could win.
Although another campaign was just about the last thing in the world
she wanted, she could tell how much *he* wanted it, and in ways that
were utterly ordinary for that time, she was used to bending to his
will. All of Tom's children cherished his company, but he wasn't the
kind of father who went to cheerleading practice or parent-teacher
conferences; he liked it best when his kids came along to whatever *he*
was doing. It was Madolyn who readied their daughters for school,
while Tom sat in the living room making his way through three newspapers every morning, and Madolyn who managed the schedule for
all of them like an air traffic controller arranging layovers and approv-
ing flight plans. In the end, he chose to run without her blessing, and
she went along with his decision, knowing that even if it would be
worse for their family, it would be better for Alabama.

Alabama, though, had already bid Tom a very grand good-bye.
Which left him facing a problem: How does a man who has publicly
bowed out of politics gracefully climb back onstage? Tom knew that
some people were likely to accuse him of overplaying the threats to
his family to win the pity vote, so he started by explaining that his
decision to withdraw had been not opportunism but overreaction. "I
did not make it as some cynics may have thought to create sympathy
for me or my family," he explained; rather, he had responded to the
barrage of threats "as a mere man might do." "I am not defensive
about changing my decision," he said, but "I think I have matured; I
hope I am a better man because of the difficult days of the past year."

Tom announced his candidacy on September 6, 1969. "This time I am in the fight for good," he told the press that gathered to cover his entry into the race. "I'm in the fight for honesty and integrity in all branches of state government. . . . I'm also in the fight for rational and progressive reform and for brotherhood and justice for all our citizens." The Democratic primary was the following May, leaving Tom eight months to charm a vote out of everyone he could in Alabama's sixty-seven counties. He went out first thing and had those Kennedyesque pictures of his family taken in Montgomery and then blanketed the state with color brochures and billboards of the resulting photographs beneath the slogan "Tom Radney Cares About You." He went to every fish fry and pig roast and county fair he could find and addressed the breakfasts, luncheons, and suppers of any civic club that would have him.

It didn't take long for Tom to start earning endorsements. The teachers' unions and labor unions backed him, as did newspapers in Alexander City, Heflin, and Anniston. In March, he promised a group of black students at Miles College to contribute his own "blood, sweat, and tears as we continue to right the wrongs that have been a hindrance to our full and complete development." In April, his hometown of Wadley celebrated Tom Radney Day, feting their favorite son with music and speeches. By May, he'd exhausted himself and his budget. The billboards alone had cost him eighteen thousand dollars. The campaign in total cost fifty thousand. Tom contributed twenty thousand dollars of his own money and accepted another ten thousand from Madolyn's parents; friends and supporters provided the rest.

Radney faced seven opponents in the lieutenant governor race, and their platforms differed sharply from his. For one thing, while they were running on law and order, he was running on education and the economy. He wanted to double the education budget, build highways to link the state's small towns, and take on power companies for polluting Alabama's waterways and failing to reliably control water levels in reservoirs like Lake Martin. But he knew that all of these measures would require increasing property taxes, which hadn't been raised in six decades. He went around singing the praises of paying one's fair share, and trying to cultivate an understanding of what governments at every level can do for their people. Opportunity was expensive, Tom argued, but a lot more affordable than the alternative, which was falling even further behind the rest of the country. "I yield to no man in the state of Alabama the love I have for the past," he'd say from the stump, "but we can't live in it."

Above all, though, Radney and his opponents parted ways on civil rights. Tom never marched and he never registered black voters. He didn't go to meet the freedom riders after their integrated buses arrived in Alabama, and when he found himself on the defensive, he wasn't above telling a crowd, "I am proud of my Southern heritage and I honor the Confederate flag as a symbol of something noble and good." But he was no believer in the Lost Cause, and he always took care to add, "I do not honor it in the 'Hell, no, never' type of defiance."

More starkly, he was a sixth-generation Alabamian who dared to say that his state was often wrong and the federal government was sometimes right, and after the courts mandated integration, he became a staunch supporter of it—not only in his public life, but in his private one as well. Once, when he heard that a local restaurant refused to serve an all-black marching band, he told Madolyn that he'd be bringing some students by for lunch; shortly thereafter, he showed up with all two hundred members of the band. On the day in 1970 that the Alexander City schools integrated, when many white families kept their children at home, Tom sat his seven-year-old daughter, Ellen, down at breakfast and told her that it would be a very special day. "There'll be busloads of black children at your school," he told her. "They are going to be scared, but you be nice, and make sure they know you are their friend." In a state where a legislator had proposed closing the public schools instead of integrating them, it was more than enough to get Tom branded as a radical.

And there weren't many registered radicals in Alabama. Although the fearless organizing of civil rights activists had increased the number of African American voters in the state from 66,000 in 1960 to 315,000 in 1970, their work had caused a backlash, in the form of a highly effective countereffort by white supremacists. The under-told and stunning story of voter registration in the South is this: in 1965, 79 percent of eligible whites were registered to vote; five years later, that figure had risen to 97 percent. In the end, there simply weren't enough votes to carry a progressive candidate like Tom into the runoff.

We like to say that some people are ahead of their time, but it is closer to the truth to say that Tom Radney was ahead of his place. On the evening that he lost the race for lieutenant governor, Tom said he felt "not defeated, only disappointed." He had wanted to bring a new kind of politics to Alabama: "the politics of reason, not race; of unity, not division; of concern for all citizens, not callous disregard of some for the sake of others." Like most liberals in the Deep South, he refused to believe that the region would never change, and spoke movingly about his willingness to work until it did. He knew that the struggle for civil rights and political equality remained unfinished and promised to keep fighting for both as a citizen. He conceded the election before all the votes were even tallied, gave by far the greatest speech of his political career, then bowed out once again, this time for good.

# 10

# The Maxwell House

THERE WERE COURTS IN ALABAMA EVEN BEFORE THERE WERE courthouses. In the early years of the nineteenth century, a judge in Baldwin County presided from the fork of an oak tree, with the jury on his right, the spectators on his left, and another oak—the one for the hangman—not far away. In Jasper, the seat of Walker County, the judge sat on a big rock, the jury on a bigger one. Over in Randolph County, the judge's bench was a stump, and those he sentenced to jail did their time in a hollow log along the Tallapoosa River. After one prisoner nearly drowned when the river flooded and carried the log off the bank with him inside it, the court turned over a wagon instead, put prisoners underneath, and had a sheriff sit on top.

When proper courthouses did come to Alabama, though, they came in style. As a rule, most southern towns are allergic to authority and resent any federal presence that isn't a post office. But all of them welcome a courthouse, no matter what court it's designed to house: city, county, district, federal, anything so long as you can put a building around it. As the Alabama chapter of the National Society of the Colonial Dames of America put it in 1860, there was no better way to advertise how civilized you were than "the erection of a courthouse in a new and virgin territory." Some of the first ones in the state were simple log cabins, but it didn't take long for even half-paved hamlets and unassuming county seats to start trying to outdo each other architecturally, with grand brick numbers, column-happy Greek Revivals, and extravagant affairs with cupolas and clock towers and gilt eagles on top. Inside were the courts themselves, together with government offices, records rooms, and space to host pretty much anything that might happen in a small southern town: Mardi Gras balls, shape-note concerts, dinners for foxhunters, Confederate reunions, campaign rallies, land auctions, Klan meetings, harvest dances. That's to say nothing of their basement vaults, where men gathered to stay cool while playing poker or dominoes.

Right around the time that Tom Radney was giving up his political ambitions, he was settling into a new law office just beside the Alexander City Courthouse. Although the county seat of Tallapoosa is over in Dadeville, Alex City has had a courthouse for more than a century, and for a long time it has split the county's circuit cases. The original one burned down in 1902, but not the bottle of rum set into its cornerstone, which was moved into the new building. This building, erected after the Great Depression, had one wing to house the court, another for city hall, and spare rooms to accommodate other uses. A person could show up at 1 Court Square to pay his taxes, register his will, sue for his inheritance, check out a library book, renew his driver's license, or marry his sweetheart. For locals, it was where you went for pretty much everything short of salvation and groceries.

Still, the courthouse wasn't the most important place in Alexander City; that honor belonged to the mills. The whole South was built on cotton, but Alex City was built specifically on athletic clothes, long underwear, and teddies. In 1902, thirty years after the town was founded, a local man named Benjamin Russell set up shop with six knitting machines, ten sewing machines, a steam-powered mill, and a dozen employees. The company barely stayed afloat on its original plan, which involved buying up yarn to make knitted shirts for women and children, but business took off when Russell switched to teddies, better known at the time as camiknickers. By 1932, the mill could move fiber all the way to finished product, and its inventory had expanded substantially. The company enjoyed another boom a decade later, during World War II, when Russell made millions by manufacturing military uniforms like the one the Reverend Willie Maxwell had worn.

Some of the people who made the clothes that made Ben Russell wealthy lived in Alex City, but many others—including the Maxwells—did not. The back roads and half-towns of the surrounding counties were full of spinners, slashers, cutters, weavers, folders, and spoolers who traveled to Alex City each day to punch in, and between Russell Mills and its competitor Avondale Mills, the whole region seemed to keep time by the work whistles. Jobs at the cotton mills were coveted, but most workers there didn't make regular wages; they were paid according to what they produced, and much of what they earned went straight back to the company, either during their shift as the dope wagon moved between rooms selling sodas, chocolate bars, sandwiches, and chips or after hours for their housing and clothing and food.

Whether or not you worked in the mills—whether or not you even lived within the city limits—Alexander City was clearly a company town. Within a dozen years of opening his mill, Russell had hired a teacher to hold classes in a church downtown, and pretty soon his employees were sending their kids to the Russell School, getting their medical care at the Russell Hospital, and buying their groceries at the Russell-owned store. Ben's brother Thomas served as mayor from 1907 until 1947, and the Russell family helped establish the Chamber of Commerce and ran one of the town's largest banks. If cotton was king, it turned men like the Russells into dukes and earls and made Alexander City lavishly more wealthy than the surrounding areas.

TOM RADNEY, WHO WOULD EVENTUALLY COUNT RUSSELL MILLS among his clients, fit in with all that prosperity just fine. He'd studied law at the University of Alabama and spent his summers with the Marine Corps at Camp Upshur, in Virginia. He was a bit younger than the Reverend Maxwell, so he missed the war, and quite a bit wealthier, so he entered the service in 1955 as a member of the Judge Advocate General's Corps. At Fort Jackson, South Carolina, Radney was promoted to first lieutenant; at Camp Chaffee, in Arkansas, he received his commission and served as assistant trial counsel.

Thanks to his time in the JAG Corps, Radney returned home

to eastern Alabama with trial experience; thanks to law school, he returned home with a partner, a friend he'd made while signing up for classes. It was Tom who proposed opening a practice in Alexander City, in part because he had some cousins there and in part because he wanted to work in a town affluent enough to accommodate his ambition. He and his friend hung up a shingle above a furniture store and waited for clients to come knocking—waited so long, in fact, that his partner eventually gave up and left private practice. But Tom stuck it out and gradually attracted enough business to move to an office on the second floor of the Alexander City Courthouse, which he maintained throughout his political career.

When that ended, though, he was ready to change just about everything else, too. After Tom lost the lieutenant governor's race, he let his hair grow out, literally: the disappearance of his signature crew cut was such a shock that it made the local newspaper. His suits got a little looser, and his cars got a little nicer. His marriage started recovering from the strain of the campaign trail. Most momentously, he and Madolyn had another child: Thomas, his only son, who was born the May after the election and irrevocably turned his father into Big Tom.

Big Tom had more money than state senator Radney, and now that he was practicing law full-time, he needed a little more office, too. He leased the land next door to the courthouse, at 56 Court Square, and built his own place, a brick building with an interior atrium and offices all around. Later, when the other big mill in town—the rumor one—started churning out questions about how exactly Radney could afford such a fancy place, people started to call the building the Maxwell House. But because it was so constantly busy, Big Tom preferred to call it the Zoo.

The office was busy in part because Big Tom believed that everyone deserved a lawyer, and he wanted every potential client to feel welcome in the building. But he also lived for conversation, and he would talk to anyone, client or otherwise, who set foot in his door—including, in a pinch, the skeleton named Harvey that lived in the office library. Over the years, the Zoo hosted farmers, governors, mill workers, judges, police officers, medical doctors, bankers, restaurateurs, rival counselors, preachers, postal clerks, janitors, juvenile delinquents, and senators. When country star Tammy Wynette came to Alexander City for the seventy-fifth birthday celebration of the Russell Corporation, she walked off her tour bus singing "Stand By Your Man" and, as just about everybody in Alex City did eventually, made her way to 56 Court Square.

Whenever clients called the Zoo, Radney's assistants knew to put them right through to Big Tom; if he wasn't there, they knew to say that he was in court, a policy he insisted they follow even when court wasn't in session. When clients showed up in person, they were marched right into Tom's office, where he'd sit them down, pull a malt ball from the candy drawer in his desk, pop it into his mouth, lean back in his green leather chair, and listen, surrounded by his own personal Louvre of Liberalism: busts of JFK, donkey cartoons, and pictures of himself with everyone from Ted Kennedy to Jimmy Carter.

While his clients talked about what kind of lawyering they needed done, Tom would think about what to charge them. He wasn't above raising rates on those he knew could afford it; for those who couldn't, he would work cases on contingency, or in exchange for blueberry cobblers and chickens, for pecan pies or, sometimes, just pecans. One bill was paid in furniture. He thought often about what his mother had told him when she sent him off to the neighbors with milk and jam, and he liked to say that no client should be charged more than he or she could manage. As with his political career, Big Tom's legal career seemed like a way to reject his father's cruelty and reflect his mother's generosity, and whenever he did work for less than what it was worth, he felt that he was using his time and talents as she had taught him and as God wanted.

He taught his own son and daughters the same lessons. Big Tom wasn't the kind of man who boasted about never bringing his work home with him; he *always* brought his work home with him. He liked to rehearse his cases with his wife and children, encouraging them to ask questions and refusing to reveal which client was his until after his family had reached a verdict; his "dinner table jury" heard every case he ever tried in a courtroom. As Ellen, Fran, Hollis, and Thomas grew older, he gave them each a pocket copy of the Constitution for their birthdays, and they all did stints at their father's law office, making him coffee, running his errands, and doing his typing, a skill he never learned. Big Tom hired other runners, too, young men and women from around Lake Martin who learned a little law and a lot of liberalism during their time at the Zoo. He wasn't above asking them to oil the office plants (he liked the leaves and fronds to shine, and baby oil did the trick) or to throw on the yellow dog costume that he'd purchased for political rallies.

Post-campaign Tom still loved going to those, in costume or otherwise. Madolyn didn't want him running for public office again, but Radney raised money for other candidates, attended just about every event a Democrat held in a five-county radius, and kept ballots handy in case he needed to show anyone how to vote a straight Democratic ticket. He even occasionally snuck himself onto those ballots, but only for party leadership, never again for general office. But if Radney missed his political career, that loss was mitigated by how much the courtroom felt, to him, like the campaign trail. Like many politicians, he had always been extroverted and charismatic, and he loved the performative aspects of being a trial lawyer. After years of trying to win over tens of thousands of voters, he found it was easier to convince twelve jurors.

THE FAILURES OF BIG TOM'S POLITICAL CAREER HAD GIVEN HIM character; the success of his legal career gave him personality. His Democratic boosterism was less threatening from the sidelines, and his liberal streak was more tolerable after he'd helped your teenage son out of a legal jam. Tom soon settled into a Big Man in Town role, gathering over lunch most weekdays with a rotating roster of Tallapoosa County businessmen, lawyers, bankers, and mill managers. They'd call around in the morning, meet at a restaurant at noon, and gossip for an hour or two before going back to their offices. One by one, the restaurants in town kicked them out for staying too long, not ordering enough, or using language that was a little much for the other patrons. Finally, when there were no restaurants left in town large enough or accommodating enough to seat them, they bought a duplex next to the St. James Episcopal Church, remodeled it, hired a cooking staff, and incorporated themselves as "The Lunch Bunch." The dues were modest, and there were only two rules: every lunch started with a round of "Strike the Jury" to determine who would cover that day's tab (guests played, but never paid; last man standing got the check, second to last man got the tip); and every lunch ended with a few hands of blackjack.

Indulgent as it sometimes seemed, Big Tom's relentless sociability was part of what made him such a remarkable trial lawyer. He knew just about every power broker in the judicial circuits where he practiced, knew what they liked to drink and what they thought of their neighbors and whether they liked the guy who cut their lawn. But he also knew the guy who cut the lawn and what *he* liked to drink. Big Tom was a walking Rolodex of bias and conflict; he knew who had been fired from what, where someone had worked before she got her current job, why one person would pardon an aggravated assault and another would want the death penalty for petty theft. He was the lawyerly version of the "old woman" in W. J. Cash's *Mind of the South,* the one "with the memory like a Homeric bard's, capable of moving easily through a mass of names and relationships so intricate that the quantum theory is mere child's play in comparison." Big Tom was a genealogist and sociologist of everyone he'd ever met, and it made him, among other things, a master of the art of jury selection. Anyone who ever saw him in action marveled at how he turned voir dire into a family reunion, catching up and chatting with potential jurors as if they were his second cousins.

Selection, though, was just the start of his seduction. Like Clarence Darrow, Radney believed that "jurymen seldom convict a person they like, or acquit one that they dislike. The main work of a trial lawyer is to make a jury like his client, or, at least, to feel sympathy for him; facts regarding the crime are relatively unimportant." Radney knew getting the right people on the jury was only half the battle; the real trick was getting them to see the right version of the case. A Casanova of the courtroom, Big Tom managed to do it again and again. His juries might not have always liked his clients, but they sure liked him. He once had a jury slip him an envelope at the end of a trial; inside it was a birthday card, signed by all twelve of them.

For every case a lawyer wins, though, someone else loses, and for someone like Tom, who stacked up acquittals like firewood, there were plenty of opposing counsels and clients who resented not only the verdict but the lawyer who'd won it. Not everyone was charmed by Tom's "country lawyer shtick," as one detractor called his folksy style. In a small town, memories are long, and grudges last longer. Some people held them against Big Tom for his success, others for his self-promotion, still others for a certain profligacy in his personal life.

Because he would happily work with minority and indigent clients, Big Tom also took some flak for the people he represented, and once the Reverend Willie Maxwell came along, he took a lot more. It was one thing to defend the Reverend against a single murder charge; it was something else to help him make money and to make money off him. For his part, Radney didn't believe in asking potential clients whether they had done what they were accused of doing, and he didn't withhold an ounce of his talent from even the guiltiest among them. He'd challenge all the evidence he could to keep it from being admitted; if it was admitted anyway, he'd go after the person who'd collected it. When Big Tom was in charge, a jury was sure to hear about it if a toxicologist had degrees in zoology or a medical examiner had previously worked as a butcher. If a doctor's testimony was damning, Big Tom would come up with a long list of patients who were now deceased and then in court inquire one by one if the doctor had treated each person and, upon getting a yes, ask where that patient was now.

As Tom won judgment after judgment and helped clients avoid conviction after conviction, his practice grew—in size, in reputation, in settlements. He defended young boys in destruction of property cases and old men for public drunkenness; he prevented the state from trying a fourteen-year-old charged with homicide as an adult, and got a guy off a robbery charge even though he'd been caught holding a marked bill from the store's till. He took care of deeds, divorces, wills, and estates; defended county commissioners accused of accepting bribes; and sued doctors and hospitals for medical malpractice and wrongful death. He tried cases in traffic court and in the federal court of appeals. No task was too small, no odds were too long, and no amount of enmity people felt toward Tom mattered if they suddenly needed him on their side. Even the police officers in town, angry about the acquittals Radney sometimes won at their expense, forgave him whenever a friend or relative of theirs needed a good attorney.

All those years of representing Maxwell, in both civil and criminal trials, hadn't endeared Big Tom to anyone around Lake Martin, but it had helped him make his name as a lawyer who could handle any case. Which is why, on the day that a man named Robert Burns shot the Reverend in front of three hundred witnesses, his brother told him not to worry and promised, "Big Tom'll get you out of this."

# 11

# Peace and Goodwill

I T WAS A HUNDRED DEGREES ON THE DAY OF THE REVEREND Willie Maxwell's wake, a week after the one for his stepdaughter, in the middle of June 1977. Lightning flashed overhead during the fever break of a summer storm, and the wind tore a dead limb from a tree across the street from the House of Hutchinson Funeral Home, sending it crashing down through all the lower branches before hitting the ground. People arriving on foot hurried toward the funeral home doors holding on to their hats, and car after car pulled up in front of the same chapel where Maxwell had been gunned down days before. However much locals might have gone out of their way to avoid crossing paths with the Reverend during his lifetime, half of eastern Alabama showed up to his wake. "They might be coming to see if he is really dead," one person speculated. "Some people say he isn't, and some say that he will be back."

Outside House of Hutchinson, reporters hung around with their notebooks and cameras. A story that had simmered for seven years on the back roads of Coosa County was suddenly burning up the front pages of newspapers around the country, and journalists from all over were wandering around the funeral home parking lot, looking for sources and shade. There was Vern Smith, a writer for *Newsweek* who grew up in Natchez, Mississippi, and Mike Keza, the white photographer who came with him to Alex City to cover the case. There was Phyllis Wesley, with *The Montgomery Advertiser,* whose colleague Lou Elliott had been following the Maxwell case since Shirley's murder and was one of the few journalists to have interviewed the Reverend before he was shot. There was Harmon Perry, who had been the first black reporter for *The Atlanta Journal* and was now the Atlanta bureau chief for *Jet*. Alongside these and other out-of-towners were Jim Earnhardt and Alvin Benn, still tag-teaming coverage for *The Alexander City Outlook*.

Nearly everyone in the crowd outside House of Hutchinson refused to go on the record. Many of them didn't want to talk at all, those that did rarely consented to using their name, and what most of them claimed to know about the Reverend often turned out to be something they'd been told second or third or fourth hand. No one had seen the Reverend Maxwell's alleged voodoo room for themselves, but everyone knew someone who knew someone who'd seen it; everyone knew that Maxwell had been involved in the deaths of five of his family members and maybe some others too, but no one had any proof or knew exactly how he'd done it. That did not stop the press from writing their stories, of course, and the rumors that had been circulating around Alex City for years now found new homes between quotation marks. "Voodooist Is Slain at Ala. Funeral" read one headline; "Death of Voodoo Shaman Lets Town Breathe Easier" read another. One unnamed neighbor of the Reverend was quoted as saying that everyone was "rejoicing" because they'd been "scared to death of him"; another, also anonymous, said that after Maxwell's death "it was like a burden was lifted off the whole town."

But not everyone felt safer after the Reverend Willie Maxwell was killed. Some thought that he might come back from the dead to haunt or harm them, and some worried that he had left behind accomplices. "There's no reason for any joy," one woman said. "There might be somebody else involved and it wouldn't be safe to say anything about what happened." A few thought that the Reverend was innocent and that therefore the real criminal, or criminals, were still around. "Will Maxwell," a friend of his said, "was killed by public opinion. I hope now that he's gone, the investigators will get to work and really find out what happened to Shirley Ellington and who was responsible."

That sentiment was echoed by the Reverend's grieving family. When Alvin Benn interviewed Ophelia Maxwell for *The Alexander*

*City Outlook* at her home on the day after her husband's murder, she insisted on his innocence and said she felt as if she were "living in a nightmare." In addition to his widow, the Reverend had left behind several children, a grandchild, his mother, three sisters, three brothers, and various nieces and nephews; a great many of them had been witnesses to his murder. So had some of his colleagues from the ministry, the mill, and the quarry. To those who believed he was innocent, Maxwell had gone from being the victim of vicious rumors to the victim of a vicious murder.

"I just hate all this publicity," the Reverend's old friend Mac Thomas said. "I don't think this is helping anything." One of Maxwell's relatives, unable to avoid the scrum of journalists outside the funeral home, shouted at them instead, saying she was sick of hearing the word "voodoo" and warning them that the family would sue any reporter who printed anything slanderous.

It was just as hot on Thursday as it had been the day before at the wake, but there were more people at the funeral, and even more press. By noon, up at the junction where Highway 9 meets Highway 22, not far from where four of the Reverend's relatives had been found dead, lawmen leaned against their cars, smoking and watching the traffic heading toward the Peace and Goodwill Baptist Church. Many of them had worked on one case or another of Maxwell's relatives, and many of them were upset about his death—not because they grieved him, but because they felt they had been deprived of the chance to finally bring him to justice. Unlike all but one of the cases that preceded it, the death of Shirley Ann Ellington had been officially declared a homicide, the cause of death had been determined to be strangulation, and the Reverend had been the only suspect. The authorities were planning to charge him as soon as the coroner's report was certified.

But it was too late to charge the Reverend Willie Maxwell now, and the agents, deputies, sheriffs, and state troopers gathered that day were only there to maintain order at his funeral. Soon enough, they got back into their cars, followed the traffic to Peace and Goodwill, and split up to patrol the parking lot and the chapel. Captain Chapman, who had worked the Maxwell case for the Alabama Bureau of

Investigation—he was the investigator who had been so frustrated all the way back when Dorcas Anderson changed her testimony about the night that Mary Lou Maxwell died and whose partner had taken the testimony of the two would-be accomplices—had brought along his son, and the two of them stood by the door, watching the bottom of men's blazers to see if they flapped in the wind or stayed still, held down by the weight of a gun. At the start of the service, Chapman went inside to join the other officers, who fanned out to guard the pulpit and all three entrances to the sanctuary.

At the altar was a silvery-blue steel coffin, open for all to see the Reverend's body, draped partly by an American flag and surrounded by wreaths of red and white carnations. From a photograph on the front page of the funeral program, the much-avoided eyes of the Reverend stared at every mourner. Inside was the service order, the list of survivors, and a bit of verse that sometimes appeared in the obituaries of country preachers: "*Their trouble and sorrow into his ears had poured. The old, young, sick, healthy, poor, rich, dark, white and everyone. His mission finished, his reward ahead, in one quiet moment for the last time he bowed his head.*"

Ophelia was seated in the front row. She and the Reverend Maxwell's mother cried as a sheriff's deputy looked on from his place beside the pulpit, and every journalist that had descended on Alex City that week watched from the back of the sanctuary. The family had asked that the press be kept out, but the presiding pastor, the Reverend Chester Mardis, had declined to bar them from the service. Instead, Mardis, who was seventy-seven and had driven the eighty miles from Birmingham that morning to officiate, had welcomed the assembled reporters, telling them "we have nothing to hide" and then spelling his own name to make sure they all got it right in print.

Between the grieving relatives, the other mourners, the curiosity seekers, the press, and the police, there was not that much peace and goodwill that day at Peace and Goodwill. At one point during the service, a folding chair slid down from where it had been propped against a wall, clanging loudly against the ground and causing all the lawmen to reach for their guns. But no one was shot at the funeral of the man who was shot at a funeral. The choir sang a few songs, some scripture and psalms were read, prayers were offered, an assisting minister sang Thomas A. Dorsey's "The Lord Will Make a Way Somehow." The eulogy came last, and the Reverend Mardis preached on the tenth chapter of the Gospel of John, reminding the congregation that Jesus the Good Shepherd leads his flock, including the Reverend Maxwell, into eternal life. Mardis then compared Maxwell to Moses, "a murderer and a fugitive" whom God used to bring freedom to God's people. "The Devil couldn't take Moses from God," Reverend Mardis said to a chorus of amens. But when he added that the Devil couldn't take the Reverend from God either, the chorus quieted, and when he said that Maxwell would be coming back to judge those who had judged him, people all over the chapel shook their heads in disapproval or alarm, and one man said audibly, "I hope to hell not."

By three o'clock that afternoon, it was over. The pallbearers carried out the casket, which was driven down the road to the Peace and Goodwill Cemetery. At the graveside, Mardis offered a few more words, those gathered recited the Lord's Prayer, and the American flag was removed, folded, and presented to Ophelia before the casket was lowered into the ground. The Reverend Willie Maxwell was buried less than a mile from his home and only a few feet from the final resting places of Mary Lou Maxwell, Dorcas Maxwell, John Columbus Maxwell, and James Hicks.

TOM RADNEY DIDN'T GO TO WILLIE MAXWELL'S FUNERAL, BUT he spoke with a lot of the journalists who were covering it. He wanted everyone to know that he wouldn't have defended the Reverend for the murder of Shirley Ann Ellington, but he also wanted to remind them that Maxwell had never been convicted and in fact had been charged only once in any of the deaths that people so persistently associated with him. The Reverend, his former lawyer was quick to tell you, had been acquitted of his first wife's murder, John Columbus drank himself to death, Abram Anderson had a degenerative disease and died of pneumonia, Dorcas Maxwell had died of respiratory distress, and as for James Hicks, well, he seemed to have died of nothing at all. In a song that he would very soon cease to sing, Big Tom pointed out that, legally speaking, the Reverend was and always had been entirely innocent.

While Tom was busy publicly defending his old client, he was privately trying to figure out how to defend his new one. He had known nothing of Robert Burns before the Reverend's murder; unlike his victim, Burns had not previously been notorious around town. In fact, he hadn't always been around town at all. Born and raised in Alex City, Burns had left after high school and moved to Cleveland, where he drove a truck, and then to Chicago, where he drove a city bus. While there, he was drafted into the army and served in the Fourth Infantry Division during the Vietnam War.

After he was discharged, he met his wife, Vera, and the couple returned to Alex City to settle down. She got a job with Head Start, he resumed his work as a long-haul trucker, and the two of them moved into a house near Horseshoe Bend. They moved home to be near family, including one of Robert's brothers, Nathaniel, who had married and then divorced the future Ophelia Maxwell. As a result, Ophelia's children, including Shirley Ann Ellington, were Robert Burns's kin, and he was close with them. On the night that Shell was killed, Burns had been hauling a load in Ohio; when the dispatchers reached him and he learned what had happened, he got into his truck and drove the eight hundred miles home.

By the time that Big Tom met him, Robert Burns was a tall, trim, handsome, self-possessed thirty-six-year-old. He and Vera had been married eight years, and together they were raising her teenage son from a previous marriage and fostering a severely disabled seven-year-old girl whose mother had rubella during pregnancy. By all appearances, Burns was an unassuming, hardworking, tenderhearted family man, right up until he pulled a gun and, from three feet away, with a whole chapel watching, shot and killed the Reverend Maxwell.

In the weeks after Maxwell's funeral, the temperature in Alexander City barely fell below one hundred degrees. June's hot spell turned to July's heat wave; the hay fields that generally had two cuttings by midsummer hadn't yet had one, cotton was a third of its usual height, the corn had dried up entirely, and most of the soybean crop hadn't even been sown. Dust devils swirled along the sides of the highways. The sun rose up every morning into an already smoldering day, scorched everything beneath it, and set into a stifling night. Clouds occasionally formed and threatened, but the rains never came. By the third week of July, the drought was so severe that President Carter declared both Coosa County and Tallapoosa County, not to mention the rest of Alabama and Georgia, disaster areas.

The heat that summer made the farmers crazy and made the loggers crazy and made the mill workers crazy and basically made everyone crazy except the iceman and the kids down in Lake Martin, which is how, one day, Big Tom settled on his defense of Robert Burns. In the middle of July, when Burns was indicted by a grand jury in Tallapoosa County, he did as Radney had told him and pleaded not guilty by reason of insanity. Then Burns walked out of the courthouse in blue bib overalls and a Caterpillar baseball cap on a ten-thousand-dollar bond.

INSANITY ISN'T AN EASY THING TO PROVE, AND IT IS OFTEN THE defense of last resort. The belief that madness can be exculpatory is an ancient one—so ancient that it was carved into the Code of Hammurabi seventeen hundred years before the birth of Christ, alongside the notion of proportional retaliation, *lex talionis,* an eye for an eye. But by the time Tom Radney invoked it, the insanity defense had been out of favor for a century. Queen Victoria tried to stifle it in the mid-nineteenth century, out of fear that it would encourage would-be assassins; a hundred years later, President Richard Nixon tried to have it outlawed. Too many defendants had turned out to be insane only until acquittal, and prosecutors and psychiatrists alike had come to worry that the defense was just a way of letting murderers get away with murder; around the country, there were examples of defendants sent to state mental hospitals after a jury decided they were insane, only to have the hospital's superintendent and staff release them after diagnosing them as sane. In response, some states—Idaho, Kansas, Montana, and Utah—banned the insanity plea entirely. But Alabama still allowed it, and Big Tom had decided that it was his best bet. In reality, it was probably his *only* bet. His client had brought a pistol into a chapel, shot a man three times in front of hundreds of people, then confessed to the police not once but twice before the body of his victim had even grown cold. A first-year law student could have successfully prosecuted the case in his sleep.

Tom's opposing counsel in the murder trial of Robert Burns was not a first-year law student, to put it mildly. By the time the trial started, Thomas F. Young had already served sixteen years as district attorney and was just starting another six-year term. He, too, went by Tom, and he was said to have tried more criminal cases than any other DA in Alabama history. He also had something to prove when it came to the Maxwell case: he'd been the district attorney who failed to bring timely charges against the Reverend in the death of his first wife. He and Tom Radney had faced off in fifty or so other murder trials, and although both men had respected records, they had very different styles.

"Radney is silk, and Young is sandpaper," Alvin Benn wrote in *The Alexander City Outlook*. Benn was a man well acquainted with contrasts: a Jewish reporter raised in Pennsylvania Amish country who came south to cover the civil rights movement and stayed to raise a family, he'd listened nervously as KKK members denounced Zionist Jews at a rally but then took him out drinking, and he interviewed the Reverend Martin Luther King Jr. and the police commissioner Bull Connor for the same story. But even Benn had seldom seen two men diverge as dramatically as the two Toms. Young wasn't about to lose a murder case when he had hundreds of witnesses, and Radney wasn't about to lose a case with the whole state and half the nation watching. Despite what potboilers and Perry Mason would lead you to believe, Benn said, "most trials resemble warmed-over grits and it takes some doing to stay awake." But the Burns case was different.

From the beginning, Big Tom knew there were two things he needed the jury to know, and two things he needed them not to know. The two things he needed them not to know were that his client had a criminal record and that he had confessed to killing Maxwell. Tom Young claimed to be in possession of an FBI file indicating that Burns had been arrested for assault and second-degree murder in Ohio, shoplifting in Maryland, and aggravated assault in Illinois. But the file was murky—the murder case had been discharged, and next to the assault charge, which lacked a case number, someone had written "incorrect," and no final disposition was indicated—so Radney filed a preemptive motion to have any mention of it excluded from the trial. The confessions were similarly complicated. Two police officers inside the chapel had heard Burns as he stood over the body of the Reverend Willie Maxwell and said, "You have mistreated my family long enough," but to Radney's mind that was closer to eavesdropping than to obtaining a confession. Burns had also confessed in the backseat of the police cruiser as he was being driven away from the funeral home—"I had to do it," he said, "and if I had it to do over, I'd do it again"—but he hadn't been read his rights until he arrived at the police station. Worse, the man to whom Burns confessed was his brother, who, although he had been a deputy sheriff in years past, had been deputized only for the purpose of driving suspects and prisoners in custody and wasn't on duty the day of the funeral.

Even if Big Tom could keep the confessions and the criminal record out of the courtroom, he would not exactly be sitting pretty—there was still the matter of those three hundred witnesses—but at least he'd be able to make his own case. That involved making sure the jurors entered deliberations with two things foremost in their minds: voodoo and Vietnam. To win, Tom had decided, he needed the Reverend Willie Maxwell to be the witchiest witch doctor and voodooiest voodoo priest the South had ever known—a man so mysteriously powerful that no force of law could touch him and so feared that no neighbor would look him in the eye. And just as Tom needed his former client to be exceptionally bad, he needed his current one to be exceptionally good: a war hero whose patriotic bravery halfway across the world had made his sensitive heart and susceptible mind vulnerable to trauma back home.

For his part, though, Tom Young needed only one thing: he needed Robert Burns to seem sane. To that end, he filed a motion to require the production of any and all medical reports on the defendant, and he began casting aspersions on the insanity defense more generally, publicly deriding the "revolving door" at Bryce Hospital, the state psychiatric institution, through which, he claimed, those acquitted by reason of insanity rapidly reentered society. There was no reason to believe Bryce was any worse in this respect than any other state institution at the time, but it was true that there was nothing a clinician could do except release a patient-prisoner who was diagnosed sane, no matter how short his stay in the facility or how heinous the crime that had sent him there. Radney responded with a motion alleging that Young's remarks had already poisoned the jury pool. All that summer and into early fall, the two lawyers sent competing motions volleying back and forth. Finally, on the last Monday of September, seven years after the brutal murder of the first Mrs. Willie Maxwell, Tom Young and Tom Radney walked through the doors of the courthouse in Alexander City to begin trying *State of Alabama v. Robert Lewis Burns*.

# 12

# Tom v. Tom

JAMES ALBERT AVARY WAS NOT THE KIND OF JUDGE WHO CARED to stand on ceremony. He didn't like to wear a robe in the courtroom, and he very much liked to smoke a cigar in his chambers, tapping the ashes into a designated drawer in his desk. Born just across the state line in La Grange, Georgia, Avary had attended prep school in New York City, studied religion at Princeton (he later wrote a "Guide to the Redneck Riviera" for a reunion of his classmates), then returned to the South to study law at Emory. After a few years with a firm in Atlanta, he'd opened his own practice in Lanett, Alabama, and ran it until he was elected judge of the Fifth Judicial Circuit. That election had taken place the year before the Burns trial; the man Avary beat for the position was Tom Young.

Mindful of the widespread interest in the case now facing him, Avary had wanted to allow cameras in the courtroom during the Burns proceedings. According to Alabama law, though, all parties had to consent, and Tom Young didn't want anyone taking photographs or filming while the trial was going on. *The Alexander City Outlook* was eager for visuals of some kind, so when Jim Earnhardt mentioned that his cousin Mary Lynn Baxter, who was already working for the *Outlook,* had a knack for drawing, she was promptly commissioned to make courtroom sketches. Judge Avary later relaxed the rules to allow photography during recesses, but Baxter's pictures constitute some of the few images of the trial as it unfolded.

Court was called to order at nine in the morning on September 26, 1977. It was a maddeningly hot day for so late in the month, made worse by the fact that the air-conditioning wasn't working and by the size of the crowd in the courtroom. Five of the several dozen prospective jurors had to be dismissed right away, because, in addition to being summoned, they'd been subpoenaed: four were character witnesses for the defendant, and one was an eyewitness to the shooting. Those dismissals were telling. As with any small-town trial, the lawyers had to weigh not whether people knew one another but how well, in what way, and with what degree of sympathy or antipathy. But Tom Young and his assistant DA, E. Paul Jones, also hoped to start making their case right away by using the jury selection to undermine the insanity plea. They asked first if any of the potential jurors had heard talk that "this man should be turned loose," and next if they would be able to judge the testimony of "so-called expert witnesses." Big Tom, who made a habit of lighting his own fuse on his way into the courtroom, immediately exploded with objections: the state was making speeches; the state was slandering his witnesses before they'd even had a chance to testify. Judge Avary waved him off and let Young and Jones proceed.

When his turn came, Big Tom set about trying to engineer the kind of jury that he thought he could win over. That meant people who believed in expert testimony and the insanity defense, but most of all it meant twelve white men: men, because Radney thought they wouldn't be as squeamish at the idea of a righteous murder, and white, so they had no connection to Maxwell or his grieving family and could be made to see the situation as Burns had—namely, that shooting the Reverend had been a necessary and courageous act.

In the end, Big Tom got what he wanted: it was two rows of six white men each who arranged themselves in the jury box. Immediately afterward, Judge Avary looked at his watch, saw that it was half past eleven, and recessed the court. With the jury out getting lunch under the watchful eye of the bailiff, Big Tom and Tom Young approached the bench and promptly started bickering. Radney brought up two of his outstanding motions. The first was for specific relief: he didn't want the state saying anything about "revolving doors" at Bryce Hospital, and he didn't want Young undermining the insanity plea by calling it an illegitimate defense. The second had to do with Burns's alleged criminal record. Quite aside from the issue of its questionable accuracy, Big Tom argued, such a record was inadmissible in a case where the defendant was pleading insanity. Judge Avary observed that keeping it out of the courtroom could be tricky if Radney planned to call any character witnesses, but when Avary tried asking Young about his plans for cross-examining those witnesses, Young lost his temper and exclaimed, "I don't like being terrorized at this point, because I don't know what's going to come out!" Then Young harangued the judge about the abuses of the insanity defense until Radney lost *his* temper and snapped, "Your Honor and I don't have time to listen to your speeches right now."

All of this yielded only partial resolution. With a lot of carts getting before a lot of horses, Judge Avary decided that the accused had a right to argue any defense, including insanity, and that the criminal record was out for the time being but could be revisited when the character witnesses began testifying. And with that, Avary decreed the lunch break over.

THE JURORS AND SPECTATORS RETURNED FATTED AND FED, A little sleepy in that postprandial way, sticky from the heat and sagging somewhat in the court's hard-back benches and chairs. The defense took their seats on the left side of the courtroom. Tom Radney's co-counsel, Lee Sims, a lawyer from Dadeville, had two stacks of law books on the table in front of him, seven volumes high. Tom sat beside him with a few pieces of paper and a smile. Robert Burns sat to the left of his lawyers, his posture relaxed, his expression serene. He was wearing light slacks and a hatch-mark-patterned shirt; the loudest thing about him was his lapels.

On the other side of the courtroom, nearest the twelve jurors and next to the area reserved for the press, were Tom Young and E. Paul Jones, and they offered the first opening statement. Young began by reminding the gentlemen of the jury that earlier in the year "a cold-blooded murder was committed in the presence of several hundred people." Now, Young said, the state would prove Robert Burns had committed that murder and that he was "nothing but a one-man lynch mob" who had no place in a law-abiding town like Alexander City.

Young got out all of 143 words before Big Tom objected. The district attorney had started to say something about the defendant's plea, and Radney jumped in to protest that it wasn't the place of the prosecutor to comment on the defense. Judge Avary sustained the objection, and Young, already sweating through his pale blue suit, went back to his remarks. "You are here to judge guilt or innocence," he would remind the jury, and asked them to deliver a verdict "you can sleep with, not for tonight or tomorrow night, but for the rest of your life."

"No, sir, we object to this," Big Tom interrupted again, this time to quibble over the responsibility of the jury in the present case. His next objection was followed by one from his co-counsel, and then another from him. Tom Young could hardly get through a sentence without one member of the defense team or the other rising from behind their table to object. Young was only a few minutes into his opening statement when he turned to the jury to complain: "I expect a lot of muddy water to be poured into the stream of justice here today!"

Big Tom was happy to have stalled the prosecution's engine at the start, but it wouldn't take long for Young to return the favor. Radney liked to deliver opening statements like a bard launching into an epic poem, narrating the life of his client all the way from birth to whatever troubles and injustices and turns of fate had resulted in everyone convening in the courtroom that day. In keeping with that strategy, Big Tom started by introducing Robert Burns as a local boy, born and raised in the northern end of Tallapoosa County. Then he walked the jury through Burns's time driving buses and trucks in Cleveland and Chicago and serving his country in Vietnam—Big Tom paused there to dwell on his client's bravery and the horrific violence he had seen overseas—and then returned the war hero to his home county, where, Big Tom mentioned, Burns had a lot of kin, including his former sister-in-law, Ophelia Maxwell.

At the sound of that surname, Tom Young jumped out of his seat. "Mr. Radney," he said sharply, "is obviously about to start out on the route that the court cautioned him about back here. He's about to go into a matter that is not in any way related to the case." Young knew that Big Tom was planning to try two cases simultaneously: defending his current client, and prosecuting his former one. Undeterred by the objection, Radney thanked Judge Avary for overruling it and then offered the jury a word to the wise. "I have to give you a little sideline," he said: "When Mr. Young stands up like that, it means he is getting a little hot under the collar."

"I was telling you, before I was so rudely interrupted," Big Tom continued, returning to his rehearsed remarks, and then went on to start enumerating all of the relatives the Reverend Willie Maxwell had allegedly killed, whereupon the district attorney interrupted him again. "Alright, if the court please," Young snapped, "the state asks for a mistrial."

It was the first of many times that the state would plead with Judge Avary to end the trial, claiming it was already too compromised to continue. After that initial request, Young asked for a mistrial four more times during Big Tom's opening statement alone. When four of those requests were denied, Young asked for a recess, which was also denied, and then he objected and was overruled.

While Tom Young was getting nowhere, Big Tom was just getting started. He had no intention of trying to deny the undeniable, he said. He was not going to claim that Robert Burns hadn't killed Willie Maxwell—only that Robert Burns had not been Robert Burns when he'd done so. Bent on establishing his ability to look the facts of a case squarely in the eye, Big Tom ended his opening statement with a grandiose admission: "We admit he killed him, and we admit he shot him three times, and we admit he shot him wherever Mr. Young says he shot him, in the head, the stomach, or wherever he says he shot him, and we admit he died as a result of the gunshot wounds that Robert Lewis Burns put in him." The defense admitted all of that but then reminded the jury that none of those facts meant the defendant belonged in prison.

With that much established, the state called its first witness, Dr. Carlos Rabren, the toxicologist who had autopsied the Reverend Maxwell. Dr. Rabren outlined his background and training and then testified about the three bullets he had removed from the Reverend's body. Everything was going well for Tom Young until the cross-examination began, at which point it came out that Rabren had worked for the Department of Toxicology for fifteen years, during which time he had handled not only the autopsy of Willie Maxwell but also those of several of his relatives. Sims, who was handling the cross for the defense team, began asking Rabren about one mysteriously dead body after another. Had the doctor investigated the death of Mary Lou Maxwell? Tom Young objected. Had the doctor investigated the death of John Columbus Maxwell? Tom Young objected again. "They are throwing mud and everything else," Young complained, not so much to convince the judge as the jury, "trying to cover up the real issues of this trial."

Judge Avary overruled the objections, and Sims went back to his inventory, using the prosecution's own witness to impugn the character of the murder victim. "Isn't it true," he asked, "that the second Mrs. Maxwell was found, along with the first Mrs. Maxwell, behind the wheel of an automobile, dead?" Well, not exactly, Dr. Rabren explained; the second Mrs. Maxwell had been found on the floorboards. Sims asked next about the death of James Hicks. Dr. Rabren said that he hadn't worked that case but that he knew something about the state's findings, or lack of findings. "Sir," he started to explain, "the department did not issue a cause of death in this case. I don't know if it's a homicide or not—"

"Voodoo, it was voodoo," Sims shouted, throwing one fist theatrically into the air. Tom Young objected again, but the black cat was out of the bag. People all around Lake Martin had been spreading rumors about the Reverend for seven years, salacious headlines had flown out over the wires the day that Maxwell had been shot, and any chance the state had of shooing all that gossip out of the courtroom had now vanished. Of Big Tom's two strategies for the trial—turning it into a referendum on the victim instead of the accused and turning the accused into a hero—he'd accomplished the first one within an hour, and not a single one of Tom Young's thirty objections during the testimony of his own witness could stop it.

THE SAME THING HAPPENED WHEN THE STATE PUT ITS SECOND witness on the stand. Tellis Hudson, another member of the Auburn crime crew, explained his ballistic analysis, which showed that the shooter had been only three feet away from the Reverend when he fired. But during cross-examination, Big Tom asked Hudson how long he'd been with the lab and then asked about the death of James Hicks. Unlike Rabren, Hudson had been involved in that case, and he confirmed that Hicks's cause of death had never been determined. "Your investigation revealed that he was a strong, healthy, twenty-two-year-old that worked in the cotton mill all night, and was on his way home and was found in his car dead, and you don't know what caused it," Radney said. "Is that correct?"

It was, Hudson said. Big Tom, never one to stop when things were going his way, asked the witness about a box of black pepper that had allegedly been in the Reverend's pocket at the time of his death, about the blood that had supposedly been painted across the front door of the Reverend's house, and about the chickens rumored to be hanging upside down from the pecan trees in the Reverend's front yard. Hudson testified that he hadn't heard about any of those things, but it didn't matter; now the jury had. Another witness, the Reverend Burpo, who had delivered the eulogy for Shirley Ann, testified that he hadn't heard those stories either but then conceded during cross-examination that Maxwell had lost all of his churches because of rumors that he'd killed his relatives.

The defense was well on its way to making Maxwell into the most notorious voodoo preacher since Marie Laveau. But Tom wanted to make another point, too—that Robert Burns was a good man who'd returned from Vietnam with a troubled mind—and when a later witness for the prosecution, Patricia Burns Pogue, took the stand, she accidentally helped him do so. Pogue, who was another one of

Robert Burns's nieces, had been sitting with him in the second pew of the House of Hutchinson chapel during Shirley's funeral and testified that he had cried the whole length of it. Burns had been so emotional that he couldn't talk. She shouted at him after he fired the first shot, she said, but he seemed to be in some kind of trance and wouldn't even look at her. And so it went: one by one, the witnesses for the prosecution were sworn in, took the stand, and wound up sounding like witnesses for the defense.

But then came James Ware. A veteran of the navy, Ware was one of the first African American police officers ever hired in Tallapoosa County; he had worked for the Alexander City Police Department for twelve years and, unlike the other witnesses, had plenty of experience testifying in court. On the day of the Reverend's murder, he had been directing traffic outside Shirley Ann Ellington's funeral and had raced inside at the sound of the first shot. He had heard Robert Burns confess clear as day in the chapel, then heard him do so again in the squad car on the way to the police station.

If any of that came out, Big Tom knew, Officer James Ware would definitely not sound like a witness for the defense. Any kind of confession would have been a problem for Radney, but Burns's particular words—"You have mistreated my family long enough" and "If I had it to do over, I'd do it again"—definitely did not sound like those of someone in the grips of temporary insanity. On the defensive for the first time since the trial started, Big Tom objected at almost every syllable from Young or Ware. When the scene in the squad car was looming, he asked Judge Avary to remove the jurors from the courtroom before Ware finished his testimony so that the court could resolve the question of whether the confessions were admissible, given the peculiar circumstances under which they were obtained.

Judge Avary assented, and once the jurors were gone, the reporters and spectators listened attentively as the lawyers promptly picked up arguing where they had left off before lunch. Big Tom contended that because Robert Burns hadn't been read his rights until an hour after he confessed, and because the only two people who heard him do so were officers of the law, the confessions were improperly obtained and therefore inadmissible. Tom Young countered that both of them had been offered voluntarily and spontaneously to anyone within hearing distance, and thus they were perfectly proper. Furthermore, Young said, although one of the people who had heard the confession, Robert Burns's brother William, might have worked for the sheriff's department in the past, he was not doing so at the time of the murder, and therefore any confession to him was admissable.

With the jury still out of the courtroom, the state put William Burns on the stand, where, to Young's dismay, it came out that the confession hadn't exactly been spontaneous after all. William had actually asked, "Robert, why did you do it?" Worse than that, when Young tried to establish William's employment record, claiming the man hadn't worked for the Sheriff in years, the court learned that, in fact, he occasionally still volunteered for the department. Tom Radney then pointed out that William had been allowed to remove his brother's handcuffs, something no one who wasn't an officer of the law would have been permitted to do. Judge Avary, convinced, ruled the confessions inadmissible.

BY THEN IT WAS FOUR O'CLOCK IN THE AFTERNOON, AND TOM Young wanted to cut his losses and call it a day. But Big Tom, who thought of jury trials like stage plays, wanted to make sure the scene changed when he thought it should, and he didn't want the jury spending all night wondering exactly what his client had said in the squad car on the way to the police station. So Big Tom objected to recessing so early in the afternoon, and Judge Avary agreed that they ought to keep going. The jury was brought back, Officer Ware went back to testifying, and Tom Young went back to trying six ways 'til Sunday to sneak the confessions into the courtroom, while Big Tom went back to objecting as steadily as a metronome.

Forty-five minutes later, everyone had had enough. Before gaveling the court to a close for the day, Judge Avary reminded the jury that they would be sequestered for the night—an unusual occurrence in a circuit where charges often ended in pleas and most trials were over in a matter of hours. With Judge Avary's apologies, the jurors weren't even allowed to go home to get clothes. Instead, they made lists of what they needed, and deputies went to each of their homes to fetch the various items from their wives and girlfriends. Judge Avary asked them to ignore the news on the television and radio and then sent them to get some rest just up the street, where Highway 22 meets Highway 280, at the Horseshoe Bend Motel.

# 13

# The Man from Eclectic

A T LEAST THE AIR-CONDITIONING WAS WORKING. THE COURT-room was cooler on Tuesday than it had been on Monday, but it was still just as packed with spectators. The rest of the Alexander City Courthouse was packed, too: the defense and the prosecution had subpoenaed each other's witnesses to keep them away from the trial until they took the stand, so the meeting room was full of the state's witnesses, the library was full of law enforcement, and the defense witnesses were milling about the hallway. Tom Young was convinced that some of them could hear the proceedings over the sound of the air-conditioning, and he kept his eye on one defense witness in particular, who seemed to be skulking about within earshot.

Early in that morning's proceedings, the state called to the stand the only other African American officer on the Alexander City Police force: a man named Joe Ennis Berry, who, along with James Ware, had been assigned to direct traffic outside House of Hutchinson the day of the Reverend's murder. Berry had been serving his country since he was a teenager. At sixteen, he'd passed himself off as eighteen, enlisting in the army early enough to follow paratroopers onto the beaches of Normandy and then serving in the air force before coming home to Alabama. In 1966, a time when few law enforcement outfits in the South were interested in integrating their ranks, the mayor of Alexander City called Berry up and asked him to join the police force.

Officer Berry had been with the department ever since, so when the defense team began to cross-examine him, they asked about the police investigations of the deaths of Mary Lou Maxwell, John Columbus Maxwell, Dorcas Anderson Maxwell, James Hicks, and then finally Shirley Ann Ellington. Tom Young objected to almost every question and again called for a mistrial, but Judge Avary overruled him.

In response, Tom Young called Officer Ware back to the stand, and hoping to figure out a way to finally get in a word about Robert Burns's confessions, he asked once more about the day that the Reverend Maxwell was shot. Tom Radney promptly interrupted him: "Just a minute, Mr. Young, you shut your mouth for one second."

"Well, I think—" Young said.

"Shut your mouth," Radney shouted. "I mean for you to shut your mouth."

"You go to hell," Young answered.

Judge Avary, used to playing referee for his two young daughters, Pye and Scottie, called a time-out for Tom and Tom. He sent them back to their respective tables, gave them a few minutes to cool off, and then began reprimanding the prosecutor. "Mr. Young," he said, "we have been over this, time and time and time again, about this statement. And I have ruled it out." Radney, playing the part of the munificent colleague, told the judge that he did not want a mistrial, just to continue so that his client's name could be cleared. Avary decided to proceed and was admonishing the attorneys to conduct themselves appropriately when Young interrupted him: "Your Honor, how can a man conduct himself in that manner when he is talked to like a dog by the defense attorney?"

Judge Avary had the jury removed from the courtroom, and then he gave the lawyers what for. He should have let those television cameras in after all, he told them; maybe then they wouldn't be making such fools of themselves. The trial had turned into a "carnival" and a "circus," and he pleaded with Radney and Young to be professional. The same went for the press and the spectators, who had already been called to order countless times by the increasingly beleaguered judge. Two hundred people had come to watch the trial of Robert Burns, and the Alexander City Courthouse was packed tight as a box of crayons. The onlookers gasped at the coroners, laughed at witnesses, and whispered among themselves during any new testimony, their benches squeaking every time they leaned over to talk with their neighbors. Again and again, the judge had asked them to quiet down. Enough was enough, he declared: from the attorneys on down, everyone had to behave.

HAVING SHAMED HIS COURTROOM INTO TEMPORARY DOCILITY, Judge Avary brought the jury back into the box, and soon the last of the state's ten witnesses took the stand. This was Jimmy Burns, one of Ophelia's sons, who testified, as expected, that he had seen his uncle Robert shoot and kill his stepfather at Shirley Ann's funeral. That was a fact no one disputed, including the defense, and the courtroom, only a few minutes ago nearly raucous, now threatened to grow bored. But during his cross-examination Jimmy Burns said something that made everyone bolt up in their seats. At Shirley's wake, Jimmy said, the family had learned that a man from the nearby town of Eclectic was going around saying that the Reverend Maxwell had tried to hire him to kill her.

Like the person from Porlock, the man from Eclectic interrupted the morning's proceedings dramatically and irrevocably. As it turned out, that man was named Alphonso Murphy, and he actually lived closer to Wetumpka now, southwest of Lake Martin in Elmore County. He was twenty-four years old and had run a saw on the Reverend's pulpwooding crew for a month. He'd quit when he learned about his employer's sordid past and began to wonder who all the Reverend might hold insurance on and whether he might be the next person found dead.

Instead, five months later, Murphy testified in court, the Reverend came by his house to say, "I'm pretty sure you done heard talk about me." Then Maxwell told him that he would make it worth his while to murder his stepdaughter. "I can give it to you any way you want it," the Reverend said. "Give it to you in cash, or a new car, or help buy you a place to put your house on." The fee was negotiable, and so was the exact nature of the job: "I can let you do it all, you can either kill her or, if you don't want to kill her, then I just want you to pretend that you wrecked the car."

Tom Young hadn't wanted Murphy anywhere near the courtroom, but Tom Radney couldn't wait to get him on the stand. He was the first witness the defense called, and he offered the most salacious testimony of the trial, as well as the closest thing to a theory of the crimes that had ever been made public. According to Murphy, the Reverend said that Shirley would be dead before she was placed in the car and suggested that Alphonso give himself a few cuts so that the "accident" would seem more realistic. All Murphy needed to do, the Reverend said, was stay there until the police arrived at the scene. That is, unless he had his own domestic issues or worried about being betrayed. "If you would be afraid of your wife telling it," the Reverend advised Murphy, "I would suggest you put her in there and knock her off, too."

IN ONLY A FEW MINUTES OF TESTIMONY, ALL THE RUMORS OF voodoo drained from the courtroom. There were no poisons or powders, no curses or charms or spells. Evil acts that for seven years had seemed supernatural now suddenly seemed all too human: a man had knocked on the door of another man and asked him to help commit murder. The collective gasp first elicited by the man from Eclectic turned into a communal whisper as the gallery recalled all of the other suspicious accidents and began to speculate about who might have helped with those.

After his examination of Murphy, Tom Radney called to the stand the one person in the courthouse who would not have been surprised by the testimony of the man from Eclectic: ABI agent James Abbett, who had taken similar statements years before from two other men about the death of James Hicks. Abbett had also been the one to interview Alphonso Murphy, and the two and a half pages of notes he had taken during that conversation proved to be far more detailed than Murphy's testimony that day in court.

According to Abbett's official investigative notes, Murphy reported the exact date of the Reverend's terrible offer: it was Thursday, May 19, and "Preacher Maxwell" had come by his house in a two-door 1974 Gran Torino to offer him a house or a trailer or cash if he would help kill the man's stepdaughter by the middle of the following month. The Reverend Maxwell claimed that Shirley had been trying to poison him with some kind of capsules and that she "had been going around asking people why he was not dead."

Paranoid and pressed for time, the Reverend had said that in addition to whatever payment Murphy wanted up front, he could have some of the insurance money that Maxwell would collect after Shirley's death. He told Murphy that he had already picked out a place to stage the accident—a spot near Wind Creek State Park, a camping area on the western shore of Lake Martin. There were plenty of secluded roads into, out of, and along the park to leave a car, and it was conveniently situated between Eclectic and Alexander City. A few days later, when the Reverend returned to see what Alphonso had decided, Murphy turned him down, refusing to play any role in the murder.

The defense couldn't have asked for a better story, or a better witness to deliver it to the jury. Abbett, who would go on to be elected to six terms as sheriff of Tallapoosa County, was professional, thorough, and authoritative. After his testimony, Radney and Young were no longer really trying *State of Alabama v. Robert Burns.* They were arguing *The People v. Willie Maxwell,* and in that trial every term of the real one was inverted: the Reverend, who had been shot and killed, was not a victim but a cold-blooded murderer; Burns, who per three hundred witnesses plus himself actually was a cold-blooded murderer, was instead a righteous vigilante, the one man in a terrorized town brave enough to do what needed to be done.

Not that anyone could come right out and say any of this, of course. The man from Eclectic went back to Wetumpka, Abbett came down off the stand, and the trial—whichever one it was—went on. Radney called the first of his two expert witnesses, a man named Julian Woodhouse, who worked at the East Alabama Mental Health Center in Opelika. Woodhouse was thirty-one and had studied psychology at New Mexico State University, then earned a master's degree in clinical psychology at Florida State University. He'd completed an internship in clinical psychology at the University of Texas, worked in the forensic psychology unit of the Florida State Hospital, and completed his course work for a doctorate but hadn't actually finished his dissertation. Like Robert Burns's brother Deputy William Burns, who wasn't really a sheriff's deputy, Dr. Woodhouse was not quite a doctor.

"I understand he is not a doctor," Young objected, the first time that Radney tried to suggest he was one. Oh, for heaven's sake, Radney countered; with all but the dissertation done, it was a distinction without a difference. Never mind that his witness had not yet gotten his degree, Big Tom maintained that the man was more than qualified to have administered and read the psychological tests to which Burns had been subjected. Radney agreed to call Julian "Mr. Woodhouse" rather than "Doctor," but within a few questions he'd forgotten the agreement and went right back to inflating his witness's credentials. "Now, Doctor," Big Tom said, and then, "excuse me, Julian," before having Woodhouse recount his extensive clinical work, including a summer at the Veterans Administration Hospital in St. Petersburg, Florida, and additional studies in England.

Young objected again. "If the Court please," he said, trying the new tack of politeness, "I don't think the gentleman is a doctor, and I know Mr. Radney wants to give all his witnesses the prestige of doctor, but Mr. Woodhouse has testified that he is not a doctor." The objection was sustained, and Woodhouse went back to what he was trying to say about the mental health of the defendant. He had evaluated Robert Burns twice that summer, for three hours each time, administering six psychological tests during the first and second week of July. For each test, the witness explained the general methodology and then the specific findings to the jury; as often as he could, Radney asked "Dr." Woodhouse to do the honors. Young objected and objected and objected, then finally gave up. Radney was an expert at the game of repeating something until it became true. By the end of Julian's testimony, in a capitulation itself worthy of a psychologist's explanation, even Tom Young was calling the witness "Dr. Woodhouse."

And when, at the end of what he had made seem like the longest, most rigorous examination ever undertaken of a human psyche, Radney asked his expert witness to describe the defendant's state of mind on the day of the shooting, it was "Dr." Woodhouse who answered: "When Robert Lewis Burns pulled the trigger on that day, he was suffering from disease of the mind, which prevented him from being able to choose from right and wrong." Radney, wanting Woodhouse to say more, asked if "irresistible impulse" was an accurate term for what Burns had experienced at the funeral home. Woodhouse agreed that it was and added that he had diagnosed Mr. Burns with "transient situational disorder."

Radney, having gotten what he wanted from Woodhouse, called to the stand his second expert witness, Dr. Frances Goodrich Gunnels. Gunnels was an old friend of Big Tom's from the Alexander City junior college, where he occasionally taught politics and history, and she had chaired the social sciences division and headed the psychology department. Young was furious when she took the stand, but, strangely, not about the obvious conflict of interest. Gunnels was the witness he had become convinced was trying to eavesdrop earlier in the trial, so he asked for the jury to be dismissed and, once they were, became apoplectic. He must have been worried that the second of Big Tom's expert witnesses was trying to make sure her testimony matched that of his first or cribbing answers for any technical questions, but instead of explaining his actual worries, he raised his fist at the judge.

"I approached the bench yesterday, and advised the Court, and the Court knows, that I was going to object to this witness, Dr. Gunnels, testifying in this case at all," he told Judge Avary. "Not only yesterday, but today she has been standing at the air vent there at the door of the courtroom," he claimed, "right by the witness stand, within eight feet of the witness stand, and listening to the evidence." But when Judge Avary questioned Dr. Gunnels, she said that while yes, she had been in the hallway the whole time, she couldn't hear anything because of the air-conditioning. Moreover, she was so hard of hearing that even if she'd pressed her ear against the vent, she wouldn't have been able to make out what was being said inside the courtroom.

Avary, once again unpersuaded by Tom Young, brought the jury back in, and Gunnels began her testimony, both about her own

qualifications—which included degrees in psychology, special education, and counseling, as well as extensive work with the Birmingham
Child Guidance Clinic and the Veterans Administration—and about
her interactions with Robert Burns, whom she had interviewed three
times that summer, for a total of six hours. Gunnels testified that
she found Burns to be of average intelligence but suffering from a
passive-aggressive syndrome whereby he suppressed his anger, making
him predisposed to "explode" after a tragedy like the murder of his
niece. She went so far as to testify that Robert Burns was "incapable
of avoiding" what had happened at House of Hutchinson.

Young began his cross-examination of Gunnels by belittling her
credentials, the same way he had done, with perhaps more justifica-
tion, to the Not-Quite-Doctor Woodhouse. "You have, in effect, been
the same as a school counselor," he said of her work at the Birmingham Child Guidance Clinic. "In essence, that's all you are, is that
true?" It was not. As Dr. Gunnels explained to Young, and to the jury,
her decade of experience as a clinical psychologist involved evaluating
and treating everything from dyslexia to schizophrenia.

Having failed to discredit the witness, Young tried to discredit
psychology in general. Was it, he asked, "an art, a science, or what?"
He had already attempted this move during his cross-examination
of Woodhouse, by asking whether one of the tests that Burns had
been administered, the Minnesota Multiphasic Personality Inventory,
"truly reflects conditions in blacks as well as whites" and whether
animal subjects like mice could reliably represent human beings. But
when he returned to this latter point with the new witness, Young
found himself outmatched; Gunnels ran a mouse laboratory at the
community college and was more prepared to defend her research
than Woodhouse.

Things got worse for Tom Young when the defense rose for re-
direct. Lee Sims asked Dr. Gunnels whether she had ever given testimony before as an expert witness. She had, it turned out—including
for the State of Alabama. Now this witness, favored by the DA's
own office, told the jury that "no man and no money could make
me say a man is insane if I don't believe he is," and she believed that
Robert Burns was not sane at the time that he shot the Reverend

Willie Maxwell. He was not a violent person, she said, and he had not committed any acts of violence prior to this one except during his military service.

Tom Young, who had the FBI file on Burns full of allegations to the contrary, sat in his seat fuming. But no matter which way he pushed, the witness could not reveal to the jury anything about the defendant's earlier episodes of violence, because Gunnels had not talked with Burns about his time in Ohio, Maryland, and Illinois and did not know anything about the crimes he had allegedly committed there. The same went for every character witness Big Tom called. They testified about what a good man Burns was; they testified about what a good family he came from; they knew nothing about any visits to Cleveland or Laurel or Chicago. As far as anyone in the jury could tell, prior to the shooting, Burns was admired and beloved everywhere he went.

To deepen that impression, Big Tom called his client's wife to the stand. Vera Burns talked about her eight years of marriage and how her husband was helping to raise their teenage son and foster daughter, the one with special needs. She also testified that Shirley Ann Ellington had been close with that daughter and that her husband had been close to Shirley. In what was perhaps her most effective testimony, she told the jury that she had heard about what the Reverend Maxwell had asked the man from Eclectic to do and that she had told her husband about it prior to the shooting. On hearing it, she said, Burns became distraught. "He told me he just felt sick, he just got upset," she testified. "And he said he was afraid Mr. Maxwell would kill the rest of Nathaniel's children" and that "he was afraid that Mr. Maxwell might even try to do something to us."

"Let me ask you, Vera," Big Tom asked, in his gentlest tone. "Was it true that every member of the Burns family was scared to death of Reverend Maxwell?"

Vera said yes, they were, and when Radney asked if she specifically was afraid of Maxwell, she said yes, too. When he asked her about voodoo, Mrs. Burns explained that there had always been a lot of talk about that. It was awful, Mrs. Burns said, everything they'd learned about the Reverend since Shell's death, and then to see him at the funeral was just too much. Her husband carried his pistol everywhere, so she hadn't thought anything of it when he took it to the funeral. She hadn't even been there when he fired it, because she'd left early with one of Shirley's sisters, who had gotten emotional during the service.

It was effective testimony, but Big Tom, who understood perfectly well that jurors can nod sympathetically and dab at their eyes but still vote to convict a man, wanted to put one more witness on the stand. A resident of Alexander City, Dorothy Moeling had been matched years earlier with Robert Burns for a letter-writing program organized by a local community group for troops serving abroad. Although she had met Robert Burns only once, she had exchanged many letters with him while he was fighting in Vietnam. "My husband and I just thought his letters were marvelous," she said on the stand. "He was very patriotic and very dedicated."

Tom Young objected, claiming that Moeling's testimony was irrelevant and asking for it to be excluded, but Big Tom appealed to a higher authority: "Every act, the Supreme Court says, from the cradle to the grave, on a plea of insanity is admissible." Avary overruled Young, and Big Tom read much of Robert Burns's DD 214 into the record, complete with his service summary, his honors, and his medals. Then he read aloud from a letter that Burns had written to Dorothy Moeling from Vietnam. After thanking her for taking the time to write to him and describing his upbringing near Horseshoe Bend, he told her that he'd been in Vietnam 134 days and still had 232 more to go. "I want you to know I don't regret one day of it," he wrote, before extemporizing on the famous words of Nathan Hale: "I only regret that I have but one life to give for my country, and people like yourself."

He was writing by candlelight, Burns continued. Two days before, his company, Action Alpha, had been in "a big fire fight, and we killed fifty-eight men and three women, and also wounded three women." "Mrs. Moeling," the soldier finished, "we are going to win this war if it costs many more lives and mine, if that's the price I have to pay." It was a deftly chosen bit of evidence, and Big Tom was right to fight for its inclusion. Whether or not the jurors thought that Burns had been a hero that day at House of Hutchinson, they were reminded that he had been heroic in Vietnam and that his military service had shaken him the way that combat can shake any man, however peaceable he was before.

AT TEN MINUTES TO FOUR IN THE AFTERNOON, TOM RADNEY rested his case. Fifteen minutes later, the state followed suit, and both sides readied their closing arguments. The assistant district attorney spoke first, revisiting the testimony of the witnesses and walking the jury through the state's straightforward argument: that Robert Burns shot and killed the Reverend Willie Maxwell, and that he had been sane all three times he pulled the trigger. Anticipating the defense's closing statement, he then reminded the jurors that while they might have convicted the Reverend Willie Maxwell had they been given the chance, that was not what they were there to do. "It matters not one bit," E. Paul Jones told them, "not one iota, if Willie J. Maxwell was guilty of all of those murders or not, in determining the guilt or innocence of this man." At the end of his closing remarks, Jones articulated the crux of the state's case and a cornerstone of our justice system. "If Willie Maxwell had confessed those crimes in open court, right here in front of all of you," he said, "that would not have given Robert Burns the right to take his life."

Lee Sims, who offered the first closing statement for the defense, proceeded to ignore everything that Jones had just said. He cataloged the accusations against the Reverend and reminded the jury of what the expert witnesses had said about the mental state of Robert Burns. Then he handed the closing over to Big Tom, who rose from behind the defense table and loosened his tie.

Trials were what Big Tom lived for, and he was most himself in that brief period of time when all of the motions and objections and testimony and evidence were over and he was standing before the jury, freed from any obligation except eloquence. The jury knew everything he did—or anyway, they knew everything that he wanted them to know—and he could finally talk with them the way he talked with his dinner table jury at home. First, he pleaded humility, saying that

Jones was wrong to say he'd "wax eloquently," because after all he, Tom Radney, was no great orator, only a simple country lawyer. Then Big Tom apologized for any offense he had caused during the heat of the trial, asking the jury to forgive him, because anything he'd done had been in the service of his client, a man whose liberty was at stake. Then he apologized to the jurors for the inconvenience of having to serve on the jury, subjecting them to a hotel stay and taking them away from their families.

Once all of that was out of the way, Big Tom reminded the jurors that Robert Burns was a good man who had served his country and whose family needed him at home and that until he'd done what he did, half of Coosa County lay awake at night wondering, "Who will the Reverend get next?" He summoned for them the images of the scales of justice and asked them to put his client, Robert Burns, on one side of that scale and the Reverend Willie Maxwell on the other. And then, finally, in what was one of Big Tom's signature closing remarks, he asked them to take their time, pointing at the defendant, saying he knew there were at least a few jurors who "would sit there forever—*forever*—before you would ever give him a day."

The final word in the case—except for the verdict—belonged to Tom Young, who used it to plead once more for law and order. "We are not living in the days of the wild and woolly west," he said. "We are living in Alexander City, Alabama," not "Lynch City, Alabama." He lashed out at the press for stirring up hatred of Willie Maxwell, accused them of being complicit in his murder, then turned his attention to the defendant and implored the jury to answer one question and one question only. It was the same question that at twenty minutes to six on Tuesday, September 27, 1977, in the Fifth Judicial Circuit in Alexander City, Judge James Avary charged them with answering: "Did Robert Lewis Burns unlawfully and with malice aforethought kill Willie J. Maxwell?"

# 14

# What Holmes Was Talking About

EIGHTY MINUTES LATER, THE JURY WAS BACK. NOT BECAUSE they'd reached a verdict, but because Judge Avary wanted an update from the foreman. L. D. Benton, a sixty-year-old army veteran who'd earned a Bronze Star and a Purple Heart in World War II and then became a supervisor at Russell Mills, reported to the judge, the attorneys, and those still gathered in the courtroom that the jury was pretty close to being deadlocked. His report must have worried both the defense and the prosecution, but Judge Avary sent him back to the jury room, said maybe dinner would help them with their deliberations, and ordered the bailiff to take their orders for hamburgers and sandwiches.

At nine in the evening, Judge Avary called the jurors back again. He was impatient and wanted to know whether they'd be able to decide the case that night, or at all. Benton reported that they still hadn't reached a verdict, but they had taken votes. Avary asked him to report their split, without saying whether they leaned toward conviction or toward acquittal. There was no reason to think that where they were then was where they would end up, but it was still a heart-stopping moment for the defendant and his counsel. An acquittal was a loss for the state, but the state had lost before, whereas a conviction of murder in the first degree would likely mean life in prison for Burns. Benton announced that they were nine and three, and Judge Avary sent the jury back, reminding them they could ask any questions that might help with their deliberations.

A few minutes later, the bailiff returned to the courtroom with a written question. "What action would be taken," the jury wanted to know, "if a verdict of not guilty by reason of insanity was reached?" Judge Avary wanted to answer the jury and suggested telling them, "I would send him to Bryce Hospital where he would be evaluated; in the event they determined he was, at this time, sane, he would be released."

For once, the attorneys were in agreement. Big Tom, worried about reviving talk of a revolving door, argued that any answer beyond the sentencing options that the jury had already been given would be prejudicial; the state, worried about a mistrial if inappropriate instructions were given, concurred. Judge Avary was convinced and sent the jurors back a note that read "It is not proper for the jury to consider this in reaching their verdict."

At ten o'clock, with fifty people still milling about waiting on a verdict, including Robert and Vera Burns, Judge Avary called the jury back to the courtroom for a fourth time. When Benton said that they were still deadlocked and that they'd already asked the only question they had, Judge Avary informed them that the court had secured rooms for another night at the Horseshoe Bend Motel. A fair and just trial, he warned them, could take days, but for now he'd give them another half an hour to deliberate before dispatching them to the motel for the night. Big Tom objected to what he considered this "dynamite charge," claiming that Judge Avary had basically threatened the jurors with confinement. For the first time since the opening gavel, Big Tom asked for a mistrial. "That was just a firecracker," Avary snapped back, denying Radney's motion. "I am holding the dynamite until later."

HE WOULDN'T NEED IT. AT THE END OF THEIR THIRTY MINUTES, almost exactly five hours after they started their deliberations, the jury sent word through the bailiff that they had reached a verdict. Tom Young had already gone home for the night, and so had the Reverend's widow, but there were still dozens of people around—including Big Tom, who had an appeal bond filled out and ready to hand to the judge. First, though, the foreman had his own piece of paper to give Judge Avary. The judge took it and read it aloud: "We, the jury, find the defendant not guilty by reason of insanity."

Robert Burns let his head fall into his hands. His wife started to cry. Cheers and applause filled the courtroom, and once the jury had left and the judge had called Burns forward to read the judgment again, friends and family raced to hug him and to shake Big Tom's hand. Judge Avary wanted to send Burns to Bryce Hospital right away, but Radney asked that he be allowed to go home with his family for the night, and Avary assented.

By the next morning, when everyone reunited in court, almost the whole town knew what Judge Avary had wanted to tell the jury in answer to their question: a defendant found not guilty by reason of insanity is sent for evaluation at a state mental hospital and is released as soon as the superintendent of that facility sees fit; there is no minimum stay, even for a killer. Tom Young, who had wanted the jury told as much but didn't want to risk a mistrial, came to court that morning with a statement for the press. "Now, a cold-blooded murderer is a hero," it read. "The plea of insanity was never proven. In fact, it was completely disproven. Any commitment of Burns to Bryce would be a complete farce and a waste of taxpayers' money. If he is sent over there, he won't need a change of clothes, but he might need to pack a lunch."

Young was wrong, but not by much. When the staff at Bryce evaluated Robert Burns, they did not agree with the diagnosis offered by the experts who had testified at his trial. That wasn't very surprising, because, by then, it had come out that those experts didn't even agree with themselves. "In a way," Dr. Gunnels later said, "killing Willie Maxwell was the sanest thing anybody did all summer." There wasn't a jury in Tallapoosa County, she continued, that would have convicted Burns, who "was just doing what the law ought to have done sooner." Then she added, without an ounce of irony, "Why, I probably would have killed that man myself."

Robert Burns was taken to Tuscaloosa on September 28, 1977, and released from Bryce Hospital a few weeks later—less time than had passed between when he committed the murder and when he was found not guilty of having done so. He was back home in time to celebrate Thanksgiving with his family.

At its core, the Burns trial had turned on two kinds of primitivism: belief in the supernatural and belief in vigilante justice. It wasn't the first time that a white jury in Alabama had heard compelling evidence of murder yet reasoned their way to an acquittal. Vengeance is as old as violence, and many white southerners can trace their moral genealogy through family feuds and gentlemen's duels, across rivers and oceans all the way back to medieval courts and biblical dynasties. Theirs was a society that not so long ago had written theft into legal treaties with Native Americans and bondage into legal deeds on the lives of African Americans; a society that until recently had believed the law elastic enough to bend without breaking, exempting lynching from the category of homicide. Like those killings, the murder of the Reverend Willie Maxwell had been witnessed by hundreds but still resulted in no conviction.

That verdict of not guilty by reason of insanity in the Burns trial exemplified what Oliver Wendell Holmes had written in his book on American common law: "The first requirement of a sound body of law is, that it should correspond with the actual feelings and demands of the community, whether right or wrong. If people would gratify the passion of revenge outside of the law, if the law did not help them, the law has no choice but to satisfy the craving itself, and thus avoid the greater evil of private retribution." When *The Montgomery Advertiser* cited that excerpt in its editorial about the Maxwell case, it said that people around Lake Martin, accustomed to living in fear of the Reverend, knew what Holmes was talking about, because the law had failed them. Yet when the jury acquitted Maxwell's killer, that same newspaper lamented the decision. Vigilantism was both romantic and repellent: too practical to condemn, too dangerous to condone. But right or wrong, the case was now closed, and if some people had scruples about what had happened, almost no one outside his immediate family and thwarted law enforcement officers grieved the end of the long, strange career of the Reverend.

Like the dam on the Tallapoosa River, the gates had closed on the Maxwell case, and ever so slowly the waters began rising. As the weeks and months passed, stories began to change, case files began to walk away, court records began to go missing. Some of these disappearances were deliberate. Would-be heroes wanted to be better known; the tarnished wanted to be left in peace; survivors of all kinds wanted the world to move on. Other losses stemmed from the inevitable ebb of memory and the erosive power of time. The present kept sliding over the past, and the past kept slipping further down, until the truth of what had transpired in the life and death of the Reverend Willie Maxwell, elusive even as it was happening, became like the stone foundations and submerged churches and sunken graves 150 feet down in a drift of silt at the bottom of Lake Martin. But before all of it vanished completely, someone came along and tried to salvage it.

The Reverend Willie Maxwell, back from his military service and already preaching at churches around Lake Martin. *The Alexander City Outlook*

A small selection of the life insurance policies taken out by the Reverend Maxwell on his relatives, including wives, brothers, aunts, nieces, nephews, and children.

Shirley Ann Ellington, a stepdaughter of the Maxwells, who was living with them at the time she was murdered.

*The Alexander City Outlook*

Newspapers and magazines around the country ran stories and wire reports about the strange life and shocking murder of the Reverend Willie Maxwell.

Pallbearers carry the Reverend Maxwell's flag-covered coffin out of Peace and Goodwill Baptist Church. *The Alexander City Outlook*

Ophelia Maxwell leaving her husband's funeral. *The Alexander City Outlook*

Mourners gather in front of the House of Hutchinson Funeral Home after fleeing the chapel where the Reverend Willie Maxwell was shot to death during the funeral of Shirley Ann Ellington. *The Alexander City Outlook*

A young Tom Radney, at work in his law office.
*The Radney Family*

Runt O'Daniel's campaign brochure from
the 1966 state senate runoff, in which he
attempted to use "the negro bloc vote"
against Tom Radney. *The Radney Family*

The Radneys
posing in front of
the State Capitol
in one of their
official portraits
for the 1970
lieutenant governor
campaign. *The
Radney Family*

From left to right, Officer James Ware, Chief Winfred Patterson, and Officer Joe Ennis Berry of the Alexander City Police Department. The first two African American officers on the town's police force, Ware and Berry both testified at the trial of Robert Burns. *Johnson Publishing Company, LLC.*

Tom Radney leaving the arraignment hearing with Robert and Vera Burns. *The Alexander City Outlook*

Courtroom sketch of the jury in the Burns trial. *The Alexander City Outlook*

Robert Burns and his family at the defense table on the first day of the trial.
*The Alexander City Outlook*

Robert and Vera
Burns await the
jury's verdict.
*The Alexander
City Outlook*

District Attorney Tom Young rises from behind the prosecution table, while Tom Radney and the defense wait out a recess on the second day of the trial. *Montgomery Advertiser, Gannett-Community Publishing*

The Radneys—Madolyn, Ellen, Big Tom, Hollis, Fran, and Thomas—around the time of the Burns trial. *The Radney Family*

Big Tom and Madolyn Radney with all of their grandchildren. Middle row, left to right: Margaret Harvey holding William Lovett; Madolyn Price Kirby holding Cecilia Radney; Anna Lee Price holding Radney Lovett; Elizabeth Harvey, and Finlay Radney. Front row, left to right: Thomas Lovett, Anderson Radney, and Luke Harvey. *The Radney Family*

Nelle Harper Lee in the offices of the *Rammer-Jammer* during her time as a student at the University of Alabama. *The University of Alabama Special Libraries Collection*

Harper Lee with her father, A. C. Lee, on the front porch of the family home on West Avenue in Monroeville. *Donald Uhrbrock/The LIFE Images Collection/Getty*

Harper Lee writing in her family's law office in Monroeville. *Donald Uhrbrock/ The LIFE Images Collection/Getty Images*

Harper Lee and Truman Capote walking up Second Avenue in New York City in 1976. *Harry Benson*

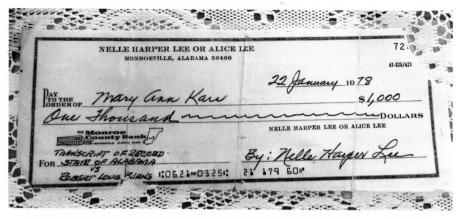

The check Harper Lee wrote court reporter Mary Ann Karr, including the thorough memo line.

The Horseshoe Bend Motel in Alexander City, where Harper Lee stayed while reporting and where the jury was sequestered during the Burns trial. *Tichnor Brothers Inc.*

Harper, Alice, and Louise: the three Lee sisters together at the Alabama History and Heritage Festival in Eufaula in 1983. *The Eufaula Tribune*

Visitors to 433 East Eighty-Second Street might never have noticed "Lee-H" beside "1E," though the writer's name was on the door buzzer of her New York City building for decades.

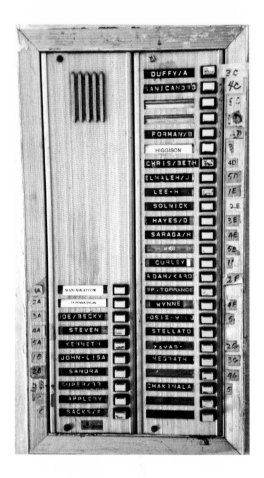

Harper Lee in her room at the Meadows in Monroeville. *Penny Weaver*

PART THREE

The Writer

# 15

# Disappearing Act

It was the damnedest thing, but Maryon Pittman Allen couldn't find a copy of *To Kill a Mockingbird* anywhere in Washington. Mrs. James Browning Allen was the second wife of the junior senator from the great state of Alabama, and in that role she was expected not only to attend the Ladies of the Senate Luncheon but to present the First Lady of the United States, Rosalynn Carter, with a book representative of her home state. It was obvious to Allen which book she should bring, since there was no Alabama tale more famous than the one about the adventures of a tomboy named Scout and her heroic lawyer of a father, Atticus Finch, but even though there were millions of copies of Nelle Harper Lee's novel in circulation at the time, Allen couldn't find a single one for sale in the nation's capital.

Allen was Lee's age, and they had both dropped out of the University of Alabama around the same time. Lee had been a student at the law school and quit to write; Allen had been a journalism student and quit to have children. Her first marriage didn't take and she had three mouths to feed, so she began working as a reporter for a handful of newspapers around Birmingham. That's how she met her second husband, who was then Lieutenant Governor James Browning Allen, a widower with two children of his own. She heard church bells on her way to interview him for a story and hoped it wasn't a sign, but four months later they were married, and four years after that they were moving to Washington for him to take his seat in the U.S. Senate. Allen didn't like to make a big production out of her role as a Lady of the Senate, but she also didn't want to embarrass her husband or her state, so she was determined to bring the right gift to Mrs. Carter. When she couldn't find the book, she went looking for its author.

Allen knew that she and Lee had a mutual friend from their Tuscaloosa days, and she thought that he might know how to get a hold of her. Nearly everyone in the state would have recognized John Forney's voice, and the half who were Alabama fans basically thought it was the voice of God: Forney had been calling the play-by-play for the Crimson Tide for over a decade. "John," Allen said when the sportscaster answered, "do you know where Nelle Lee is? I've simply got to find a copy of her book." After she explained why, Forney told her that Lee was in Alexander City.

Allen knew Alex City well; her first husband had been born and raised there. In the years when her own father was building levees on the Mississippi River and living with her mother in a tent on its banks, her ex-father-in-law had been hobnobbing in the Alabama State Senate. After that, J. Sanford Mullins had gone to Alex City to serve for more than three decades as the town's attorney. As best as Allen could remember, the most exciting thing that had ever happened around Lake Martin was her father-in-law climbing into the bed of a truck to deliver one of his speeches, unfailingly fiery numbers that could draw an audience from three counties. But the Oratorical Wizard of Channahatchee Creek had long since died, and she couldn't imagine what would entice a world-famous author to Tallapoosa County. "What in the world," Allen asked Forney incredulously, "is she doing in Alex City?"

Lee was there writing, Forney said, but if Allen could give him a little time, he would try to get in touch with her. A few hours later, Forney called back and said that he'd tracked Lee down at the Horseshoe Bend Motel—maybe she knew it, it was that hexagon-shaped number on Highway 280—and that he had been given the go-ahead to give her the writer's private telephone number. "It was like she was hiding behind damn trees down there," Allen remembers, "but I got the secret number, and we talked for over an hour."

They talked about small-town lawyers, since Allen wondered if Lee knew anything about her ex-father-in-law, and they talked about journalism, since Lee was a regular reader of Allen's syndicated column, "Reflections of a News Hen." When Allen finally got around to asking why Lee was hanging her hat in Alex City, the author wouldn't say much—just that she had been there for a few months, working on something that had to do with a voodoo preacher. Lee did say, though, that she would make sure that a copy of her novel got to the nation's capital by May 15, 1978, in time for the luncheon.

True to her word, Lee sent a first edition of her book, inscribed on the front page "To Rosalynn Carter," along with a verse from one of the hymns to wisdom in the book of Proverbs: "Her ways are ways of pleasantness, and all her paths are peace." Mrs. Allen presented the book to Mrs. Carter at the Ladies of the Senate Luncheon—which, as it happens, was the last of those Allen would ever attend. Two weeks later, after she and her husband had returned to Alabama for the summer recess, Senator James Browning Allen died of a heart attack at their beach house in Gulf Shores. Not long after that, Governor George Wallace appointed Maryon Pittman Allen to her husband's seat, making her the state's second female senator. Overwhelmed both personally and professionally, she forgot all about the Pulitzer Prize winner holed up at the Horseshoe Bend Motel.

It was easy enough to forget about Harper Lee in those days. *To Kill a Mockingbird* had come out eighteen years before, and in all that time Lee had published almost nothing else. Three short essays for two glossy magazines, two tiny profiles that were favors for her friend Truman Capote, one satirical recipe for crackling bread in a novelty cookbook: in nearly two decades, that was the only writing she had put into the world. No second novel had followed the first, and she hadn't given an interview in fourteen years. The last time she had so much as agreed to be quoted in print was another favor for Capote. In 1976, he had asked Lee to sit with him during an interview for *People,* which was running a profile of him. She had said a total of twelve words on the record, seven of which were, "We are bound by a common anguish."

*To Kill a Mockingbird* had made Lee extravagantly wealthy, but you wouldn't have known it to look around her life. When she was in New York, she lived in a small, rent-controlled apartment on the

Upper East Side; when she went back to Alabama, she stayed with one of her sisters in a modest brick ranch house in their hometown of Monroeville. No matter where she was, she avoided the press, her fans, and anything that seemed too literary; she tried to live her life as if she had never published one of the most popular novels in American history. In 1962, the year the film adaptation of her book came out—the one that earned Gregory Peck an Oscar and further fixed her portrait of a small southern town in the nation's collective memory—Lee told a reporter for *The Mobile Register* that she wanted to disappear, and she basically had.

Now, alone in a motel in the middle of nowhere, with the world no longer watching, she was nearly as free as she had been in the tiny flat where she had written *To Kill a Mockingbird*. That was what she chose not to tell Maryon Pittman Allen that day on the phone: Harper Lee was in Alexander City because finally, all these years later, she was going to write another book.

# 16

# Some Kind of Soul

FOR THE FIRST THIRTY-FOUR YEARS OF HER LIFE, SHE WENT BY Nelle. It was "Ellen," backward: the name of her maternal grandmother, Ellen Rivers Finch. Her middle name, and the one she would make famous, was the surname of a pediatrician in Selma who had saved her older sister's life. When it came time to publish a book, Lee chose to leave one of her two family heirlooms off the cover. "We must confer on which name/names I'm to 'come out' under," she wrote to her agents the summer before *To Kill a Mockingbird* was published. "I've signed myself 'Harper Lee' simply because the spelling of my first name is peculiar, and most people call it 'Nellie' when they read it (on checks + job applications)—something I can't abide. I lopped it off just to avoid confusion." As it turned out, that choice only swapped one kind of confusion for another, setting Lee up for a lifetime of having some readers assume she was a man. But the chain-smoking tomboy who played football with the boys and slept in men's pajamas was used to confusing those around her.

Born in 1926, a year after the Reverend Maxwell and six years before Tom Radney, Nelle Harper Lee was the fourth child of Frances Cunningham Finch and Amasa Coleman Lee. Even by the elastic standards of southern eccentricity, the Lees were a curious bunch. Descended from a Confederate soldier, but not that one, Amasa, who usually went by A.C. and sometimes by Coley, was raised on a farm in Florida and had just a few years of formal education. He knew early, though, that he did not want to spend his life in the fields; instead, before he was out of his teens, he passed the examination required to become a teacher, then began working in the schools he'd barely gotten to attend. After that, he became a sawmill clerk and later a bookkeeper, which is what brought him to Monroe County, where he met his wife, a Finch of the Finchburg Finches. The couple married in 1910 and eventually settled in Monroeville, where A.C. managed a neighboring railroad line for a local law firm, Barnett & Bugg.

The seat of Monroe County, Monroeville had originally been called Centerville, but that name was enough of a lie that the town finally changed it. Supposedly, the surveyor tasked with finding the center of the county had been persuaded with liquor to move it a few extra miles, but after the death of President James Monroe, the residents gave up on the ruse, and voilà: Centerville became Monroeville. By the 1930s, the town had just over thirteen hundred people—a little more than Nixburg, but a lot fewer than Alexander City. Far from both the river and the railroad, Monroeville was hard to get to and easy to get stuck in.

While A. C. Lee was working for Barnett & Bugg, he began teaching himself law, and he kept working there once he had passed the state bar exam—a thing you could do back then without first earning a degree. After he made partner, the firm became Barnett, Bugg & Lee, and it prospered, even during the Great Depression. In 1929, when so much of the country was going bankrupt, A.C. bought the local newspaper, *The Monroe Journal,* which he owned until 1947, and won a seat in the Alabama House of Representatives, which he held until 1938.

Money does wonders for misfits. Thanks to their father's prominence, the Lee children could be as odd as they pleased. That oddness started with their ages: Nelle, the baby of the family, was six years younger than her closest sibling, a brother named Edwin Coleman Lee; a decade younger than her sister Frances Louise Lee, known as Louise; and fifteen years younger than her oldest sister, Alice Finch Lee. The long gaps between children were partly a result of the difficulties their mother had experienced after Louise nearly died in infancy. The stress had left her with a "nervous disorder" too difficult for local doctors to treat, so she went away to a specialist in Mobile.

It would be nearly a year before she found her way home to Monroeville.

Because of their age differences, all four of the Lees grew up feeling a little like only children. By the time that Nelle learned to read, her oldest sister had left for college; the year that she got a bicycle for Christmas, her second-oldest sister got a husband. By fourteen, she already had a nephew. She was closest with her brother, while her older sisters were more like mothers to her. Her actual mother, made into an aesthete by years of boarding school, taught Nelle to play the harpsichord, got her hooked on crossword puzzles, and read aloud to her, but only when she was well, and she wasn't well often. Frances had terrible allergies that made a misery of life in the agrarian South, which, with its coal trains and cotton gins and dusty seasons, could be as bad as the industrialized North, and her mental health never fully recovered from the collapse she suffered after her second pregnancy. She sometimes went away for long stretches, and when she was in Monroeville, she didn't manage the household, delegating that job to her older daughters and a series of African American maids. The Lee children all say that their mother was gentle and kind, but their patience with her fragile health was not shared by their town or their times. Neighbors gossiped about Frances playing piano at odd hours, shouting from the front porch, repeating herself often, and, conversely, sometimes staring off in silence, incapable of the pleasantries expected of southern women.

With her mother ill and her father at work all day and intermittently away at the legislature in Montgomery, Nelle's early years were low on supervision. But that wasn't unusual for children in Monroeville, who were allowed to find whatever trouble they could, so long as they came home in time to wash their hands before supper and tame their cowlicks before church. It was an era when young people were not merely permitted but expected to entertain themselves. Those who had the rare ten cents to pay for a movie were obliged to reenact the entire thing for all the other kids afterward. (Nelle, too young to see Boris Karloff's *Frankenstein* when it came out, was terrified by one of her sisters' rendition, and amazed, many years later, by its accuracy.) Mostly, though, the things they did for fun they did for free. They turned cornfields into the battlefield of Gettysburg, and cattails into the jungles of West Africa. If they stared at the ground, they were leading brigades of ants over field and mountain; if they looked to the sky, they were flying like Amelia Earhart or Lucky Lindy across the Atlantic. When there were enough of them together, they played electricity, ostrich tag, looby loo, hot grease in the kitchen, and witch in the ditch; when they were alone, they got bored, and got used to it.

Even when life wasn't boring, it was seldom all that exciting. Monroeville was the kind of town where if your sister served cake on a Friday, she would be featured in the newspaper for having "entertained," and if your friend's eighth birthday party included fruit punch and prizes, it might merit its own headline plus five column inches. Open almost any issue of *The Monroe Journal* from the 1930s and 1940s, and you'll find a mention of the Lees—not just because their father owned the paper and authored many of its editorials, but because there were plenty of pages and not enough news to fill them. Louise went all the way to the National 4-H Club Camp in Washington, D.C.; Edwin and the rest of the championship football team were feted with a banquet; the Epworth League of the Methodist Church met for a lecture on the Crusades, followed by an address on the state of the world, delivered by a twelve-year-old Nelle, titled "What Is the Cause of This Confusion?"

Those were what passed for big days in a small town. For children, only school cut into the number of hours you had for doing nothing. The sleepy-eyed, towheaded Nelle went to the public schools of Monroe County, which were still segregated; it's unlikely that she or any of her siblings ever set foot in the town's Rosenwald School, one of the five thousand designed by Booker T. Washington and funded by the philanthropist Julius Rosenwald for the education of black children in southern states. Nelle's own school was right by the Lee house, but her classmates never made her feel at home. She wore the wrong sorts of clothes; her hair was too short; she wrestled with the boys and didn't like playing with the girls. When neighbors looked out their windows, they often saw Nelle, clad in overalls, running around whooping as if she were one of the Red Sticks fighting Old Mad Jackson in the Creek Wars.

Nelle didn't fit in with her peers socially—even in class pictures, she is out of line with them, literally—and she was years ahead of them academically, chiefly because of how early she had learned to read. She had started with Rapunzel, the Rover Boys, and Uncle Wiggily Longears, then moved on to the Bobbsey Twins and the adventures of Tom Swift, and before long she was going to Avonlea with Anne of Green Gables and attending meetings of the Fair and Square Club with Seckatary Hawkins. By the first grade, she could be counted on to have read both *The Monroe Journal* and *The Mobile Press,* a feat not many adults in Monroeville managed.

IF NELLE WAS AN UNUSUAL CHILD, SHE WAS NOTHING COM-pared with her best friend, the little boy who had appeared one day like a changeling at the house next door. His mother, Lillie Mae Faulk, had grown up in Monroeville with four cousins but left at seventeen after marrying one Archulus Persons, a blond-haired, bottle-glassed lawyer by training who made his living as a pint-size P. T. Barnum— managing a boxer, booking tour groups on steamships, and staging a variety show with a performer the posters described as the "World's Foremost Man of Mystery." (When Persons brought the show to Monroeville, he buried the man of mystery in a grave at the elementary school Nelle attended and left him there for two days breathing through a pipe; interested parties paid one dollar to look down the hole at him.) To no one's surprise except Lillie Mae's, they ran out of money before their honeymoon ended. She got pregnant and wanted an abortion; he wanted a son, and won. When the boy arrived, his father named him Truman, after an old school friend, and Streckfus, after a steamship line on the Mississippi.

Truman Streckfus Persons came into the world in 1924 and lived mostly in Monroeville from 1928 until 1932. The cousins of Lillie Mae's who had taken care of her before the wedding took care of her son after, and they lived in the house next door to the Lees. There was just a low stone wall between them, and by the time that Nelle was out of toddlerhood, she and Truman had become partners in crime and just about everything else. They flew kites, staged baptisms in his family's fishpond, and whiled away hours together in the tree house her father had built in a chinaberry tree in the backyard. Before they could read, Nelle's brother read to them, then all three of them would act out the plot, vying for the best roles based on age, size, or stubbornness. Eventually, Nelle and Truman started reading for themselves, and once they ran out of stories to read, they started writing them, finding their heroes and villains in familiar figures on South Alabama Avenue. When Nelle's father gave her a beat-up typewriter, she spent hours every day typing out poems and scenes, occasionally consenting to share the contraption with Truman.

School might have sometimes been miserable for Nelle, but it was worse for Truman Streckfus Persons, a boy half the size of his name and twice as strange. Nelle was younger, but taller, fiercer, and more inclined to fight back, so what protection he got, he got from her. Mostly, though, they kept close to each other and away from others; they were both "apart" people, as he would explain much later, when the world knew him as Truman Capote. His parents had divorced after his mother ran away with another man, Joseph Garcia Capote, a Cuban office manager who worked for a firm on Wall Street, and after a nasty court fight Lillie Mae, now going by Nina, got full custody of her son. She moved him to New York and changed his surname, but still sent him home to her cousins for long stretches in the summers. "Master Truman Capote of New York City arrived Sunday," *The Monroe Journal* reported of one such visit in June 1935, "to spend several weeks in Monroeville with the Misses Faulk."

The loss of Master Truman as a full-time neighbor was a blow to Nelle, but summers were better than nothing, and now whenever Truman crossed the Mason-Dixon Line, he brought the whole world with him: subway tokens, skyscrapers, prep schools, tuxedos, foreign languages. But when he went away again, the world was just Monroeville, and Monroeville, for Nelle, was mostly just her family: the attentive love of her father and the distracted affections of her mother; the watchful, encouraging eye of her oldest sister, Alice, whom she called "Bear" because of an early visit to the Montgomery Zoo; the protective presence of Ed, who was on his way to becoming a military pilot; and the adoration of her sister Louise, known as Weezie, who moved across the state to Eufaula to start a family when Nelle, who was known to the family as Dody, was barely in her double digits.

When Nelle Harper Lee finally found another friend in high school, it wasn't a classmate but a teacher, Gladys Watson Burkett, who wore her eyeglasses around her neck and her passion for literature on her sleeve. "She is one of the few teachers I've known who has an absolute love of her subject," Nelle said. "She taught me all I know about English." Burkett lived across the street from the Lees and took such an interest in Nelle that the two stayed close until Burkett died. "She is my closest friend in Monroeville and has been all my life," Lee once said, revealing not only the appetite she had for intellectual friendships but also the deep estrangement of a bright young woman from her hometown.

WHEN THE TIME CAME TO GO TO COLLEGE, CAPOTE DID NOT. He knew that he wanted to be a writer, and he didn't see the point in studying how to do it when he could just hurl himself at the task instead. Nelle was two years his junior, and by the time she faced the same decision, he was already living on Park Avenue, working as an office boy at *The New Yorker*. He walked the halls of 28 West Forty-Fourth Street like a ballerina, carrying pencils and wearing a cape; the first time the editor in chief, Harold Ross, ever saw Capote, he asked, "What's that?"

The answer, soon enough, was a staff writer. Nelle wanted to be a writer, too, but her parents were as present as his were absent, and they expected all of their children, especially the girls, to get an education. As a result, in 1944, Lee left Monroeville to attend Huntingdon College.

Situated on a beautiful campus not far from where F. Scott and Zelda Fitzgerald lived during their Montgomery years, Huntingdon was a small women's school run by the Methodist Church. Alice had attended and loved it, but Nelle found it small and stuffy: there were five hundred girls on a fifty-eight-acre campus, and they were required to gather early every morning for chapel. She joined the Chi Delta Phi literary honor society and the glee club but never quite settled into student life. It was grade school all over again: whatever her peers were doing, Nelle didn't want to do, and whatever she did want to do, they did not. She wouldn't wear hats or makeup, and she didn't dance or date; she smoked constantly, stayed awake all night reading the Victorians, and cursed like the boys her classmates' mothers warned them about.

The only place Nelle Lee was at home was on the pages of campus publications. During her year at Huntingdon, she reviewed Bertita Harding's *Lost Waltz* (the novelist, she griped, was too gentle with the house of Hapsburg) and Norman Cousins's *Good Inheritance* (whose academic prose "is something of a relief from the so-called 'realistic' writings of the day"). She also published her first two works of fiction in *The Prelude*, the student literary magazine. "Nightmare" was about a young girl who watches a lynching through a crack in a fence post; "A Wink at Justice" was a courtroom scene where a judge lines up eight African American defendants accused of gambling and examines their hands to see whose were rough enough to prove they had been working instead. Although clearly juvenilia, both stories were foretastes of the feast to come: the lynch-mob mentality that would overtake so many residents of Maycomb, and the courtroom as a theater of morality.

Never quite happy at Huntingdon, Nelle left after a year for the University of Alabama. During her time there, its campus in Tuscaloosa had more than eight thousand students, and she liked it better from the start because of the hours she could keep: with no mandatory chapel, she could stay awake as late as she wanted, getting by on three or four hours of sleep, sustaining herself with cigarettes, candy, and hot showers. Her idea of heaven, she told the student newspaper, was "a place where diligent law students and writers ascend after death and can stay up forever without Benzedrine."

Lee pledged the Chi Omega sorority, but its members were just as puzzled by her as the women at Huntingdon had been; no pledge before her had been so bold as to correct the pronunciation of her soon-to-be sisters during an initiation, and most of them teased their hair more than their professors. Soon enough, Lee ditched the sorority house for one of the regular dormitories. It didn't much matter where she kept her toothbrush, though, because she practically lived at the Union, the building that housed all of the student publications.

It was a sanctum for someone like Nelle, the first place she'd found, outside her own home, where no one felt the need to comment if she stayed hunched over a typewriter all day or looked askance if she invoked Childe Roland or recited long stretches of Swinburne. The Union was also the place where she made one of her closest friends—once again not a fellow student but a professor named James McMillan. Jim was the director of the newly formed University of Alabama Press, which had its office in the Union as well, and most mornings when he got to work and started a pot of coffee, all-nighter Nelle would come stumbling down the hall for a cup. They'd talk about history, botany, literature, and linguistics, about what she was writing or what he was editing, and then eventually she would head back to her dorm for a few hours of sleep.

When she first got to campus, Nelle had tried getting on the newspaper but found it was harder to do so when your father wasn't the editor. She was, however, able to get something in the humor magazine, the *Rammer-Jammer,* right away, and she got herself on its masthead by the end of her first semester; a year later, in the fall of 1946, she became the editor in chief, a position that attested to her talents but also to the times, since in college journalism, as in every profession, four years of sending men abroad for World War II had created opportunities for women. In addition to running the show, Nelle still wrote pieces for most issues. These included a campus version of *Romeo and Juliet,* a mock-country newspaper called *The Jackassonian Democrat* that wasn't so unlike her father's *Monroe Journal,* and an *Esquire* send-up that she called "Some Writers of Our Times," which cataloged all the things a writer supposedly needed to be successful: a sadistic father, an alcoholic mother, "some kind of soul," and, most essentially, to have been born in a southern town. That piece included a cameo by her friend Truman Capote, who lisps his way through a diatribe about his masterwork in progress: "Honey, I'm thuck. My novel ith about a thenthitive boy from the time he'th twelve until he ith a gwown man." The best of her contributions, though, was "Now Is the Time for All Good Men . . . ," a one-act play about the Boswell Amendment, an actual attempt in 1946 to prevent black Alabamians from registering to vote; in her parody, the Honorable Jacob F. B. MacGillacuddy, chairman of the Citizens' Committee to Eradicate the Black Plague, has designed a literacy test so onerous that not even he can pass it, leaving him to plead for an exemption from the U.S. Supreme Court.

The pieces Nelle wrote for the *Rammer-Jammer* were mostly silly and all sophomoric (appropriately so, under the circumstances), but they weren't bad, and there were a lot of them, which was enough to snag her a column on the student newspaper, *The Crimson-White*. Anyone who hadn't encountered Nelle Lee's acerbity in a classroom got to know it through her "Caustic Comment," which excoriated everyone from campus security to the registrar. One of her columns absolutely flayed the philistines on the library staff who first refused to give a friend of hers a copy of *Ulysses* and then made him settle for one without the "Penelope" chapter.

WHILE NELLE WAS PILING UP CIGARETTE STUBS AND TYPEWRITER ribbons, her sister Alice, back home with their parents, had earned her own desk in the offices of Barnett, Bugg & Lee. She had followed A.C. into a legal career and developed a knack for tax law, buoyed partly by the Victory Tax that came after the war and left everyone, even those without much income, needing help with the Internal Revenue Service. Between her father and her sister, Nelle had spent years listening to cases in the Monroe County Courthouse. Movies might have cost a dime, but trials were free. The rolled-tin ceiling gleamed from above and the gum-tree floors gleamed from below as she eavesdropped on cases that ran the gamut from mischief to murder.

Even before Nelle was old enough to read a law book, her father had started talking about renaming his firm "A. C. Lee and Daughters, Lawyers." Whether or not that dream ever had any appeal for her, Nelle had always been eager to please her father, and after one year at Alabama she applied for early admission to the law school. By 1947, she was officially a law student, losing even more sleep to contracts and torts. She would later say that she had enrolled only to get access to the law library, but at the time she told her family that a legal education would provide the discipline she would need as a writer and that studying the law would teach her how to think.

By the next summer, Nelle Lee had thought herself right out of Alabama. She had been accepted to the International Education Exchange at the University of Oxford, and on June 16, 1948, right around the time the Reverend Willie Maxwell headed home after his army service, she set sail for Southampton on the *Queen Elizabeth*. She spent that summer at Lady Margaret Hall, reading widely in British literature and traveling around what seemed, to someone born and raised in the vast open spaces of the Deep South, a tiny curio of a country. Like so many southerners, Nelle regarded the United Kingdom as the cradle of civilization, and she obsessed over its history all the way down to the level of obscure Whig politicians and minor Anglican bishops. She loved the English countryside so much that when her courses finished, she rented a bicycle and pedaled around solo, staying in hostels. When word of her adventures reached Monroeville, her neighbors were alarmed, but the Lees, who had long since made peace with Nelle being Nelle, simply looked forward to the next installments of A Tomboy Abroad, which included an account of cycling into London and running into Winston Churchill while having tea.

It was a memorable encounter, by any measure, but when it came to meeting people, her friend Truman Capote, then and ever, put her to shame. Capote was in Europe that summer, too, but instead of studying literary giants, he was palling around with them: dining with Noël Coward, Somerset Maugham, and Evelyn Waugh in England, then dashing over to Paris to meet Gertrude Stein's partner, Alice B. Toklas, and, allegedly, to sleep with Albert Camus. It was an enviable itinerary, or anyway a glamorous one. Lee was still a coed, but Capote was already well on his way to becoming an international celebrity. He came home on the *Queen Mary* the first week of August with Tennessee Williams, rubbing elbows on board with Clark Gable and Spencer

Tracy. She caught the same steamer two weeks later, encountering no one except a few other students who had been enrolled in exchange programs like hers.

Nelle arrived in New York on the last day of August. She took the Crescent Limited back to Alabama, where constitutional law and civil procedure awaited her. While she paid to sit through lectures and fret over exams, people were paying Capote for every word that he wrote. He was a peacock strutting about the globe; she was a pigeon pacing the roost. Whatever she had told herself before about law school—about acquiring discipline or fulfilling her father's dreams—it wasn't enough anymore. Six weeks shy of graduation, Nelle Lee dropped out. It had become obvious to her that a writer is someone who writes, and also that sooner or later everyone disappoints their parents: better, she figured, to get started on both.

# 17

# The Gift

NELLE LEE WAS TWENTY-THREE YEARS OLD WHEN SHE MOVED to Manhattan. By the time she arrived, Truman Capote had already grown sufficiently bored of New York that he had taken off on another one of his fabulous grand tours. In Morocco that summer and unable to welcome her, he went to the British Post Office in Tangiers and wrote to another friend to ask him to look after her. Michael Brown had moved to New York two years earlier from Mexia, Texas, to try to make a career as a lyricist, and he felt that the code of displaced southerners obliged him to go meet the young woman who had once lived next door to Capote in their tiny Alabama town.

"Nelle and I were instant friends," Brown said. Along with both being southerners, they had a lot else in common: he, too, had mostly been raised by a much older sister, after his mother died; he, too, idolized his father, a physician who had supported the family and helped put him through college and graduate school. And he wanted so badly to shed his small-town identity that he began, as Nelle later would, by changing his name. Born Marion Martin Brown, he came to New York after World War II—having served in the U.S. Army Air Forces, like Nelle's brother—and introduced himself to everyone as Michael.

Brown was writing songs on book jackets and paper towels while earning a living as a typist, and soon enough Nelle found a day job, too. In the spring of 1949, she went to work as an assistant editor for a trade magazine called *The School Executive*, a monthly publication of the American School Publishing Corporation. For three dollars a year, readers of *The School Executive* could keep up with trends in pedagogy, new textbooks and teaching aids, commentary on education policy, and profiles of school systems around the country. But working at the magazine required the regions of Nelle's brain that she most needed for her own writing, and she left after only six months. She then took a job as a ticket agent, first for Sabena Belgian Airlines and then with the British Overseas Airways Corporation. Air travel was expensive and exciting in those days (to her delight, she had once taken a call from Sir Laurence Olivier, who needed a flight home to London), and Nelle thought that in addition to paying the bills, the position might help her, like Olivier, get a ticket back to England. It turned out, though, that she would use the employee passes only to return to Alabama, the very place she had tried to leave behind. Like the *School Executive* job, the ticket agency work was adjacent to yet removed from the life to which she aspired.

Around the same time, Lee moved into an apartment at 1540 Second Avenue, in the Yorkville neighborhood of the Upper East Side. The apartment was a few blocks from the East River and what must have felt like a million miles from Monroeville: far enough away that she could wear tennis shoes and blue jeans without attracting stares, far enough away that she could forget about the law degree she had failed to get, far enough away that she could try to do something with words. When she wasn't working for the airlines, she was writing— short scenes and sketches like those from her college days—and when she wasn't writing, she was whistling Dixie with other southern expats, including friends from the University of Alabama like John Forney, who'd come to the city to work for an ad agency and wound up producing Joe DiMaggio's local television show.

Those expats did not include Capote, who was still abroad, working on another novel. His first, the one Nelle had parodied in the *Rammer-Jammer*, had come out in January 1948, under the title *Other Voices, Other Rooms*. It was a gothic tale set in Louisiana and Mississippi, and Capote quickly followed it with a collection of short stories. Now he was trying to write another novel, this one about Monroeville and the Misses Faulk who had helped raise him. Even though the pages of *The Grass Harp* would be filled with the china trees, cotton bales, blackberry wine, gypsy moths, dropsy cures, and catfish of Monroe County, Capote mostly wrote it on the island of Ischia, near Naples, while looking at the Strait of Gibraltar from Morocco, and in the shadows of Mount Etna on the island of Sicily. He was living with his partner, Jack Dunphy, plus an ever-growing entourage of beasts— two parrots and a Siamese cat, along with a little green frog they considered quite tame—and they were more often away from New York than not.

Capote was writing full-time, and his stories seemed to move effortlessly from his mind to the pages of magazines and the shelves of bookstores. But Nelle was busy earning a living, covering the costs that even the most frugal New York City existence incurs, and she had become distracted by the city itself. Like a lot of small-town bookworms, she was too well-read to be a true country bumpkin, but too country, even after Montgomery and Tuscaloosa, to be anything but mesmerized by Manhattan. She had enough books to read—and movies to see, and museums to visit—to last her several lifetimes. The city overwhelmed and delighted her. In a single letter from those early years, she described falling in love with the Met, even though it was "a mess"; reading a six-volume history of Judaism, because she "just wanted to find out something about the Jews"; and seeing a documentary about Mount Everest that she deemed "sublime." She was less impressed by a film adaptation of "The Fall of the House of Usher," which she improved with her own voice-over, provoking a fit of laughter in a friend and a reprimand by the management.

NEARLY TWO YEARS INTO HER TIME IN NEW YORK, NELLE WAS wrenched back home to Monroeville. Her mother had become sick with something that wasn't allergies or nerves. Unable to determine what was wrong, her local doctor sent Frances Lee for tests in Selma, where her husband dropped her off on his way to a conference for the Methodist Church. By the time A.C. returned, Frances had been diagnosed with cancer of the liver and the lungs and told that she had only a few months to live.

While Nelle had moved away, all three of her siblings were still in Alabama. Alice was living in the family home and practicing law at the family firm. Edwin, a distinguished pilot who had survived both the European and the Pacific theaters of World War II, had started a family in Monroeville but was called back into active duty at the start of the Korean War, so he was stationed in Montgomery at Maxwell Air Force Base. Louise was living with her husband and their two children over in Barbour County. All three were within driving distance of their mother, but Nelle was a thousand miles away.

Nelle got the call about her mother on a Friday night, but her father told her to wait before making any travel arrangements until they knew more. On Saturday morning, while Nelle waited by the telephone in New York, the rest of the Lees met at the Vaughan Memorial Hospital in Selma, a towering brick building with tall columns out front, not far from the Alabama River. They visited for hours, then finally left to get supper; while they were gone, Frances had a cardiac episode. By the time the family returned to the hospital, she was unconscious; by that evening, only a day after being diagnosed, she was dead.

Nelle was never more grateful for her day job than that Saturday, June 2, 1951, since the airline flew her home in time for the services. She was there for the funeral and the burial, watching as her mother became the first of the Lees to be lowered into the family plot. Nelle was twenty-five years old, and the loss was tremendous. Years later, when everyone in the world thought of her as her father's daughter, Nelle's older sister Louise said that Nelle belonged equally to their mother: "Daddy is practical; mother was impractical." Their mother, an artist of sorts who, by choice or necessity, defied the expectations of southern femininity, had given her daughters permission to be who they were. Although A.C. had made sure that Nelle had "one foot on the ground," it was Frances, Louise insisted, who had made her "a dreamer."

The loss of her mother marked the beginning of a difficult stretch for Nelle Lee. She had returned to New York and barely resumed her routine of airline shifts during the day and writing at night when another telephone call came from Alabama, this one more awful than the first. On July 12, only six weeks after her mother's death, her beloved brother suffered a brain aneurysm and was found dead in his barracks at the air force base in Montgomery. Once again, Nelle flew home from New York in a state of shock and grief. The loss of her mother had been terrible; the loss of her brother, at just thirty years old, was unbelievable, and unbearable. He had been the only sibling she had truly grown up with, the one who had read stories to her and listened to the stories she wrote, who had played with her in the tree house and sat at the table with her for breakfast, dinner, and supper day after day. All her life, she had called him not Edwin or Ed but simply Brother: the only one of those she would ever have. Not long after she lost him, she lost the home they'd shared as well. As if he couldn't stand to be in the place where they had once been a family, A.C. sold the house on South Alabama Avenue and moved with Alice into a smaller one a few streets away.

Leeched by these losses, Nelle returned to New York and tried once again to pour herself into her work. She had already wanted to write about her childhood, to preserve in words a lifestyle she felt was slipping away; now her desire to memorialize acquired new urgency, and new emotion. But, as seemed to always happen in those years, her oldest friend got there first. Capote had returned from Europe that August, and in October he published *The Grass Harp,* the novel he had been working on based on his years in Monroeville. Nelle watched as their shared front-porch fables and backyard games charmed the rest of the world, and she longed to do the same thing for her brother and the small-town childhood they had shared.

Instead, Lee struggled to write anything at all. She had never taken a class in creative writing, and although she had written for all those campus publications, she had never produced anything longer than a few pages. Composing a single sheet of prose to her satisfaction could take an entire day. "I am more of a rewriter than a writer," Lee said, and explained that everything she wrote, she wrote at least three times.

She claimed that while there could be "no substitute for the love of language, for the beauty of an English sentence," there was also "no substitute for struggling, if a struggle is needed."

FIVE YEARS DISAPPEARED INTO THAT STRUGGLE, INTO THE SEE-saw of perfectionism and despair, with nothing to show for it but the pay stubs from jobs she didn't like. Lee was still living on the cheap, now at 1539 York Avenue, in a third-floor walk-up that lacked not only hot water but a stove on which to heat any. Worse, as far as she was concerned, it didn't have a desk, so she fashioned one for herself by dragging a discarded door up from the basement and resting it on some apple crates.

When she couldn't write, she painted, an outlet for a visual appetite she had last exercised in high school, when she had studied photography and learned her way around a darkroom. It was easier to move a brush than a pen, and Lee calmed the emotional storms of her life by fixing placid images on canvas, imitating Edward Hopper's barren rooms and bleak natural scenes. A seascape from those days went home to Bear; an empty, expressive bench beneath a window went to Weezie.

While Lee was living off peanut butter sandwiches, her friends were not only finding fame, like Capote, but starting families, like Michael Brown, who had gone, in his own words, from "the gloomiest guy on this side of Charles Addams" to the "Laughing Boy of Tin Pan Alley" after falling in love with the only American ballerina in the Ballet de Paris. Joy Williams wore Michael's Phi Beta Kappa key around her neck like the Hope Diamond, and once his career took off, the Browns bought a town house and started having children.

All her days, Nelle would seek out the company of married couples and families, delighting her nephews with spontaneous renditions of the comic operas of Gilbert and Sullivan and hiding out with the children when she wanted to escape the drear of any adult gathering. Her friend's brownstone life appealed to her far more than the bohemian one that Capote had made for himself. Truman had first lived in Manhattan, on Park Avenue, but he liked hanging around a house in Brooklyn on Middagh Street that was variously occupied by W. H. Auden, Richard Wright, Benjamin Britten, Gypsy Rose Lee, Carson McCullers, and a chimpanzee. When the owner moved into another house on nearby Willow Street and started recruiting similarly unconventional characters, the literary wunderkind and son of a carnival barker took a basement room and started calling Brooklyn Heights home. Nelle could walk down to the end of her street and look south toward Capote's borough across the East River, but it was Alabama all over again: cliques she wasn't part of, parties she didn't like going to, an endless distraction from writing. Like many self-exiled people, she was betwixt and between—wanting to write about Alabama when she was in New York, and wanting to be in New York whenever she was home in Alabama.

And she was going back home more than she ever expected. Her father had developed arthritis and needed more assistance than Alice could provide, and after he had a heart attack, Nelle returned to Monroeville to help. Cortisone shots for his pain had caused internal bleeding, and an ulcer affected his ability to eat; his recovery came one jar of baby food at a time. It was a shock to Nelle that summer of 1956 to see how much her father had aged—and how much, in aging, he had regressed. "I've done things for him that I never remotely thought I'd be called on to do for anybody, not even the Brown infants," she wrote to a friend. Her father, who had been as wise as Solomon when she was small, suddenly seemed as aged as Abraham. "I found myself staring at his handsome old face," she wrote once while sitting with him at the kitchen table, "and a sudden wave of panic flashed through me, which I think was an echo of the fear and desolation that filled me when he was nearly dead."

But for all that she adored her father, she found being home trying. She started signing letters from Monroeville as "Francesca da Rimini," after the young Italian woman who, in *The Inferno*, makes Dante faint from pity when he finds her trapped in Hell, and "The Prisoner of Zenda," after the hero of a nineteenth-century novel who is drugged and imprisoned on the eve of his coronation to try to keep him from claiming his throne. It wasn't just her father's failing health that taxed her. She didn't enjoy her peers any more at thirty than she had at ten: "Sitting & listening to people you went to school with is excruciating for an hour—to hear the same conversation day in & day out is better than the Chinese torture method." Even worse, she confessed, "I simply can't work here." "Genius overcomes all obstacles, etc., and this is no excuse," she said with characteristic self-deprecation that summer, but she also wanted, with increasing desperation, to be back at her makeshift desk in her make-do apartment, making things.

In a way, though, Nelle was making things in Alabama. Her city friends were rapt by her missives from Monroeville, and when she came back to New York that fall, Michael Brown demanded that she go talk to a literary agent, or at least the sort of agent he happened to know. "Annie Laurie Williams, Inc." was actually a drama and motion picture agency, wherein the eponymous Annie Laurie Williams sold stage and screen rights, while her husband, Maurice Crain, worked as a literary agent next door. Crain and Williams, who had met at the Texas Club in New York, favored southern stories and southern storytellers, and Brown thought they might take pity on an aspiring writer from Alabama whose accent was still so strong she claimed to be afraid of consonants.

Nelle showed up at the agency on November 27, 1956. Its offices were on East Forty-First Street in midtown, half a block from the New York Public Library and the grand stone lions that guard it, Patience and Fortitude. Low on both, Nelle had to walk around the block three times to summon the courage to go in. When she did, she was too timid to do anything but mention that she was a friend of Truman Capote's and leave some stories with Annie Laurie Williams. There were five of them: "The Land of Sweet Forever," "A Roomful of Kibble," "This Is Show Business," "The Viewers and the Viewed," and "Snow-on-the-Mountain." None of them survive, but whatever was in them made Maurice Crain, whose time as a prisoner of war in Stalag 17 had left him with a somber demeanor that the agency staff lovingly mocked by calling him "Old Woodenface," break character and come dashing out of his office, exclaiming over what he had just read.

Crain was particularly impressed by "Snow-on-the-Mountain," a story about a woman with cancer and her prized camellias, but when he and Lee finally met, he suggested that she stop tinkering with short things and try for something longer. It was easier, he explained, to sell a novel than to place short stories. "Why don't you write one about the people you know so well," Crain said encouragingly.

It was the first week of December, and Lee had never been so hopeful, or so hopeless. It had taken her seven years to write those stories; now Crain wanted her to write a whole novel. She didn't know how to do so, and she barely had time around her airline shifts to even try. She told the Browns about the meeting and then made plans to see them for Christmas, since Advent was a homesick season for her and she wouldn't be going back to Alabama for the holidays.

She spent Christmas Eve with the Browns in their town house, and when one of their boys woke her early in the morning, as little boys do on Christmas Day, she accompanied him downstairs. It was nice to be surrounded by a family, even if it wasn't hers, and to be in a real house, even if she didn't own it. The boys unwrapped their toy rockets, while Nelle honored the family's tradition of presenting the best gift she could find for the least amount of money, giving her Anglophile friends a portrait of the Reverend Sydney Smith, an obscure English cleric, and the complete works of Margot Asquith, a countess and slightly less obscure English writer. When it finally came time for Nelle to open her gift, the Browns pointed to an envelope hanging among the tinsel and ornaments on their tree. Inside it was a sizable check made payable to Lee, together with a note that read, "You have one year off from your job to write whatever you please."

IT WAS THE MOST SHOCKING CHRISTMAS GIFT OF LEE'S LIFE and, as it would turn out, one of the most momentous in the history of American literature. The Browns weren't rich, but they'd had a good year, and they suspected that if Nelle could focus on her fiction as much as she focused on selling airline tickets, she'd be able to write something magnificent. It was an ancient model of patronage, imported to Manhattan—a way to help an artist work without worrying about where her next meal would come from or how to keep the lights on. "They'd saved some money and thought it was high time they did something about me," Nelle explained years later in an essay about their generosity for *McCall's*. "They wanted to show their faith in me the best way they knew how. Whether I ever sold a line was immaterial. They wanted to give me a full, fair chance to learn my craft, free from the harassments of a regular job."

Nelle promptly quit that regular job and settled in to write. As she told a friend back home, she pulled out three pairs of Bermuda shorts to wear for the entire year, on the theory that she'd be working so hard she wouldn't leave her apartment. The Browns "don't care whether anything I write makes a nickel," she said, "they want to lick me into some kind of seriousness toward my talents." She wanted that, too, and made plain both her joy and her gratitude. Yet she also sounded a curiously dark note for someone whose greatest wish had just been granted. Taking her writing seriously, Lee wrote, "of course will destroy anything amiable in my character, but will set me on the road to a career of sorts." "I have a horrible feeling," she continued, "that this *will* be the making of me."

It was. With the confidence of her friends for a tailwind, she sailed through more pages in a matter of weeks than she had produced in entire years. By the time that she met with Crain again in January, she had already finished a new story for him, "The Cat's Meow," that she thought he might be able to place in a magazine. More promisingly, though, and almost unbelievably, she had already drafted the first fifty pages of a novel. It drew its title from a grand bit of Isaiah's prophecy about the fall of Babylon, but *Go Set a Watchman* told the story of a small southern town and a lawyer there named Atticus. Its narrator was his twenty-six-year-old daughter, Jean Louise Finch, who went by Scout, and the novel opened with her on a train, leaving New York for home, where she would find her aging father, together with all their white neighbors, up in arms about the mandate from the federal government to integrate their schools.

Crain loved it and begged for more. Mondays with Maurice became a standing appointment for the young author, and she showed up with fifty more pages the week after that first meeting, and another fifty pages the week after that. She took the first week of February off, but came back the following Monday with pages 153 through 206, managed almost forty more by the next week, and then, finally, on February 27, 1957, showed up with the last forty-eight pages of a now-complete manuscript.

It was an incredible thing. In seven years, she'd written almost nothing; in two months, she'd written an entire novel. A day after she turned in the last section, on the last day of February, Crain sent it off to G. P. Putnam's Sons, but an editor there rejected it a few weeks later. In April, Crain tried Harper & Brothers, but a month later they disagreed with his cover-letter claim that "Miss Lee" had written "an eye-opener for many northerners as to southern attitudes, and the reasons for them, in the segregation battle." The day they declined, he sent the manuscript to J. B. Lippincott.

While *Go Set a Watchman* was still out on submission, Lee retrieved her short stories "Snow-on-the-Mountain" and "The Cat's Meow," and by the end of May she'd incorporated them into the one hundred and eleven pages and counting of another novel that she was calling *The Long Good-Bye*. This second novel was better than the first, Crain thought, and he encouraged her to keep working on it. When she finished a full draft by the middle of June, he sent that manuscript along to Lippincott, too. It featured what Crain called in his cover letter the "childhood stuff" of Scout Finch, which was "wonderfully appealing" and he thought "would make a better start than the one you have." Lippincott agreed, turning down *Go Set a Watchman* but expressing interest in the untitled book.

Crain arranged for the editorial staff to meet Lee as soon as possible, but as it turned out, "interest" was, as it often is in publishing, a kind word for a complicated feeling. If Lee walked into Lippincott more confidently than she'd first walked into her literary agency, it was only because she didn't know how little most of the editors there thought of her manuscript. The house's lone female editor had been the only one charmed by the characters, and during their June meeting Therese von Hohoff Torrey was charmed by their creator, too. Tay Hohoff, as she was known, wore pinstriped suits and a tight bun; her voice was sandpapered from smoking cigarettes, and her gray hair betrayed how long she'd been in the business of editing. Born and raised in Brooklyn, she had worked with other southern authors, including Zora Neale Hurston, whose novels and anthropological studies of folklore and voodoo had been published by Lippincott two decades before.

Hohoff wasn't ready to buy the novel right away, she told Lee, but she was intrigued, and she sent the writer home with some edits. Lee, cowed, hung on every suggestion, said she would make the changes, and yes ma'amed her way back out the door. She sent some revisions in July, though she complained to Maurice Crain and to the Browns about how difficult it was to combine the narratives of *The Long Good-Bye* and *Go Set a Watchman* into one novel. Crain had an elegant if infuriating solution: stop trying to make two books into one, and just keep writing Scout's childhood. By August, she was making headway; by October she had a new version. Impressed that the aspiring author hadn't chafed at the task of revising, Hohoff read the new manuscript and saw that "the spark of the true writer flashed in every line." She also saw, however, that structural flaws left it with "dangling threads of plot," and the draft was "more a series of anecdotes than a fully conceived novel." She still loved the characters, and in the end it was chiefly the four of them—Scout, Dill, Jem, and Atticus—who sold the book.

Hohoff offered Lee a thousand dollars for the manuscript they were calling *Atticus*—not a large sum for the publisher, but a fortune for the author. By the end of the month, Lippincott had paid her the first quarter of it; she would get the next installment, Hohoff explained, whenever she delivered a version the publisher found acceptable. Lee couldn't believe her luck, or her life. Only ten months had passed since the Browns had told her to quit her job, and she'd already sold the book they'd made it possible for her to write. Her patrons, however, had no trouble believing it at all. "She was a writer to the depths of her soul," Michael Brown would later say of that astonishing year. "It would have happened with or without us—all that we did was hurry it up a little."

ALL TOLD, IT TOOK ANOTHER TWO YEARS FOR TAY HOHOFF TO convince Lee of the structural, political, and aesthetic changes necessary to rework *Go Set a Watchman* and *The Long Good-Bye* into the book that would ultimately be called *To Kill a Mockingbird.* "We talked it out," Hohoff said, "sometimes for hours. And sometimes she came around to my way of thinking, sometimes I to hers, sometimes the discussion would open up an entirely new line."

The trickiest thing turned out to be the point of view. The protagonist of the story was always Scout, but how much she knew about herself and the community in which she lived changed significantly between drafts. Lee had first written an adult Jean Louise who returned to Monroeville and suffered the loss of innocence associated with seeing one's childhood world through grown-up eyes. But Hohoff had correctly identified the scenes with children as the strongest parts of *Go Set a Watchman* and *The Long Good-Bye,* and she thought that the young Scout would make the best narrator. Lee, who had written her first novel in the third person, wrote her second in the first, and then finally settled on the stereoscopic first-person voice of child and adult that appears in *To Kill a Mockingbird.*

Other choices followed from that one, not always quickly or easily, but necessarily. Although the setting of the novels never changed—it was always a red dirt town in the Alabama Black Belt, modeled on Monroeville; even in *Watchman,* Jean Louise only *thinks* about New York—the time frame narrowed and narrowed, until finally, instead of two and a half decades of Jean Louise Finch's life, the plot was confined to a period of three years in her childhood, from the summer of 1933 through the autumn of 1935.

Not following the plot forward into the 1950s spared Lee two difficult things. For one, she didn't have to write a romance—a relief, since the relationship between Jean Louise and Henry Clinton in *Go Set a Watchman* seemed to have been written by someone who had never been in a real relationship, which, as far as anyone knows, it was. For another, it meant that Lee's readers would encounter a book set two decades in the past, leaving the civil rights movement to hover virtuously in the novel's margins instead of clashing with any of its characters.

That, in turn, enabled the most crucial change of all: unlike *Go Set a Watchman*, *To Kill a Mockingbird* could have a hero as well as a heroine. In the first version, Jean Louise goes home to visit the father she has always idolized as humane and egalitarian and is horrified to find him participating in the White Citizens' Council and opposing the work of the NAACP. By restricting the perspective to the younger Scout, Lee could let Atticus stand as a moral exemplar, the lawyer who defends an innocent black man from a racist mob. To his daughter, Atticus was a man ahead of his time, but in *Go Set a Watchman* it not only catches up but passes him by; in *To Kill a Mockingbird*, he stays heroic forever.

There's no question that Tay Hohoff helped Lee make a better book, but Maurice Crain had been right that her first novel, although wildly flawed, was eye-opening in its analysis of southern racism. Hohoff might have found it difficult to imagine segregationists who despised the Klan, but Lee knew that the South was full of them. She had known countless men like the Atticus of *Watchman*, who would defend a black man in court only to bar him from the ballot box, not to mention the neighboring booth or bar stool. In fact, the majority of whites in Alabama would never have joined a lynch mob, yet openly opposed the integration of schools, or anything else. But Lee's efforts to convey that complexity had turned *Watchman* into a didactic stage play between "Enlightened Daughter" and "Benighted Father," and the characters could not bear their political weight.

Hohoff wanted to free Lee's fiction from its sanctimony, and she argued that a palliative plot stood a better chance of reaching readers than a moralizing one. A Quaker who was, at the time, writing a biography of John Lovejoy Elliott, a social activist with the Ethical Culture movement whose great uncle had been murdered by a lynch mob, Hohoff wanted Lee to tell a redemptive story of tolerance. And what she wanted, she generally got: not by accident was Hohoff known around New York as "the Quaker Hitler." It was easier, Hohoff argued, to structure a plot around someone like Bob Ewell, the poor and shiftless white man who everyone could agree was villainous, than to try to convince naive and self-justifying readers of the racism of seemingly respectable people like Atticus. Better, Hohoff insisted, for the Maycomb County courtroom to host a crusading trial than a racist rally, and best to convert readers to the cause of racial justice with a child's loss of innocence than to condemn them through the disillusioned voice of an adult daughter.

During the two years that Lee went back and forth on the page with her editor, she also went back and forth from New York to the Deep South as her father's health worsened. It was hard on her work, but it meant interacting more with her source material—both the place she was from and the other people who had grown up there. She and her sister took turns with their father, Alice working at the law office during the day and then spelling Nelle at night. "She would go home to look after Daddy, and I would come down here to write," she said of the Barnett, Bugg & Lee offices. Those offices were right on the courthouse square, in a Monroeville that she was turning into Maycomb while the world around her slept. By then, she had committed to Scout's perspective so deeply that she was living it. "I was sitting here one night writing the last chapter where the old boy chases the kids," Lee later said, "and I got so scared I ran home."

By November 1959, it was finally all there: Jem's broken arm, Calpurnia's church home, mean Mrs. Dubose with the pistol under her shawl, Aunt Alexandra and Uncle Jack, Atticus and his pocket watch, the pint-sized Merlin who lived next door, Tom and Helen Robinson, the ramshackle porch of the Radley house, the oak tree with its knothole full of mystery, the balcony of the courthouse, and Scout, that Hail Mary of a heroine. On the tenth of that month, Lee picked up what she thought might be her last check ever from Lippincott, and waited to see what the world would make of Maycomb.

# 18

# Deep Calling to Deep

HARPER LEE WASN'T CAPOTE'S FIRST CHOICE. HE'D WANTED to bring along his friend Andrew Lyndon, another young southern writer, but when Lyndon said he couldn't do it, Capote turned to Lee instead. He was headed out of town for a story, he explained, to a part of the country he barely knew, and he wanted someone to be his "assistant researchist." It would involve helping him conduct interviews and gather material, and it would require traveling with him to Kansas.

On November 15, 1959, in the tiny community of Holcomb in the southwestern part of the state, a farmer named Herb Clutter, his wife, Bonnie, their sixteen-year-old daughter, Nancy, and their fifteen-year-old son, Kenyon, were found murdered in their home. The Clutters were a wealthy, well-regarded family, and the news was so shocking that the murders made it all the way into *The New York Times,* albeit in abbreviated form. Capote had seen that sliver of a story and decided that he wanted to turn it into a bigger one for *The New Yorker:* not just a description of the crime or a portrait of the victims, but a profile of the entire town.

"He said it would be a tremendously involved job," Lee later remembered, and by a coincidence of timing she was tremendously available. The Clutters had been murdered five days after she turned in the final manuscript of *To Kill a Mockingbird,* and she had no idea what she was going to do next. It turned out that handing in a book, like selling a manuscript, still left you a long way from seeing it in bookstores: it was like pregnancy, except that right when you think you're done, there's *another* nine months of waiting. Lee had just begun that long limbo, and she didn't want to go back to work for the airlines, but she didn't have many other options. Capote's "assistant researchist" offer would give her something to do, and helping him with a feature for *The New Yorker* might make it easier to land her own assignments. "She had been thinking about doing a nonfiction book," he said, "and wanted to learn my techniques of reportage."

Capote, self-aggrandizing as ever, seemed to have forgotten that his friend was the daughter of a newspaper editor and already knew a thing or two about journalism. Although her time in Kansas later proved a kind of trial run for her time in Alexander City, it was no apprenticeship to Capote. Instead, it was more like a return to childhood for them both: once again, although more literally than before, they became partners in crime. "It was deep calling to deep," she'd say later, quoting the psalmist. "The crime intrigued him, and I'm intrigued with crime—and, boy I wanted to go." They settled on her fee—nine hundred dollars, almost as much as she'd been paid for her novel, plus expenses—and boarded a train together at Grand Central Terminal, its ceiling of stars a tiny sample of the ones they would soon see over the Great Plains.

It was a long way from the Manhattan they left to Manhattan, Kansas. Once they arrived there by overnight train, they were still a four-hundred-mile drive from Garden City, the nearest town of any size, to Holcomb, the village of 270 people where the Clutters had been killed. They had plenty of time on the way for talking, planning, and reminiscing. Lee had long been, as she said, "intrigued with crime," real and otherwise; she'd grown up surrounded by stacks of the magazine *True Detective Mysteries,* cut her teeth on Sherlock Holmes, and still loved murder stories. She had also watched all those trials from the balcony of the Monroe County Courthouse, and unlike Capote she had studied criminal law.

Capote, however, was the one who had previous firsthand experience with a murderer. One summer when he was staying in Monroeville, a sixteen-year-old girl had come to visit relatives and took a liking to Capote, much to the annoyance of ten-year-old Nelle. ("I was jealous," she said later, "of all the time Truman was spending with Martha—the exotic older woman.") Eventually, the girl convinced Capote to run away with her to a town some miles distant. The caper didn't last long; Capote got dragged home, and the girl was sent back to her parents. Thirteen years later, Martha Beck committed a series of murders with a man she met through the classified ads, a former inmate and professed voodoo practitioner; together, they became known as "the Lonely Hearts Killers."

By the time Lee and Capote got to Garden City, the town where they'd be staying, seven miles down the Arkansas River from Holcomb, which didn't have any hotels, they were ready to play the roles that his partner, Jack, had jokingly assigned them before they left: Perry Mason and his secretary, Della Street. They arrived just a few weeks after the murders, in an area still so mired in fear that the locals left their lights on all night long. "At first it was like being on another planet," Lee wrote, "a vast terrain indifferent to the creatures that walked upon it, an untrusting populace suspicious of anyone alien to it."

They checked into adjacent rooms at the Warren Hotel. Anticipating the limitations of anywhere that wasn't New York, Capote had packed a whole footlocker full of food. From the get-go, he was wary of Kansas, and Kansas returned the favor: most of the people of Garden City had no idea what to make of the orchid that had suddenly invaded their wheat fields. At first, no one would talk to him. His voice was odd, his clothes were off-putting, and for all the people of Finney County knew, he was connected to the murderers. Capote, indifferent but not oblivious to the impression he made, had been warned by a friend that the people of Holcomb might not appreciate a "little gnome in his checkered vest running around asking questions about who'd murdered whom."

Still, Capote hadn't anticipated the level of resistance he encountered. He'd expected to interview everyone in a few days and hadn't brought enough food for more than that. He and Lee had planned to set out each morning to report, then convene each night at the hotel to prepare their notes: she planned to type hers out while he wrote his longhand, and then they would review and revise them together, just as they had when writing stories together on South Alabama Avenue. Capote liked to say that he was a human tape recorder (although disproving his own point, he variously claimed to have 95, 97, and 99 percent recall), but Lee was close to being a human video camera: she had an excellent ear for dialogue, but also an eye for scenes and settings. Lee took care to note what someone was wearing or how he held his hands or what was on the television in the background, and it was Lee who drew diagrams, made lists, tracked itineraries, and constructed chronologies from multiple sources.

They arrived in town on Tuesday, December 15, and began making the rounds the very next day. They went first to the Finney County Courthouse, where they tried to interview Agent Alvin Dewey of the Kansas Bureau of Investigation, who was having none of it. Other reporters had already been on the story for three weeks by then, and many of them were locals. To Dewey and nearly everyone else in Garden City, *The New Yorker* sounded like some kind of regional publication, and the man claiming to work for it seemed just as likely to be a writer for *The New Martian*. Dewey told Capote to come back for the regular press conference and to bring his credentials with him when he did.

This created something of a crisis. However good his "techniques of reportage" might have been, Capote had shown up in Kansas without any proof that he was a journalist, and law enforcement officers weren't inclined to take him at his word. The case they were working was sensitive, and they wanted to protect both the integrity of the investigation and the privacy of the two surviving Clutter daughters, who were in their early twenties and already living away from home when the rest of the family was murdered. Capote made some calls and got someone at Random House—almost certainly the editor in chief, Bennett Cerf—to try to intercede on his behalf with the Federal Bureau of Investigation. A call to the bureau was duly placed, but unfortunately for Capote the FBI checked its files, consulted *Who's*

*Who in America,* and decided he wasn't sufficiently "legitimate" for them to intervene with the local field office.

Capote didn't have any better luck pleading his case directly with Dewey, so he and Lee did what they could without access, gathering clippings from local newspapers, collecting tourist brochures from around town, and eavesdropping on locals in cafés and at the post office. Lee set about learning what she could about the setting of Capote's story, from its agricultural history to its social and religious traditions to its most famous quack—one John Romulus Brinkley, who performed surgical goat-gland transplants on men as a kind of early-twentieth-century Viagra and whose wife had blasted Bertrand Russell for promoting free love while she and her husband were trying to sell it.

But background was one thing; the tragedy itself was another. When Lee and Capote tried approaching a few promising sources, including neighbors of the Clutters and relatives of the two teenage girls who had discovered the bodies, they were rebuffed or ignored. Under the best of circumstances, the shibboleths of a tiny town like Holcomb are hard to master, and during a time of such immense fear and grief residents were going out of their way to shield themselves from outsiders. But to the apprehensive locals, Lee was everything Capote was not: warm, empathetic, and familiar enough that they felt their stories were safe with her. "Absolutely fantastic lady. I really liked her very much," Harold Nye, one of the KBI agents who worked on the Clutter case, said of Lee, but of Capote he confessed, "I did not get a very good impression of that little son of a bitch."

That impression was surely affected by the fact that when Nye and three other agents arrived at the Warren Hotel to introduce themselves, Capote was wearing a pink negligee. But neither the lingerie nor the lesbian bar in Kansas City where the author later took Nye and his wife could dull the shine the couple took to Lee. Crucially, Agent Dewey, the lead investigator on the case, came to feel the same way. "If Capote came on as something of a shocker, she was there to absorb the shock," Dewey said. "She had a down-home style, a friendly smile, and a knack for saying the right things." Dolores Hope, a local newspaper writer and the wife of Clifford Hope, the Clutter family's lawyer, explained, "Nelle sort of managed Truman, acting as his guardian or mother. She broke the ice for him."

CHARMED BY THE SENSIBLE SOUTHERN LADY AND CURIOUS about her unusual friend, the town that had resisted sharing its shock and grief with strangers now began welcoming the two out-of-towners into its living rooms. And other rooms, too: Lee and Capote were soon permitted to tour the Clutter family home, even though it was still an active crime scene. They followed the stairs up to the children's bedrooms, where mother and daughter had been found, and back down to the basement to where father and son had been killed. All of the blood had been washed away by four of Herb Clutter's friends who had come the day after the murders with mops, scrub brushes, rags, and pails, but there were still the shadows of stains where the bodies had been, and the house felt like a crypt.

Capote and Lee drove the fifteen minutes back to town and retired to the Warren Hotel to work. He made three pages of notes that evening; she made nine, including details on every one of the Clutter house's fourteen rooms. Lee recorded the height of the kitchen cabinets and the titles of the books, the color of the walls and the patterns of the linoleum, the gauges of the shotguns in the closet, the autographs on framed pictures, the presence of a Ping-Pong table but the absence of Ping-Pong balls. She drew floor plans of the first story, the second story, and the basement, along with maps of the property and the landscaping.

Inevitably, Lee began drawing conclusions about the family that had lived there, too. In many ways, the Clutters were like the Lees, and she could intuit things about them that Capote could not. She had lived the liturgical cycles of their years in the Methodist Church, and like the Clutter children she had made record books for her 4-H Club. More strikingly, she had grown up in a family not unlike theirs: a self-made father whose sterling reputation crossed county lines, a troubled mother whose mental health alternately made her seek treatment in faraway cities and kept her mysteriously homebound, and children of disparate ages—two of them old enough to be out of the home, the third an anxious striver whose diary showed her struggling to please her father and appease her mother, and the fourth a loner who kept books by his bed.

For Capote, they were a story; for Lee, they were a family. She was already building a psychological portrait of the victims, and her ability to think of them as people brought her closer with those in town who had known them. During the third week of December, the Hopes called the Warren Hotel to invite Lee and her friend to Christmas dinner, worried that they would have nowhere else to go. For their part, the writers had been worried that they wouldn't be able to get anything done that week, but if the courts and everything else were closed for the holiday, the people were finally open.

After the Hopes welcomed the odd couple from Alabama, everybody else in town wanted to meet them, too, including the Deweys. Capote and Lee had nicknamed Agent Dewey "Foxy" because of how closely he guarded information about the investigation (and possibly also because he was attractive, a characteristic Nelle recorded, complete with schoolgirlish hearts, in a letter to her agents). But his wife, Marie, a native of New Orleans, was prepared to extend her southern hospitality even to big-city journalists and invited the writers to dinner. While they were getting to know the family, including the Deweys' two young sons and a giant tiger-striped cat called Courthouse Pete, Mrs. Dewey plied them with avocado salad, country-fried steak, shrimp, sauterne, and a Cajun dish with rice and navy beans and bacon. As it turned out, though, none of that was the main dish. While Capote and Lee were over that night, a telephone call came for Agent Dewey: the men who murdered the Clutters had been arrested in Las Vegas, a thousand miles away.

That news was a relief to the residents of Finney County, who could finally turn off their lights when they went to bed and pull the ten-penny nails out of their window frames, but it complicated matters for Capote. Originally, he hadn't planned to see the investigation through to its end; on his first day in town, he'd callously commented that he didn't even care if the murders were ever solved. He and Lee had already interviewed dozens of people, and he had reams of notes ready to take back with him to New York—more than enough raw material for the story he had pitched. Now that the suspects had been arrested, though, Capote knew he would need to tell their story, too, and that meant he and Lee would need to stay in Kansas a while longer.

In early January, the two writers were waiting outside the Finney County Courthouse, her feet numb and his ears red from the blistering cold, as Perry Smith and Dick Hickock emerged in handcuffs from police cars. They watched the next morning, too, as the two men were arraigned on first-degree murder charges, Hickock sounding like a cowboy as he waived his preliminary hearing, Smith sounding more like a cleric. On the next Monday, Capote paid fifty dollars each for an interview with the killers, and Lee came along. Perry Smith, the son of a Cherokee mother and Irish father, wouldn't sit until Lee was seated, and then he wouldn't say much at all, beyond allowing that he would think about talking with them for their story. By contrast, Dick Hickock, a blond, tattooed mechanic born and raised in eastern Kansas, began cooperating right away; he addressed Lee as "ma'am," answered every question the pair had, and would have kept talking all day if Agent Dewey hadn't returned him to his cell.

One week later, both men came back to Dewey's office for another interview, and another fifty dollars. This time, Smith was more forthcoming, and Hickock was even more garrulous than before: both talked about why they had targeted the Clutters (a false rumor that Herb Clutter kept a safe full of cash on the property) and where they had traveled while on the lam (a complicated itinerary that crossed several state lines and the Mexican border). Lee could already tell that Capote was overly drawn to Perry Smith, partly because of a certain physical resemblance but mostly because of their common emotional experiences. Both men were the size and shape of a crab apple, and both had fallen from the same sort of tree: their fathers were absent, their mothers alcoholic. It was obvious to Lee that the balance of Capote's authorial intent was already shifting from elegy to apologia; there wouldn't be much complexity allotted to the victims, because he would need all of it for his new protagonists, the men who killed them.

Capote knew plenty of the why of those murders from the inter-

views with the accused, and Lee had cadged him excerpts of the inter-
rogation transcripts from Agent Dewey, which added the when and
where and how. All told, Capote figured he had enough material
to start writing what he was now calling a "nonfiction novel"—an
attempt to use the techniques of fiction to tell a true story—and
together with Lee he left Kansas the next day. They splurged on the
luxury train, spent a night in Chicago, and got back to New York on
January 18, 1960. At Grand Central, they parted ways, Nelle heading uptown and Capote going back to Brooklyn. By the end of the
week, he had already talked the editors of *The New Yorker* into letting
him turn his Kansas story into a multipart series and signed a book
contract with Random House.

NOT LONG AFTER THEY GOT BACK TO THE CITY, NELLE MOVED.
She didn't leave Yorkville, but she upgraded her apartment to one a
handful of blocks south, at 403 East Seventy-Seventh Street, where she
could have heat and hot water both. While Capote was celebrating
his latest book deal, she was dotting the i's and crossing the t's on her
first one, literally: she arrived home to page proofs for *Mockingbird*
that had to be reviewed. But she also had other work to do. Partly
to make money, having long since spent the advance on her book
and not knowing if it would ever earn royalties, and partly to do
Capote a favor, since they both knew that he would need to stay in
the good graces of everyone in Kansas, she had taken her own assignment related to the Clutter case. Before becoming a KBI agent, Alvin
Dewey had worked for the FBI, and Lee had agreed to write a profile
of him for one of the nichiest magazines in the nation: *The Grapevine*,
the newsletter of the Society of Former Special Agents of the Federal
Bureau of Investigation.

The house style of *The Grapevine* hovers somewhere between
alumni notes and an autopsy report, and Lee's profile of Dewey is no
exception. Her piece was sandwiched between head shots of agents
who had retired or died and announcements about conferences and
events, and either by design or by brute-force editing, it came out
sounding just like the rest of *The Grapevine*. It was unremarkable,

unsigned, and mailed out to former G-men on mimeographed pages, but it was still her first clip since college.

A gossip sheet for the organization least inclined to gossip, *The Grapevine* is basically unknown to those outside the FBI, and Lee's article came and went in the March 1960 issue without much of a fuss. Even if it had been signed, almost no one at the time would have recognized its author's name, but the profile served its purpose of keeping Capote close with the Deweys, and it kept Lee close, too; later that spring, when Capote went back to Kansas for the sale of the Clutter family farm and the trial of Hickock and Smith, she went with him. This time, they brought along the photographer Richard Avedon, best known for his fashion shoots and celebrity portraits.

Although she didn't appear in any of the pictures that later ran in *Life* magazine, Lee shows up in Avedon's contact sheets from that trip, and she showed up every day to report, too, as she had during the previous visit. In fact, this time, she proved even more valuable, because she had spent her entire life around courthouses and was only one semester short of a law degree. When Smith and Hickock went to trial on March 22, Capote and Lee were both in the courtroom, but only she made any notes about the jurors—who, seven days later, after less than an hour of deliberation, found both men guilty and sentenced them to death. "Why they never look at people they've sentenced to death, I'll never know," Lee wrote of the jurors in her notes, echoing a sentiment she loans to Scout in *To Kill a Mockingbird*. A few days later, the judge set the date of execution for May 13, 1960.

It was, in the most terrible and literal way, a deadline. Capote was going to write this book the way he had written his last one: in the Mediterranean, far from the social temptations and professional obligations of New York. Lee did what she could to help her friend, readying all of her material from their time in Kansas and presenting him, before he left, with more than 150 pages of typed notes. These she divided into ten sections: one on the town, one on the landscape, one on the crime, one on each of the four victims, one for the two surviving daughters, one on their interviews, and one on the trial. She also included a dedication, offering up her work "To the Author of The Fire and the Flame and the Small Person Who So Manfully

Endured Him"—a tender nod to some of Capote's juvenilia and an acknowledgment of the three decades they had already spent collaborating before they ever set foot in Kansas.

Those notes formed the template for how she would organize her own crime reporting almost twenty years later in Alexander City. At the top of almost every page, above the substance of the interviews themselves, Lee noted the date that each one was made, or the date to which it corresponded on the timeline of the Clutter investigation, plus whom they had talked with and where they had done so. Wherever she could, she also set a little scene, so that however much time passed before Capote returned to the notes, he could be transported back to the living room or dining room or courthouse where the interview had taken place. She also did Capote the favor of starting to put all of the voices they'd heard in conversation with one another, gathering into separate sections what each of their many sources had said about Mrs. Clutter, Mr. Clutter, Kenyon, and Nancy, and adding questions and theories about the crimes along the way.

Lee pinned more than fifty people on the page this way, including some she interviewed and Capote did not: friends of the Clutter children, neighbors of the Clutter family, the county coroner, agents of the KBI, detectives, clergy, the judge, the sheriff, the jury, the gossips at the café, and the worrywarts at the post office. Her notes were full of sources who had talked about the Clutter case only because they were talking to her. Bobby Rupp, Nancy Clutter's boyfriend and the last person to see the family before the murders, said that if it had been only Capote conducting the interviews, he "would probably have walked out of the room."

More than mere transcripts, Lee's voluminous notes are those of a careful observer, a keen legal mind, and a tragicomic chronicler of American history. She recorded for Capote the height of Mrs. Clutter's socks and the length of Nancy Clutter's mirror—registering even the reflection that wasn't there and exactly how much of herself the girl could have taken in every morning before school. She summarized the court testimony, explained legal strategies, and offered psychological portraits of the jury. And she gave Capote the gift of notes on things that had nothing to do with the murders but everything to do with the place where they occurred—its cats, customs, charlatans, and seasons. More than most field notes, hers were a book waiting to be written.

But juries aren't the only ones who have trouble looking directly at the damned. It would take years for Hickock and Smith to run out of all their legal options and arrive, finally, at the gallows, and it would take Capote just as long to figure out a way to write about the Clutter case without blinking. In the end, after both men were dead, he finally finished *In Cold Blood,* and it became the best seller he had always hoped it would. But that was five years away, and by then Harper Lee had already published one of her own.

# 19

# Death and Taxes

O F ALL THE REASONS A WRITER MIGHT STOP WRITING— addiction, anxiety, depression, the vitriol of critics, the distraction of love, the arrival of children, a lack of ideas, an avalanche of doubt—perhaps the least likely is taxation. Yet before *To Kill a Mockingbird* was even available in bookstores, Harper Lee claimed that the Internal Revenue Service was keeping her from working.

That unusual claim was first recorded by Dolores Hope, the newspaper columnist Lee had met in Kansas. As the author of "The Distaff Side," an almost daily feature of the *Garden City Telegram,* Hope wrote up everything from cookbooks to diets to a proposed "Girdles Day," and after she met Capote and Lee in 1959, the writers started making regular cameos in her column. The following year, when the pair came back for the trial of Hickock and Smith, Hope wrote about Lee's forthcoming novel. It was two weeks before Tax Day, and Hope revealed that although *To Kill a Mockingbird* wouldn't be published until July, it had already been purchased by the Literary Guild and Reader's Digest for reprinting and sale through their services. For most authors, Hope wrote, "this is what is known as hitting the jack pot in a large way," but not for Lee, who would no longer be freelancing because "she can't afford to make any more money." Instead of praise for her book, Hope continued, Lee "jokingly asks only one bit of recognition—that her name be inscribed on a future rocket. Because, she says, she figures to pay for one." That was a wild exaggeration, but it's true that the affluent were aggressively taxed at the time; America's postwar prosperity was fueled partly by tax rates that could reach as high as 90 percent. According to Hope, Lee griped that "the government will get at least 70 percent of her earnings."

It was, you might say, rich: poor, penniless Harper Lee, who had been living without hot water, writing on a makeshift desk, walking to avoid paying bus fare, begging her agents for more money from her advance to cover expenses, flat-sitting for Truman Capote and Jack Dunphy to save on rent, and surviving on peanut butter and whatever meals she could filch from friends—that same Harper Lee was suddenly so wealthy that she couldn't work. Very few people ever knew exactly *how* wealthy, beyond her agents, her editor, and her sister Alice, whose expertise in tax law had suddenly become extremely convenient. But if Lee expected to be taxed at a 70 percent rate that year, she had probably already earned somewhere around $700,000 in today's money—a huge amount for a novelist even now, and seven hundred times the size of her advance.

And that was before the book even came out. *To Kill a Mockingbird* was published on July 11, 1960. It hit the best-seller list immediately, then kept moving up it, propelled by glowing review after glowing review. In December, it made all the end-of-the-year roundups and rankings; in January 1961, the film rights sold, and not long afterward the public learned that Horton Foote would write the screenplay and Gregory Peck would star as Atticus Finch. Publishers in France, Germany, Italy, Spain, Holland, Denmark, Norway, Sweden, Finland, and the Czech Republic bought foreign rights. In May, it won the Pulitzer Prize. By its first anniversary, *To Kill a Mockingbird* had already sold half a million copies. The film opened on Christmas Day in 1962, was nominated for eight Oscars not long after, and won three of them in April 1963. There was no lull in the accolades, no slackening in sales, no shortage of royalties, and no end to the taxes.

Alice could advise her sister about financial planning all she wanted, but no one could teach Harper Lee to render unto Caesar that which was Caesar's with gladness. When the esteemed professor Hudson Strode, who had taught Lee Shakespeare at the University of Alabama, wrote to say how much he'd loved her novel and to ask if Mr. Atticus Finch might not be Mr. A. C. Lee, she wrote back to say, "Yes, Atticus was my father. He is now teaching me to pay my taxes cheerfully, but with little success!" When a reporter followed Lee around Hollywood as she visited the set of the film adaptation, she complained so much that he ended his piece by writing, "Success hasn't spoiled Harper Lee, but it has changed her life. She can't quite convince people that the book hasn't made her an instant millionairess. The fact of the matter is that tax laws can be great for sharp-minded movie stars and oil men but are hell on authors." Her agents found themselves in the unusual position of apologizing to a client for how many checks were coming in: "We can't stop them, once they get started, and we know you will do everything you can to keep some of the money. We hate to think of so much of it going out in income tax." More than fifty years later, when Lee was well into her eighties, she wrote to congratulate the distinguished Alabama historian Virginia Van der Veer Hamilton on her memoir—*Teddy's Child: Growing Up in the Anxious Southern Gentry Between the Great Wars*—and to warn her it had better sell under three million copies: "If it sells more, you will have tax collectors hounding you!"

It was, as Dolores Hope had noted, the sort of problem most authors can only dream of having. Within a few years of its publication, *To Kill a Mockingbird* was selling a million copies a year. Lee got all the royalties from those books—and from all the foreign editions and special editions, too—plus a cut of the hefty film profits, because Annie Laurie Williams had negotiated a sweetheart deal where Lee took less cash up front in exchange for a larger percentage of the film's royalties in perpetuity. Rarely has a double bet paid off so lavishly. The film became an American classic, and the book has scarcely waned in popularity since its annus mirabilis; to date, some forty million copies have been sold.

THE BETTER *TO KILL A MOCKINGBIRD* FARED, THE WORSE ITS author seemed to, and if Lee resented the taxes, she loathed the publicity. The summer of the book's release, she wrote to a friend that she had been "in New York, where I became Famous; in Connecticut, where the Famous go to get used to it; in East Hampton, where the

Famous go after they've gotten used to it." But Lee never got used to it. There was a profile of her in *Newsweek,* written from an interview conducted at the Algonquin Hotel, where she played dumb about her own celebrity. There was a whole spread in *Life,* after a long, awkward photo shoot around Monroeville, where she played kickball in her old schoolyard, posed on the balcony of the Monroe County Courthouse, pretended to be typing at Barnett, Bugg & Lee, addressed her favorite teacher Gladys Watson Burkett's class, golfed with some friends at the local course, sat reading with her father and sister on their front porch, and peered into the windows of a house taken to be the model for Boo Radley's home.

Every bookstore wanted Lee to come for a signing, and every classmate, teacher, neighbor, waitress, librarian, soda jerk, landlord, and golf caddy she'd ever encountered wanted her to autograph their copy of her novel. They also all wanted in on her story: in a pattern of distortion that would last the rest of her life, a few minutes with almost any member of the Lee family became an epic interaction, and near strangers suddenly began passing themselves off as close confidants.

Lee herself had no patience for this budding Harper Lee Industrial Complex. But even when she started declining interviews and refusing events, there was still the matter of mail. Most of the letters she got were complimentary, but some were coarse indictments of a southern lady who had sold out her ancestral land or a white woman who had betrayed her race. The letters came by the dozens every day, and Lee found herself wanting to respond to all of them, less out of appreciation than out of obligation. Her young admirers, especially, seemed to her to merit replies; you could stock a whole library with the notes that Harper Lee wrote back to children who had read her novel.

As a result, in the year after *Mockingbird* came out, Lee wrote more letters than anything else, but she did manage to eke out a few small pieces. There was the essay for *McCall's* that described her friends the Browns and their Magi-like gift. There was that farcical crackling bread recipe for *The Artists' and Writers' Cookbook,* which sounded like something from her *Rammer-Jammer* days. "First, catch your pig," it began, then proceeded to advise would-be chefs to "ship it to the *abattoir* nearest you," variously fry and bake what comes back, and combine it all with cornmeal, salt, baking powder, egg, and milk. What you finally remove from the oven, she cautioned, will have cost you $250: "Some historians say by this recipe alone fell the Confederacy."

There was a two-page story for the April 15, 1961, issue of *Vogue* called "Love—in Other Words," which, in his files, her agent Maurice Crain aptly retitled "The Gospel According to Nelle Harper." Ostensibly an essay on love, it was, instead, an appealing jumble of all the texts and authors bouncing around in her brain: Cervantes, Shakespeare, Paul's first letter to the Corinthians, and Lytton Strachey's biography of Queen Victoria. But it was autobiographically revealing in other ways as well. Tucked into it was a vignette about a sixteen-year-old grandson sneaking his dying grandfather hamburgers in the hospital. The boy was one of her nephews, and the man in the hospital was Lee's father, whose health had once again taken a turn for the worse.

LEE WAS STILL DIVIDING HER TIME BETWEEN NEW YORK AND Alabama, and in the fall of 1960 she went home to see her father and sister in Monroeville, then her other sister in Eufaula. In both places, she was feted like a prodigal daughter. Her comings and goings were front-page news; unfortunately for her, pictures were de rigueur, and she seldom liked the process or the results, especially because she was no longer the slip of a girl she'd been in childhood. Having decided that she weighed more than she wanted, she began the cycle of "reducing" that would continue over the next decade through extreme diets.

In New York, the friends who had watched Lee struggle to become a writer since her *School Executive* days were over the moon for her. One of those friends was also now her next-door neighbor at a new apartment on East Eighty-Second Street: Marcia Van Meter, a fellow Chi Omega and glee clubber from Massachusetts, had rented an adjoining apartment. They were together one night, doing laundry in the basement, when they rescued a polydactyl kitten; they rushed him to a veterinarian, nursed him back to health, and then delivered him in an Abercrombie basket to Tay Hohoff, who named him Shadrach, made him a permanent resident of her home, and later gave him prime real estate in her memoir *Cats and Other People*.

Marcia Van Meter worked some as an editor for the College Board and then for *The New Yorker*. She and Lee traveled together, took in baseball games in the city, and watched over each other's affairs. When Annie Laurie Williams and Maurice Crain sent a telegram to Lee on the one-year anniversary of the publication of *Mockingbird*, it was sent care of Van Meter: "Dear Nelle—TOMORROW IS MY FIRST BIRTHDAY AND MY AGENTS THINK THERE SHOULD BE ANOTHER BOOK WRITTEN SOON TO KEEP ME COMPANY. DO YOU THINK YOU CAN START ONE BEFORE I AM ANOTHER YEAR OLD."

Lee was already trying desperately to do just that, but writing a second novel was proving more difficult than writing the first. She needed quiet, and even in the best of times she could take all day to do something as simple as move a character across a room; now she had too little time and too many interruptions. She had already started complaining about "the second-novel doldrums" in August 1960, and by September of the next year she told a friend, "If I'd had any sense, I'd have done a J. D. Salinger," warning that "you can spend the rest of your life simply having lunch, cocktails, and dinner with people who simply MUST meet you."

She found some respite at an old farmhouse in Connecticut owned by her agents, and she went there whenever she could rent a car or catch a ride with them, sometimes spending weeks away from the city. But her father's health had continued to worsen, and late in 1961 she rushed home again after he had another heart attack. She stayed two months to take care of him. That was while the movie version of her book was being made, and in November its art director came to Monroe County to have a look around. Lee took him to see the almond trees and collard patches, the shacks where black families lived, fancier houses that might pass for the Finch place, and the courthouse that would soon be the most famous in America. In January, Gregory Peck came down, and she showed him around real-life Maycomb, too.

The mash notes followed her home, especially when her fans realized that just about all it took to get a letter to her in Alabama was a postage stamp and the surname Lee on the envelope. Truman Capote, who was greener with envy than all of the pine trees in the state, nonetheless registered the toll that success was taking on the Miracle of Monroeville. To a mutual friend, he confided that "not long ago she wrote that she was going to Alabama for a few weeks rest-up: poor darling, she seems to be having some sort of happy nervous-breakdown"; to the Deweys, he wrote, "Poor thing—she is nearly demented: says she gave up trying to answer her 'fan mail' when she received 62 letters in one day. I wish she could relax and enjoy it more."

WHEN LEE FINALLY RETURNED TO NEW YORK, IN THE MIDDLE of February, she tried to return to her work as well, but she had barely settled back into life there when her father had another heart attack. It was April 12, 1962. Harper Lee was, by then, thirty-five years old—a decade past the death of her mother and her brother, a decade into carrying the burdens of her father's poor health. For years, she had worried when his fatigue kept him from going into the office and dreaded the day his arthritis would make it impossible for him to check the time on his famous pocket watch or turn his familiar pocketknife over and over. She had come and gone from Monroeville to help Alice and Louise take care of him so often that when the call came in, she knew all eleven hundred of the miles she had to cross to get to his bedside. This time, however, there would be no coming back from the hospital, no long, slow recovery where he eased into walking with a cane in one hand and a daughter or grandchild steadying the other. Harper Lee's father died three days later, early in the morning on Palm Sunday.

At the time of his death, A. C. Lee was eighty-two years old. His disappointment at his youngest child not becoming a lawyer had disappeared, and with the publication of *Mockingbird* his fears about her chosen vocation had turned into pure pride. "I never dreamed of what was going to happen," he had told *The Monroe Journal*. "It was somewhat of a surprise, and it's very rare indeed when a thing like this happens to a country girl going to New York." He'd taught Nelle to read and given her books her entire life, but he never imagined that she would write one of the world's most beloved ones or that he would be the model for its hero. Before his death, A.C. had taken to answering to Atticus and signing his name that way when anyone asked him to autograph his daughter's novel; the year after he died, Gregory Peck carried his pocket watch as he accepted the Academy Award for best actor.

*To Kill a Mockingbird* wasn't a biography of Nelle Lee's father, yet she had fixed some essential part of him on the page, sharing his virtues at the very moment when readers most wanted to believe that there were noble white men in the South and that good men could remain that way even in bad times. That fall, she gave money to Monroeville's First Methodist Church, where all her family's funerals had been held, to cover the cost of a renovation and expansion in memory of her parents and her brother. But her real memorial to her family would always be her work, and when she returned to the city, she tried to find her way back into the habit of writing.

She tried in Connecticut, at her agents' Old Stone House; she tried on Fire Island, where the Browns had a summer cottage in Saltaire; she tried in West Brattleboro, Vermont, where her friend Lucile Sullivan, who worked for Annie Laurie Williams, rented a summerhouse and then an apartment. But her grief followed her everywhere, and so did the publicity demands of what she had taken to calling "the Bird," as if it were alive and had an existence apart from her own. On top of all that, there was pressure from her publisher. Although other Lippincott editors remember Hohoff as "a junkyard dog," ferociously protecting her most famous author, no one thought it was good for Lee to go more than a few years without producing another book.

Meanwhile, Capote was delayed with his book, too, though not because he was having trouble writing it. Endless delays and appeals had kept Perry Smith and Dick Hickock alive. He and Lee had visited them in prison the previous year, just after Gregory Peck had come to visit her and tour Monroeville. Capote felt he wouldn't have an ending until their fate was decided. He had drafted almost all of what he was already calling *In Cold Blood,* and in April 1963 he and Lee made their final visit together to Kansas. Capote had bought a new Jaguar, which he called his Fabergé on wheels, and he came to fetch her from Monroeville, where she had been staying since the holidays and where he hadn't been in eight years. His relatives threw a party, and forty friends came to celebrate the hometown authors.

Between them, Capote and Lee had one surviving parent. Her mother and father were dead, while his mother had overdosed on Seconal and scotch. Nostalgic from his time in Monroe County, Capote took a meandering route to Garden City, stopping first in Shreveport, Louisiana, to visit his father, whom he hadn't seen since his mother's funeral almost a decade before. While just about every journalist in the country was headed to Alabama to cover the civil rights movement there, Lee and Capote were leaving it behind, driving west toward Kansas; they arrived in Garden City while Martin Luther King Jr. was writing his "Letter from Birmingham Jail." The two writers stayed a week, mostly for Capote to check in with sources, then took the long way home, stopping in Colorado Springs to celebrate Lee's thirty-seventh birthday at the Broadmoor resort.

It had been more than three years since the two had first arrived in Kansas. Capote was nearly finished with his book, which his editor was already calling a masterpiece, but Lee had seen her only other fiction submission rejected. "Dress Rehearsal" was a story that *Esquire* had requested but then turned down partly because it was overly didactic, but also because of its complicated depiction of southern racism. Like *Watchman,* it featured, in her words, "some white people who were segregationists & at the same time loathed & hated the K.K.K." The *Esquire* editor seemed to her to regard that premise as "an axiomatic impossibility," a concern that Lee, in turn, regarded as ridiculous: "According to those lights, nine-tenths of the South is an axiomatic impossibility."

She was right, and not just about the South. The kinds of people she described in her story weren't only possible; they were prevalent. A 1961 Gallup poll found that less than one in four Americans approved of the freedom riders' attempt to integrate buses, even though the Supreme Court had already declared segregated interstate transit unconstitutional. The overwhelming majority who opposed them included a lot of people who didn't know a klavern from a kleagle, or who knew of the Klan but disapproved of its activities; indeed, it included Lee herself. When asked about the freedom riders during a press event in Chicago, she said, "I don't think this business of getting on buses and flaunting state laws does much of anything. Except getting a lot of publicity, and violence." (That was even after the photographer and reporter who had come to Monroeville to profile her were beaten by a mob in Montgomery while trying to cover one of the freedom rides.)

*Mockingbird* had been read as a clarion call for civil rights, but Lee's real views were more complicated than any editor wanted to put in print. She maintained that her novel was more than the sum of its antidiscrimination parts. "My book has a universal theme," she insisted. "It's not a 'racial novel.' It portrays an aspect of civilization—not necessarily Southern civilization." Despite the book's deep roots in Alabama, Lee called *To Kill a Mockingbird* "a novel of a man's conscience, universal in the sense that it could happen to anybody, anywhere people live together."

Just as her novel sidestepped the debate over integration by retreating in time to the 1930s, Lee herself stayed curiously silent on the subject of civil rights. Although her voice could have been one of the most powerful ones in the country, she did not lend it to the movement, even when it came riding through Alabama on buses, marching on Alabama's streets, and registering African American voters in rural places exactly like Monroe County. In a private letter, she joked about being a member of the NAACP but she never aligned herself publicly with the organization; although she was at the White House on the day that the Senate ended its long filibuster against the Civil Rights Act, Lee was only there to join Lyndon Johnson in congratulating a batch of high school students who had been designated Presidential Scholars; she said nothing to the press during or after about the monumental legislation. Years later, she would inscribe a copy of *To Kill a Mockingbird* to Morris Dees, the co-founder of the Southern Poverty Law Center—who, she wrote, would "be remembered as the one who spoke when good men remained silent, and the one who acted when good men did nothing." But she herself did not speak out; she let her novel do the talking.

TO BE FAIR, LEE LET HER NOVEL DO THE TALKING ABOUT ALMOST everything. In 1964, when *Mockingbird* was four years old and she was thirty-seven, she embarked on a fifty-year silence. Her final interview of any length was with a book critic named Roy Newquist who had also sat down with Jessica Mitford, Ian Fleming, John Fowles, Doris Lessing, Lillian Ross, and scores of other notable writers for his radio program, *Counterpoint*. Newquist met Lee at the Plaza Hotel, turned on his tape recorder, and, for the next hour, asked her questions about her childhood and education, literary craft and discipline, her life in New York City and her ambitions as a writer.

"I've been writing as long as I've been able to form words," Lee told him. She also said that her vocation was a kind of regional specialty, like grits or collard greens; the South, she claimed, "naturally produces more writers than, say, living on 82nd Street in New York." But for all that she'd always been a writer, she had been utterly unprepared for the avalanche of praise that greeted her novel; it was like "being hit over the head," and it left her in a state of "sheer numbness." That feeling was starkly at odds with the conditions she regarded as essential to writing. Good writers, she said, treated work "something like the medieval priesthood" and sequestered themselves to do it well. "He writes not to communicate with other people," Lee said of any writer worth his salt, "but to communicate more assuredly with himself."

Newquist was the best interlocutor Lee encountered during the handful of years when she obliged publicity requests, and she found herself saying more than she ever had about the demands and difficulties of writing. "Sometimes I'm afraid that I like it too much," she claimed, "because when I get into work I don't want to leave it. As a result I'll go for days and days without leaving the house or wherever I happen to be. I'll go out long enough to get papers and pick up some food and that's it." Writing, Lee argued, was a never-ending self-exploration for the writer, "an exorcism of not necessarily his demon, but of his divine discontent."

Her own self-explorations had by then turned into four years of wandering in the wilderness, and by the time Harper Lee gave that interview, it was clear that she had turned in on herself. Although it is true that she was always pounding away at her typewriter, she had nothing to show for it. The summer before, her sisters had both come up to see her, inaugurating what would become a semiannual adventure in which they toured some part of the country together. That year, they went together to New England and then to Quebec, and Lee was finally able to introduce her actual family to her literary family, Annie Laurie Williams and Maurice Crain. Unbeknownst to her, however, those two worlds were meeting not by chance but by design: both sides were worried about her. Alice was still handling all of her contracts and royalties, which meant that she had a reason to be in touch with Williams and Crain, and their letters gradually became less about signatures and balance sheets and more about strategies for managing their suffering artist. Together, they began looking after her travels, trying to make sure that she had a place to work and supervision to see that she did so. They shepherded her back and forth between Connecticut and New York as well as New York and Alabama; they let her say no to more and more of the publicity requests that came her way. Yet none of it seemed to be working. Crain and Williams were so concerned that they recommended Lee not be alone for any more winters.

In January 1965, while Lee was down in Monroeville for the holidays, she burned herself while frying chicken. The grease had caught fire, and when she tried to put it out, the flames seized her right hand. For weeks, it was bandaged, and when she got back to New York, she saw a plastic surgeon, who decided that she needed surgery. Distress of all kinds can manifest itself strangely, and more than a few friends wondered if Harper Lee's inability to write hadn't made itself literal in the injury. The accident was bad enough that Lee had to give away her harpsichord; eventually, though, she was able to hold a pen again.

Truman Capote mentioned Lee's burn in a letter to Perry Smith and Dick Hickock, but her own correspondence with them had slowed, and when they asked her to come to their execution on April 15—the third anniversary of her father's death—she ignored their telegram, then refused by telephone when Capote found her at the Old Stone House. That fall, as if trying to revisit her earlier, more unfettered years, she took her high school teacher Gladys Watson Burkett on a trip to England; the pair boarded the *Queen Elizabeth* on October 7 and spent a month touring the houses of all the famous English writers they'd read.

While Lee was away, Annie Laurie Williams wrote to Alice to discuss their mutual ward. Before heading overseas, Lee had been on Fire Island for a long stretch of the summer with the Browns and then in Connecticut at the Old Stone House, but there was still no manuscript. "I told her that I thought it was better the way things turned out about her second book," Williams wrote to Lee's sister. "It doesn't have to be written according to the publisher's schedule." She went on to suggest that Lee take her time and ignore the book until she had returned to Alabama. "*But she is a writer,*" Williams added emphatically, as if to convince herself as much as anyone else, "and her next book will be a success too, and will have some of the flavor of the first one. I am saying all of this to you, because I want you to know that she was depressed when she didn't come back from Fire Island with a finished manuscript."

From her agent, from her publisher, from her sisters, that was what the world heard: Harper Lee was at work on her second novel. Every so often, though, the writer herself emerged to say something more grim about her progress. While visiting Sweet Briar College in Virginia for a rare public event, something she agreed to do only because one of her former history professors had been named the college president, Lee told the students, "To be a serious writer requires discipline that is iron fisted. It's sitting down and doing it whether you think you have it in you or not. Every day. Alone. Without interruption. Contrary to what most people think, there is no glamour to writing. In fact, it's heartbreak most of the time." That was in October 1966, just two and a half years after Lee had told Newquist that she couldn't stop writing because she loved it so much.

Grief, heartbreak, suffering: it was in that register of profound loss that Harper Lee now spoke of her work, when she spoke of it at all. That November, when Capote invited her to his famous Black and

White Ball, she didn't go. She did agree to sit on President Johnson's National Council on the Arts and went to Tarrytown, New York, to attend the meetings, but she seldom spoke in front of the group. She still went up to Vermont and Connecticut to try to write, but even those visits began to slow. Maurice Crain had developed lung cancer, and the kind of sorrow that had plagued Lee in her twenties and thirties returned to join the pain she was experiencing around her writing.

Crain had survived untold horrors while he was a prisoner of the Germans during World War II, but he would not survive this. A year before he died, Lee drove him home to Texas for the last time, reuniting him with his family and their farm in Canyon before he got so sick that he could not get out of bed. He'd lost his appetite and then his strength; eventually, he required constant care. Crain, who had grown so close to Lee that some said he was in love with her, was happy to have her minister to him during the day while Annie Laurie Williams kept the agency open. It was a different bedside, but a familiar routine: Lee tended Crain the way she had her father, trying to bar the door against death, hoping it wouldn't find a way inside. Inevitably, it did. Crain died on April 23, 1970, eight years and a handful of days after the death of A. C. Lee.

The next year, Annie Laurie Williams, doubled over with arthritis, recovering from a fractured rib, and still grieving her husband, closed the offices where the young Nelle Lee had nervously dropped off a batch of short stories fifteen years before. The New York that Harper Lee had known was changing, as it does for so many, one friend and one building at a time. By then, she had lived there for twenty-two years, almost as long as she had lived in Alabama before moving to the city to start a new life as a writer. That summer, she was mugged and confided afterward to a friend that she was planning to spend less time in Manhattan. "I'm tired of fighting dope addicts and too old to pretend that NY is the center of the universe," she joked. More bleakly, she told him, "Harper Lee thrives, but at the expense of Nelle."

TO ANYONE WHO KNEW HER, THAT HAD BEEN OBVIOUS FOR some time. Lee wasn't just struggling with a second novel; she was struggling with everything. For a while, her sister Alice had told an unlikely story about how a manuscript had been stolen from Lee's Manhattan apartment while she was away, but soon even Alice stopped saying much about her sister's writing, and eventually everyone but the press stopped asking. There were only a few people left in the world with whom Lee could talk about writing, and soon she would lose one of the most important of them. In early January 1974, Tay Hohoff, who had retired from publishing, died suddenly in her sleep. When her daughter and son-in-law came to the apartment the next morning, they had to rescue Shadrach, the polydactyl kitten that Lee and Marcia Van Meter had found in their basement, now an aged polydactyl cat.

For Harper Lee, a time of turning inward had turned into a time of losing and being lost. By setting her novel during the Great Depression, she had published a book that seemed two decades older than it was; now its author seemed just as anachronistic. Most of New York had forgotten that she even lived there, or was still living at all. Friends in her building remembered, though, and when someone banged loudly on their door late at night, they knew it was her, because she had done so before, drunk and despairing. Those friends included George Malko, a writer who had learned about the news business from his mentor Studs Terkel, and his wife, a graphic designer named Elizabeth. They had met Lee when they moved into the same building, and like so many they were alternately charmed by her remarkable wit and saddened by the private sorrows that stymied her talents.

"She was drinking at that time," George Malko said years later. "It is not for me to wonder about her demons, but we knew they were there and they were brutal." Morning martinis weren't unheard of for her, but one night she came asking the Malkos for vodka. When George lied and said they didn't have any, Lee pleaded her case: "I just threw three hundred pages of a manuscript down the incinerator." That impulsiveness, part of her temperament in the best of times, could take over when she had too much to drink, as friends could attest after fielding angry telephone calls in the middle of the night. Truman Capote, afflicted by the same demons and more, once con-

fided to a reporter that his friend "would drink and then tell somebody off—that's what it amounted to. She was really a somebody.
People were really quite frightened of her."

By then, Capote and Lee were no longer in close touch, but one
day in 1976 he called her out of the blue. *People* magazine was profil-
ing him, not for the anniversary of *In Cold Blood*, but for his new
project—a tell-all of sorts, only what Capote was telling was other
people's secrets. He had signed the contract for the book ten years
before and renegotiated it over and over again, but like his friend
he hadn't been able to finish it. He was calling it *Answered Prayers*, a
phrase Lee would've recognized because he'd borrowed it from Saint
Teresa of Ávila: "More tears are shed over answered prayers than unan-
swered ones."

It took a few telephone calls, but finally Lee agreed to sit with
Capote for the interview and meet the photographer Harry Benson
near Capote's apartment at the UN Plaza. The old tree-house friends
walked around Second Avenue, talking in what Benson remembers
was an almost private language, sweet and loving, like siblings. A lot
had transpired between the two of them by then, including no small
share of envy and anger and disapproval, but there was no mention
of any of it that day: gray-haired now and moving more slowly, the
pair walked around New York together as if it were the old, familiar
courthouse square. Lee had turned fifty that year, and Capote fifty-
two, but they could summon their childhood as if it were yesterday.
A kindergarten teacher had whacked Capote's hand with a ruler for
reading too well, Lee remembered to the reporter, a small episode
but one that said plenty about the lives of brilliant misfits in their
small southern town. It was in that interview that Lee said of them,
evocatively and enigmatically, "We are bound by a common anguish."

Anguish, shared and otherwise, had constrained and darkened
Lee's life for over fifteen years. Her editor was dead, her agent was
dead, and a year after that *People* interview Annie Laurie Williams
died, too. By May 1977, with the exception of the author, everyone
who had helped bring *To Kill a Mockingbird* into the world was gone.
If Lee had worked on serious writing projects since then, they had

been stolen from her apartment or burned to nothingness or simply hadn't amounted to much on the page.

But Lee wasn't done. Maybe it was the unexpected sweetness of her reunion with Capote, resurrecting the childhood joy of starting to write and wanting to do so forever, or the artistic rivalry between them, stirring in her the desire to do better what they had done before in Kansas. Or maybe it was just a strange story she happened to hear that July. Not long after seeing her friend Capote, Nelle had received an invitation from another Alabama friend, Ned McDavid, to attend a party at his restaurant on the Upper West Side, the Library, where the books were for decoration and the drinks were all that circulated. She showed up, uncharacteristically, and downed gin and tonics with some three hundred other folks from down home, most of them in town to nominate Jimmy Carter for the presidency. It was the 1976 Democratic National Convention, and McDavid was hosting a party on the night before the official events began; friends since their Crimson Tide days, he'd convinced Lee to put in an appearance. Governor George Wallace was a no-show, but every twenty minutes or so the restaurant's speakers blasted a recording from 1924, when an earlier governor, "Plain Bill" Brandon, nominated another of Alabama's own for the presidency: "Allabhammah casts 20-foah votes for Oscuh Dubyee Undahwood." Almost as often, a delegate from Alexander City would tell anyone with ears, "Kennedy broke the religion barrier and Carter is doing the same thing to the anti-Southern barrier."

It was Big Tom's first convention since the nightmare of Chicago, and it was where he first crossed paths with Nelle Harper Lee. The next year, when violence was breaking out in New York under the cover of the worst blackout in the city's history, he wrote her a summary of the strange life and shocking death of the Reverend Willie Maxwell. Whatever Lee thought of Radney himself, she heard in his case of a lifetime the kernel of a true-crime book and headed home to Alabama to write it.

# 20

# Rumor, Fantasy, Dreams, Conjecture, and Outright Lies

IT BEGAN WITH A BANG. MURDER IN AMERICA, AT LEAST AS FAR as its European citizens were concerned, started when John Billington fired a musket at one of his neighbors in 1630. Billington had arrived at Plymouth Plantation ten years earlier on the *Mayflower* and came to resent some of the other residents, including John Newcomen, the unfortunate target of his musket shot. Plenty of people had died by violence in the Americas by then, but no colonist had bothered to document indigenous deaths, whereas the residents of Plymouth noted in great detail the demise of Newcomen, who was shot in the shoulder and, several days later, succumbed to gangrene. Billington was convicted and hanged, thereby earning the dubious distinction of becoming the first recorded murderer in the New World.

From the time there were murders in America, there were writers trying to write about them. The earliest accounts of homicides were generally produced by those directly involved: the accused penned pardon-seeking confessions, law enforcement officers wrote self-aggrandizing stories of derring-do, relatives wrote tell-alls, and ministers who preached at the gallows published their execution sermons. Court reporters, who weren't yet salaried, cobbled together wages by printing up their trial transcripts and peddling them directly to the public. Murder, they knew, would always sell, and its early American salesmen found that pamphlets were an ideal form. They could be printed cheaply, distributed widely, and marketed for anywhere from a few pennies to a quarter.

Those pamphlets typically had salacious titles and grisly covers, with bold fonts and bolder declarations about roguish rogues, horrid homicides, fiendish fiends, and crimes of the century. Rival printers produced their own versions of whatever trial captivated the public, and a single case could produce more than a dozen pamphlets. When the Reverend Ephraim Avery was tried for the murder of a factory worker in Tiverton, Rhode Island, in 1833, the tale was told in twenty-one separate pamphlets. Readers could choose between a brief narrative, the full narrative, an authentic narrative, particulars of the seduction and murder, a report on the examination of the accused, a report on his trial, an explanation, a facsimile of letters belonging to the victim, strictures on the case, and a vindication of the trial's result. When Avery was acquitted, first by a criminal court and then by an ecclesiastical one, he felt the need to publish something of his own—an exonerative pamphlet called *The Correct, Full, and Impartial Report of the Trial of Rev. Ephraim K. Avery.*

THESE PAMPHLETS ARE THE ANCESTORS OF WHAT WE NOW CALL true crime, but they weren't the invention of the American colonists. Trial narratives are as old as the *Oresteia,* Aeschylus's account of the murders of Agamemnon and Clytemnestra, and as famous as the Gospels, which culminate in an account of the prosecution, conviction, and execution of Jesus, and trial pamphlets had long since taken hold in England. But they flourished in colonies established as experiments in the possibility of moral living and populated by a peculiar mixture of refugees from religious persecution and from prison. Crime in America had a ready audience and a nascent legal community eager to learn from records of court procedures, which at the time could be cited as case law. An emergent national literary culture likewise took note of the way literal transcripts could be edited into stories, learning one trial at a time how to shape public sympathy while tracing the course of a crime from its commission through to exoneration or execution.

Trial pamphlets proliferated in America as printing presses arrived in ports and were distributed around the country, and began to decline only when newspapers started to take over, offering frequent accounts of a trial as it was unfolding rather than a single summing-up at the end. Soon enough, a canon of American crime writing began to take shape. In addition to lawless cowboys and legendary bank robbers, that canon included heavily politicized murderers, or alleged murderers, like Bartolomeo Vanzetti and Nicola Sacco, the anarchists accused of killing two people during a shoe factory robbery in 1920, as well as heavily psychologized murderers, like the students Nathan Leopold and Richard Loeb, who killed a fourteen-year-old in an effort to prove that, like Nietzsche's *Übermenschen,* they were intellectually superior and above the law. So feverishly did journalists cover these and other murder trials that they became a perverse form of entertainment and, in short order, created a massively lucrative publishing market.

BY THE TIME THAT LEE AND CAPOTE HEADED TO KANSAS WITH their notebooks and without any press credentials, true crime had been a popular genre in America for well over three hundred years. But it was *In Cold Blood* that would make crime writing respectable. Back in the 1930s, a librarian turned crime reporter named Edmund Pearson had written a few murder stories for *The New Yorker,* as had the humorist and occasional journalist James Thurber around that same time. Yet it was only when Capote's articles on the Clutter killings appeared serially in four issues of the same magazine that true crime became something critics and scholars took seriously.

The obstacle, before then, hadn't been homicide itself. The murder plot, like the marriage plot, had long been a favorite of highbrow literature (*Crime and Punishment,* for example, to say nothing of *Macbeth*), and noir films like *Laura* (1944) and *Sunset Boulevard* (1950) had been rewarded with Oscars. Yet journalists, before Capote, rendered crime stories only a few column inches at a time, leaving it to novelists, playwrights, and screenwriters to turn violence into murder mysteries, detective stories, spy thrillers, and courtroom dramas.

"Journalism is the most underestimated, the least explored of literary mediums," Capote declared, then set out to make himself into the Marco Polo of his profession. Building on the work of John Hersey, Joseph Mitchell, and Lillian Ross, Capote borrowed the strategies of fiction writers in his nonfiction, rendering settings that were more than just datelines, crafting characters who were more than just quotations and physical descriptions, and identifying within his reporting, or imposing on it, moods and themes that made a story more than the sum of its parts. Although he called the resulting work a "nonfiction novel," he insisted—despite the obvious questions raised by the "novel" part—that every line of *In Cold Blood* was pure fact.

That, in itself, was not a fact. Yet Capote's panoptic account of what had happened in Holcomb—his profile of the town, the crime, the victims, the killers, the survivors, and the system that adjudicated all of their fates—permanently changed the way that writers wrote about crime and readers read about it. What people had long admired in the work of Wilkie Collins, Edgar Allan Poe, Arthur Conan Doyle, Agatha Christie, and Theodore Dreiser, they now expected to encounter in nonfiction accounts of criminality, too: misdirection, symbolism, suspense, and the psychological portraits that had previously been the purview of novelists alone.

Not everyone was happy with this novelization of crime, and not everyone was convinced by Capote's declaration that his book was strictly factual. A month after its publication, a journalist for *The Kansas City Times* re-reported most of it, discovering along the way a series of inconsistencies, from the fact that Bobby Rupp wasn't a basketball star to the actual price paid for Nancy Clutter's horse. A month later, a writer for *Esquire* named Phillip Tompkins also went looking and found far more substantial concerns. "In Cold Fact," which appeared in June 1966, challenged Capote's insinuation that the murders were not premeditated and the idea that either of the killers had experienced remorse. None of those present for the executions, Tompkins learned, would confirm the apology that Capote claimed Smith had uttered from the gallows, and he argued that even a cursory read of the case files—in particular the confessions—revealed very different murderers from those Capote conjured in the pages of *In Cold Blood*.

Other sources, closer to the original case, also questioned the integrity of Capote's book. In addition to pointing out various errors, Agent Harold Nye, one of the lead investigators with the KBI, objected to how *In Cold Blood* portrayed his interview with Hickock's family—which, in real life, did not take place at night, did not include both parents, and involved three agents, not just Nye himself, all of whom, contrary to Capote's claim, were honest with the suspect's mother about the crimes her son stood accused of committing. Perhaps most critical of all the responses was the one that came from the two surviving Clutter daughters, who declined nearly all interviews afterward, saying once, "Truman Capote made a similar request to write an article for the *New Yorker* magazine that he said would be a 'tribute' to the family," but then failed to honor his promise that they would be able to read what he wrote before publication. Capote, the sisters said, produced a "sensational novel, which profited him and grossly misrepresented our family."

Capote had waited until Hickock and Smith had been executed before publishing *In Cold Blood,* which meant that its two main characters, at least, could not offer any corrections or voice any objections. But Harper Lee was alive and well, and she had been with Capote on four reporting trips and in the room with him for almost every interview he had conducted, including with the killers. That meant that she, more than anyone, could see how the facts they had gathered in Kansas had become the flesh and bones of *In Cold Blood*—and also how many fictions her friend had used to hold it together at the joints. For all his public insistence that his novel was 100 percent true, Capote, in private, was not coy about those fabrications. "Do you remember telling me that the first time you ever heard of Hickock and Smith was when Alvin came home one night and showed you their 'mug-shots,' the ones with the vital statistics on the back?" he asked Marie Dewey in a letter he sent to her and her husband from Palamós, Spain, in August 1961. "Well, I want to do this as a 'scene' between you and Alvin. Can you remember anything more about it (not that I mind *inventing* details, as you will see!)?"

———

HARPER LEE, HOWEVER, MINDED VERY MUCH. CAPOTE'S INVEN-
tions were legion, going far beyond the ones uncovered by *The Kansas
City Times, Esquire,* and others. They included the claim, vehemently
denied by its ostensible source, that Perry Smith had cried in his jail
cell and, perhaps most gallingly, the wholly fabricated scene in the
cemetery between Agent Dewey and Susan Kidwell that Capote used
to end his book. Lee never aired her objections to those falsehoods
or any others publicly, but in letters to Sandy Campbell, who had
been Capote's fact-checker at *The New Yorker,* and Campbell's partner, Donald Windham, she lamented, "Truman's having long ago
put fact out of business had made me despair of 'factual' accounts of
anything."

Unsurprisingly, perhaps, that rift over the meaning of nonfiction corresponded to one between Capote and Lee. For years, people
speculated that what had ended their friendship was his enormous
and spiraling envy of all the success she had found with *To Kill a
Mockingbird*—of the Pulitzer, the Oscars, the seemingly endless sales.
Yet the two of them traveled back to Kansas together in 1962 and 1963,
after the novel and the movie had both already earned extravagant
accolades, and she wrote a glowing profile of him in 1966 for the *Book-
of-the-Month Club News* to help promote *In Cold Blood.* "For over five
years," Lee wrote admiringly in that piece, Capote "gave Kansas his
best—identification complete, involvement total."

There and elsewhere, she suppressed, in public, her objections to
his work, as well as her disapproval of his increasingly self-destructive
habits. But Capote still pulled away from her. Even though he lived
just two miles south of her in the city, they saw less and less of each
other after his book came out. Later, she confided to Windham and
Campbell, "Truman did not cut me out of his life until after *In Cold
Blood* was published. I never knew why he did it, the only comfort I
had was in the discovery that he had done the same to several others,
all faithful old friends. Our friendship, however, had been life-long,
and I had assumed that the ties that bound us were unbreakable."

What Capote had done with *In Cold Blood* gave Lee qualms and
compromised their friendship, but it also presented her with a challenge: whether she could write the kind of old-fashioned, straitlaced

journalism she admired, and whether it could be as successful as the fact-bending accounts of her contemporaries. Capote, after all, was part of a whole movement of writers trying to make nonfiction read more like fiction, a movement whose members included Norman Mailer, Gay Talese, and Joan Didion. The stories they wrote had their foundations in reportage but often included upper floors of psychological speculation, sociological exploration, or political manifesto. Swaths of dialogue in some of these authors' works were wholly or largely invented, and the narrative perspective sometimes hewed impossibly close to the consciousness of the characters. But readers, for the most part, loved them. By 1973, when Tom Wolfe co-edited an anthology of *The New Journalism,* he could write with some credibility that nonfiction had eclipsed the novel and that it was "the most important literature being written in America today." Yet Lee would never identify with the New Journalists. At the Union Building, where she had spent so many late nights and early mornings while a student at the University of Alabama, the nonfiction publications were physically divided from their fictional counterparts by a row of filing cabinets, and she always maintained that same division in her own mind and work.

That commitment would determine not only her style but also her subject. With *In Cold Blood,* Capote had chosen an exceptional crime. "Of all the people in all the world," he quoted one of the investigators on the case as saying, "the Clutters were the least likely to be murdered." That was true, and much the same could be said of the victims in most popular works of true crime that followed; except for accounts of domestic violence, not many of the murders described in those books were representative of violent crime in this country. Their victims were typically wealthy and white, while murder victims, statistically speaking, are more likely to be economically disadvantaged and people of color; their killers were often calculating or deranged outsiders, while most homicide victims are killed by someone they know. Capote, in particular, had gone looking for what amounted to a horror story in the heart of white America: the murder of an entire middle-class household by total strangers.

Lee, by contrast, found a case where the only white characters were the lawyers and law enforcement officers. To portray the victims, the killers, and the survivors, she would be writing about black lives and black deaths, black families and black communities—an unusual move for the genre even today, and a challenge for her, as the black characters in *To Kill a Mockingbird* are essential to the plot but hardly as realized as their white counterparts. But she had already demonstrated her ability to depict crimes that confronted readers with their own prejudices and those of the criminal justice system, and she'd wanted to go even further before Tay Hohoff discouraged her. *To Kill a Mockingbird* featured two parallel stories about violence: in one, a black man, Tom Robinson, dies because he is falsely accused of rape; in the other, a white man, Arthur "Boo" Radley, is spared from even being charged for a murder the authorities know he committed. The former portrayed the power of a mob to enforce a distorted vision of justice, the latter portrayed the prerogative of law enforcement to exercise personal preferences, and both dramatized the way that the biases of society are reflected in the criminal justice system. Although Atticus Finch has to be talked into sparing his son, Jem, and their neighbor Boo Radley a trial for the murder of Bob Ewell, it takes only a few pages for Sheriff Tate to convince him of the expediency of vigilantism: "There's a black boy dead for no reason, and the man responsible for it's dead. Let the dead bury the dead this time, Mr. Finch. Let the dead bury the dead."

The Maxwell case had a vigilante, too, but he was black and heralded as a hero not only privately but publicly. That made the politics of her new book less palatable than those of her previous one, and its plot contained far more complexities: an alleged black serial killer who was also the victim of violence; a crusading white attorney who was also profiting off black death; crimes that looked like murder but were mostly tried like fraud; white and black lives that existed almost side by side in small southern towns but were worlds apart. Yet because the story Lee had found was fact, not fiction, no editor could tell her it wasn't believable or insist that she simplify it for her readers.

By the time Lee learned about the Reverend Willie Maxwell, she already knew something about Alexander City. The summer before the shooting in the funeral home, her niece—one of her late brother's children, Mary McCall Lee, known as Molly—had married a native, John Robert Chapman Jr., known as Bobby. But it was not only her relatives in town who made Lee feel at home in Alex City when she showed up for the trial of Robert Burns. Everything down to the oppressive heat that fall would have felt familiar to her; as a child, she had chipped ice off the block kept on the steps of the Monroe County Courthouse for that purpose, crunching it to stay cool while listening to cases. Like all children, she had been expected to be unobtrusive back then, and she chose to conduct herself that same way in Alex City. She didn't sit with the press in their reserved row near the prosecution table, and she kept a low enough profile to observe without being observed.

If you are in the market for facts, as Lee was, trials are an excellent place to find them. As Calvin Trillin noted in *Killings,* a collection of his true-crime stories from around the country, reporters love trials because they "are transfixed by a process in which the person being asked a question actually has to answer it. He cannot say he would rather not comment. He cannot tell an anecdote on a different subject. He has to answer the question—under oath that he is telling the truth." Lee knew that whatever transpired over the course of *State of Alabama v. Robert Lewis Burns,* the case was likely to be one of her greatest troves of facts, and when she was informed that no recording devices were allowed in the courtroom, she introduced herself to the court reporter, Mary Ann Karr, and asked whether she might buy a copy of the transcript.

Karr had followed her heart to Alabama from Ohio. Her husband was a local boy, but unable to find work, he had moved to Youngstown to take a job at a steel mill during the day and an ice cream parlor in the evenings. Karr had seen him working there, liked how he looked, and turned over her water glass; when he came to her table to clean up the mess, she asked him out. Eventually, they married and moved to Tallapoosa County, where the private-schooled, college-educated Karr learned that her in-laws weren't just poor; they were no-electricity, no-running-water, use-the-outhouse-out-back poor. Her own mother worried that Mary Ann had "died and gone to Hell," but Karr took to Alabama, and she adored her husband. Years into their marriage, they were still so smitten that they had lunch together as often as they could, which is why, when Harper Lee introduced herself, Karr brought the writer home to her house on Lafayette Street.

"You wouldn't think she had two nickels to rub together—she was dressed like a pauper," Karr remembered. The court reporter found that Lee wore her wealth lightly in other ways, too. She was "really about the nicest person I ever met in my life," Karr recalled, "just down to earth and humble." Karr's husband made them bologna sandwiches, and the three of them sat down to talk about the case and the circuit. At the time, Karr had been working as a court reporter for five years, following Judge Avary around the Fifth Circuit to cover criminal trials and anything else on his docket. That meant she was in a good position to regale Lee with stories about the judge, the jury, and pretty much everyone else involved in the Burns case.

She also agreed to provide Lee with a transcript when the trial was over, though she warned that it would take some time. Karr did her court reporting in shorthand—the particular kind invented by John Robert Gregg almost a hundred years earlier, which looks less like English than an EKG—and she typed it up only if a case was appealed. That process was slow, and the Burns trial was already proving to be a long one, but Lee agreed to pay Karr whatever it cost and wait however long it took.

HARPER LEE WASN'T IN A HURRY, BECAUSE SHE WASN'T GOING anywhere. After she got interested in the Reverend, she had her niece Molly arrange for her to stay for a few months in a cabin on Lake Martin. It was one of the six hundred or so cabins built by Ben Russell, the founder of Russell Mills, with lakeside land he'd gotten from a trade with Alabama Power after giving up on a dam he himself had wanted to build at Buzzard Roost Shoals, north of Cherokee Bluffs. Russell rented the cabins to employees and friends, including Sara and Joseph Robinson, who owned an iron foundry in town. Mrs. Sara, as her students knew her, taught in the Alexander City schools and loved the idea of hosting the novelist; the novelist, in turn, never met an English teacher she didn't love.

The Robinson cabin was on the northern side of the lake with a clear view of the River Bridge between Alexander City and Dadeville. A rustic number, it was equal parts pine, tin, and screen, much like the one near Kowaliga Bridge that Hank Williams had stayed in twenty-five years earlier when he came to Lake Martin to dry out. For both artists, their isolated idylls of clear nights and calm waters held the promise of serenity and sobriety, although Lee was not always alone. Early during her stay, the novelist adopted a stray black cat that she took to calling the Reverend; later, her friend Marcia Van Meter came down from the city to see how the book was going and to meet the feline incarnation of its central character.

Eventually, Lee swapped her lakeside digs for a room at the Horseshoe Bend Motel, not only because it was the nicest place in town (it was where the sequestered jury had stayed), but because it was owned by her niece's husband, Bobby Chapman. The fifty-room facility, which was built in 1958, sat just a few miles down the road from the battlefield for which it was named, right at the corner of Highway 22, which runs between Rockford, Alexander City, and New Site, and Highway 280, which runs from Birmingham all the way across the Georgia line. Its location made the hotel popular with travelers heading to or from Atlanta and with tourists who couldn't afford a cabin but wanted to go swimming, boating, or fishing on Lake Martin. In 1967, Chapman's parents bought the place from its original owners, and three years later, when Bobby finished his studies at the University of Alabama, he came back home to run it.

The Horseshoe Bend Motel was shaped like a hexagon, with an office at the base and five lengths of rooms that angled their way around a swimming pool in the center. Bobby eventually turned its restaurant into a convenience store, where day-shift Russell employees got their coffee and biscuits before work, and opened a lounge called the Stable Club, where those same workers returned at the other end of the day for entertainment—provided partly by Bobby's liquor license, a novelty since Tallapoosa County had been dry until 1968, and partly by the local and regional acts that regularly performed shows there. "The Stable Club became something of a local 'Cheers,'" Chapman said later. "If I looked back on it, I could probably say we had our Norm and Cliff and maybe a Sam and a Carla or two." For Lee, the Stable Club was a real improvement on the café at the Warren Hotel in Kansas—not least because, unlike in Finney County, she could order more than coffee.

In other ways, though, Lee's early days in Alex City were a lot like the ones she'd spent with Capote in Garden City. Many locals were at first leery of saying anything at all about their infamous neighbor, and like many of the white reporters who came to chase the story of the voodoo preacher, Lee met with lots of resistance. "If the Reverend was alive," one of the second Mrs. Maxwell's friends said, "nobody would talk to you." Even three months dead, he still managed to spook plenty of people; stories about his posthumous powers proliferated, as did the fear that he would take revenge from beyond the grave. "Around town the talk is he's already back," Curtis Jones, a relative of Shirley Ann Ellington's, had said, "folks say he's been seen in town driving a car." People also said that the Reverend Willie Maxwell voted in an election after he was too dead to pull the lever, and that at night a mysterious light shined above his grave.

Lee also had another problem, one that she hadn't faced in Kansas but that became unavoidable in Alex City the minute anyone realized who she was. The author of *To Kill a Mockingbird* was not just famous in Alabama: she was famously rich and famously connected to Hollywood. How much would she be willing to pay for their story, almost everyone she tried to talk to asked her, and who would play them in the movie version of whatever she wrote? Lee, who had thought the chief challenge to her journalistic ethics would involve maintaining absolute fidelity to the facts, instead found herself warding off people who wanted to sell her their grandmother or sell themselves to the highest bidder. She complained that even the Reverend's neighbors thought they could sell their stories to television producers. The same went for some of the most important characters in the saga. Someone had tried to negotiate a fee for Robert Burns's cooperation, and Fred Hutchinson, the funeral director, told Lee that he could get her an interview with the Reverend's widow, for the right price. Eventually, though, after Lee had made it known that she was not in the business of buying her interviews, or paying for anything except official copies of documents like transcripts and death certificates, people relented and began to talk.

Not that their talk was always reliable. Although the Reverend was famous for a very different reason, the way people told stories about him must have reminded Lee of the way they had embroidered their stories about her since *To Kill a Mockingbird* was first published: inserting themselves where they had never been, intimating deep truths from glancing interactions, and inventing information entirely when the need arose or the mood struck. Soon enough, the issue wasn't that she did not have enough material; the busboy who delivered her dinners at the Horseshoe Bend Motel in exchange for fifty-cent tips watched as stacks of papers piled ever higher on her desk. The issue was that she had, as she would later say, "enough rumor, fantasy, dreams, conjecture, and outright lies for a volume the length of the Old Testament"—exactly what Harper Lee was hoping to keep out of her book.

# 21

# Coming Back Until Doomsday

NOTWITHSTANDING THE RUMORS TO THE CONTRARY, BY THE time Harper Lee came along, the Reverend Willie Maxwell was not available to give an interview to even the most resourceful of reporters. One of her other subjects, however, was all too happy to talk to her. No one found Lee more charming than that charmer Tom Radney, and in the months she spent around Lake Martin, he often came by the Horseshoe Bend to have a drink with her, talk about the case, suggest people for her to interview, and check on her progress.

It was easy to get along with Big Tom, and to Lee he was a familiar type. Even though he was slightly younger than she was, he had a lot in common with her father: both were country lawyers who served in the state legislature; both were lay leaders in the Methodist Church; both were members of the Masonic Lodge and the Chamber of Commerce; both were the sorts of men known to everyone in town, and liked by most. Their politics, however, were oil and water: many of Tom's letters to the editor of *The Alexander City Outlook* defended the very federal government that A.C. had attacked in his editorials on states' rights for *The Monroe Journal*. And while Mr. Lee was never seen without a jacket and hat, except on the golf course, Big Tom was a man who liked to loosen his collar.

For his part, Big Tom initially found Harper Lee to be a "shy, reserved, matronly lady" but, after watching her interact with sources, found that she was "quick to smile and make friends." The two had a shared love of travel: just as she had gone abroad to Oxford, Big Tom had hopped a ship to Europe after his army service and made his way around France and England before going to Russia to see what he called "the communist threat." They also loved politics. Lee's views fell somewhere between civil libertarian and uncivil curmudgeon, but she saw Radney's JFK cocktail party story and raised him one about JFK's presidential motorcade, which she had once waited hours to see at the United Nations. What Radney did not know about the Corn Laws, she could supply for them both, and they shared a hagiographic affection for Thomas Jefferson, Jefferson Davis, and Robert E. Lee.

Big Tom was thrilled to have the state's most famous author interested in one of his cases, and he did everything he could to see to it that the book in which he would appear got written. He tossed all of his files on the Reverend Maxwell into an enormous leather briefcase—really, more of a valise—and told Lee to keep it for as long as it took to write the book. All told, it amounted to hundreds of pages of material, including enough insurance paperwork for her to open her own agency: dozens of applications, forms, policy sheets, fee schedules, and legal briefs, not to mention a lengthy court of appeals case.

It was a gold mine, worth more to Lee than anything that had come out of Devil's Backbone or Hog Mountain the century before, when Tallapoosa County experienced its own blink-and-you-missed-it gold rush. To Lee's delight, Radney had squirreled away copies of just about every piece of Reverend-related paperwork that had crossed his desk or required his signature, including letters, indictments, witness lists, jury lists, and other documents related to the criminal cases going all the way back to when District Attorney Aaron had tried and failed to get a conviction for first-degree murder in *State of Alabama v. Willie J. Maxwell*. Radney had even saved a copy of the handwritten slip of paper that the foreman had handed the judge in the first murder trial—"We the Jury find the defendant Willie M. Maxwell not guilty"—and its perverse twin, the one six years later, that acquitted Robert Burns.

Although Big Tom specialized in acquittals, he insisted to Lee, as he had to every other journalist who asked, that he would not have tried to get another one for the Reverend in the murder of Shirley

Ann Ellington. A few days before the preacher's death, he claimed, Maxwell had come by the Zoo wanting to know if Radney would represent him, and Big Tom had refused. The Reverend was so angry when he left that he threatened a reporter in the parking lot, telling her that he would run her over with his car if she didn't move out of his way. Lee, well aware of all the lawyering Radney had done for the Reverend over almost a ten-year period, starting with a land transfer in 1967, had reason to doubt these claims. She had already seen the Maxwell House, and she was learning just how lucrative a client the Reverend Maxwell had been; moreover, Big Tom's story undermined his long-standing and admirable insistence that every client, regardless of guilt, deserves a lawyer.

Lee was not entirely convinced by Tom's story, and she was dubious about his motives for making himself look so noble. "He seemed," she later said, "to see himself as a cross between Atticus Finch and Robert Redford." To be fair, Big Tom might have started seeing himself that way the day that Lee picked up the telephone in front of him and called Gregory Peck, joking with the actor about what role he would play in the film version of the book she was working on; maybe, she teased, he would be cast as a Baptist preacher. It would not have been unreasonable for Radney to think that Peck might prefer to play the defense attorney who had gotten an acquittal for a murder that had been witnessed by three hundred people, reprising the sort of role that had won him an Oscar. Even the small chance of that was enough to make Radney eager to cooperate, and whether or not Lee's book was ever made into a blockbuster, it was sure to be a best seller.

But Big Tom was not only motivated by self-interest. Even without encouragement or incentive, he could be generous and gregarious with anyone, and when Lee showed an interest in his life, he gladly invited her into it. He took the author to see his family's farm—a parcel of land, originally part of the Quarters, that he had bought back not long after he started representing the Reverend. There in Daviston, Radney had built a cabin, put in a swimming pool, and filled a red barn and pasture with horses, chickens, goats, sheep, and, briefly, an emu. Like the Lee family, the Radneys had a beach property down in Destin, on the Florida panhandle, but Big Tom preferred to spend the days he wasn't at the office at the farm. The Quarters was the closest thing to ancestral land he had, and it wasn't far from his childhood home in Wadley or his family's church. Everyone who came out there with him, Lee included, was liable to be subjected to the line he'd used in speech after speech when he was campaigning: "Never forget from whence you came."

She understood that, of course, because it was something they had in common. Both were southerners unwilling to leave a region that would have preferred to do without them: an unmarried, unconventional literary woman; an in-your-face progressive. She could have stayed in Manhattan; he could have started a fresh political career almost anywhere north of the Mason-Dixon Line. But Harper Lee returned over and over again to the town where she was born, and Big Tom never really left; both of them were deeply loyal to the South, even when it disappointed them or disapproved of them.

The South would gladly have done without the Reverend Maxwell, too, but unlike them he had very little chance of getting out of it, even if he had wanted to. Six million African Americans went north and west during the Great Migration, but many millions more stayed behind. Among them was Maxwell, who lived in one of the many small towns the civil rights movement seemed to have passed by. What Harper Lee knew about Tom Radney's South instinctively, she could have learned about Willie Maxwell's South only through patient research and ongoing conversations of the kind that very few white Americans, then as now, ever have.

She sought out some of those conversations, but the ones with Big Tom came easier, and she got to know his whole family. Madolyn couldn't spend endless hours at the Stable Club with her the way her husband could, but she was delighted that Alabama's most famous author wanted to meet her children: Ellen, who was already fourteen; Fran, who was twelve; Hollis, who was ten; and six-year-old Thomas. In the years since Big Tom had given up politics, Little Tom had outgrown being a homemade home plate when the family played kickball in the driveway, and was now big enough to pedal around in the fire truck that Radney had bought for his children when none of them won the one being raffled by the Alexander City Fire Department. The girls, meanwhile, were old enough to know who Lee was, and when one of them said to her, "I never read anything by you except *To Kill a Mockingbird,*" the author's retort tickled them all: "Nobody else has either."

Like Big Tom, Madolyn liked Lee a lot. She remembers "just sitting back and listening to the conversation" whenever Lee and Radney got to talking about case law or the Creek Wars or whatever else one of them dredged up from the depths of their erudition. Madolyn also noticed what just about everyone who ever met Harper Lee did—namely, that she "didn't care a whit about the way she looked." While most women at that time had to mind what went into their mouths and what came out of them, Lee smoked and drank as much as any man and, as Madolyn said, "had several four-letter words she'd contribute to any conversation."

Unlike the three Mrs. Maxwells, who had all been pastor's wives, and Mrs. Radney, who was a politician's wife, Lee was no man's wife. Instead, like those men, she was defined by her work, and free to spend all of her time reading and writing. No one could tell her what kind of reporting she should be doing, as they most certainly would have; true crime had plenty of female victims and the odd female murderess, but almost no female authors. She could devote an entire day to thinking if she wanted, or spend six hours with Sergeant William Gray and his wife, going over crime scene photographs that he had stashed at home, then stay up all night transcribing her notes on his memories of the death of the second Mrs. Maxwell. She was nowhere near as anonymous as she was in Manhattan, where hundreds of thousands of people came and went every day and no one noticed if your apartment light was on all night or you didn't leave the building until late afternoon, but in Alex City, unlike in Monroeville, Lee could still find relative peace. She came and went as she pleased, since her cabin was remote and the rooms at the Horseshoe Bend had their own private entrances. She wore down her tires driving from one tiny village to another, learning the byways and back roads of the three counties around Lake Martin, and talking with anyone who knew anything about the Reverend Willie Maxwell.

ALONG THE WAY, LEE TRACKED DOWN THE BYLINE THAT HAD interested her most when she reviewed the earlier coverage of the Maxwell case in *The Alexander City Outlook* and *The Montgomery Advertiser*. Of all the reporters who had covered the story, only one was present on the day the Reverend was shot. Lee called the newsroom of the *Outlook,* got the editor, Alvin Benn, on the phone, explained who she was, and asked if she could speak with one of his reporters, Jim Earnhardt. Unfortunately, right at that moment, she could not, he informed her, because Earnhardt was out obeying Benn's motto: there's no news in a newsroom.

When Earnhardt got back to his desk and found a note on his typewriter saying that Harper Lee had called, he thought it was a prank. But when he returned the call, there was Lee on the other end of the line, hoping to talk with him about his reporting. An avid reader of novels, histories, and just about anything else he could get his hands on, Jim was thrilled to speak with her, and the two hit it off right away. Soon enough, they met in person, and Jim, like Big Tom, ended up giving Lee everything that he had on the Reverend—in his case, a scrapbook that his mother had made for him of all the articles about the case. The red cover was unmarked except for a gold border, but inside, protected by plastic sheets, were all of the stories Jim had written about Shirley Ann Ellington, the Reverend, and Burns, plus clippings his mother had saved from other newspapers.

Later, after Lee had come for supper with Earnhardt's parents, she mailed them a letter to say how highly she thought of their son. She was the same age as Jim's father and a little older than his mother, but she took a shine to the bearded, bespectacled twenty-two-year-old reporter, and it was easy to see why: Jim was just as comfortable reconstructing the rise of the Russells in Alex City as discussing Faulkner, whom Lee had never met, and Steinbeck, whom she knew because they shared a literary agency. What Jim couldn't reciprocate in the annals of celebrity, he could match in the annals of Alabama arcana: like Alice Lee, he could rattle off all sixty-seven counties in the state, together with their seats. He had wanted to be a reporter since he was twelve and had grown into one with as strict a sense of ethics as Lee herself; with no prompting from her, he cast aspersions on "nonfiction novels" and other "pseudo-journalistic practices."

Perhaps most important of all, Earnhardt intuited the quality that Harper Lee valued most in her friendships: discretion. He didn't cover her comings and goings in the *Outlook,* never pried into what she was or wasn't writing, and would answer anyone's questions about the Maxwell case, so long as they had nothing to do with her. Lee and Earnhardt struck up a correspondence that next spring that lasted for decades and included half a dozen visits in Manhattan. When Jim came to the big city, Lee worried like a mother about him getting mugged, introduced him to the man who ran her local newsstand, took him for drinks with Marcia Van Meter, and made him stay at the Algonquin the way real writers did. They ate Persian food at Teheran and Chinese food at Mayor Koch's favorite restaurant; she even took him to Sardi's, where she used to eat with Maurice Crain, and for burgers at Jackson Hole, after which the daughter of the Great Depression took the leftovers home for "Aunt Lily," the older woman who lived on the same floor of her building.

Like Lee, Earnhardt loved music, so when he came to town, she took him to the symphony. Once, during a performance of Mozart by the pianist Alicia de Larrocha, Jim saw her "politely correct a young man seated next to us who was moving his hand to the music in the wrong time signature." They also both loved books, of course, so his visits inevitably involved sojourns to bookstores. Lee directed him to the Strand, but also to the Bryn Mawr, one of her favorite shops, where she'd once found a rare edition of Whitman's *Leaves of Grass* in the gardening section and where he found a first edition of Eudora Welty's *Delta Wedding* for a dollar. Their literary adventures took other forms, too, including a pilgrimage to Woodlawn Cemetery in the Bronx, where they paid their respects to Herman Melville. After Jim left the *Outlook* for *The Montgomery Advertiser,* he wrote a column about their graveyard adventure in the only way that Lee wholeheartedly endorsed: so anonymously ("My friend, an Alabamian who has lived in New York for many years") that when her sister Alice sent along the clipping, she wrote, "This is the way I like to read about you; identifiable only to the author, her sister, and the subject."

Earnhardt was as trustworthy with his reporting as he was with his friendships, and Lee soon found that he was the rare source who never fabricated a memory, even around the edges. He recalled for her with precision everything he knew about the Reverend and readily admitted when she needed to look elsewhere for information. That turned out to be an unusual quality. Like a lot of places in Alabama, if you asked a question around Alex City, you could expect an entire epic, with all the narrative liberties the word implies, or no answer at all. Lee had committed herself to a book built from facts, but when it came to the story of the Reverend Maxwell, those were hard to come by and harder still to verify. Many of the people she talked to never really knew the details of the case, some had already forgotten them, and others had reason to lie about them.

Worse, some of the most crucial facts of the case had never been established: of all the deaths associated with the Reverend Willie Maxwell, only two had ever been declared homicides, and neither of those had resulted in convictions. Plenty of people had theories about what the Reverend had done—including, eventually, Lee herself—but it just wasn't possible to say for sure what had happened in the other four deaths, absent exhumations or perhaps innovations in toxicology. Nonetheless, Lee armed herself with so many autopsy reports, death certificates, and interviews with the experts who'd prepared them that she joked about being "up to my neck in funerals."

She was also up to her eyeballs in other paperwork. From the county courthouses at Dadeville and Rockford, she pulled marriage certificates and the Reverend's military service record. When she found out that the Maxwells had worked for Russell Mills, she got someone to copy down the employee records for the Reverend and his first wife. She even had cocktails with Ben Russell, Benjamin Russell's grandson, at the Willow Point Country Club, where the Radneys were members. And one day, Lee obtained a copy of the "Declaration of Legitimation" that the Reverend had filed for the daughter he had fathered in 1969.

As a result, when Lee went to interview the first Mrs. Maxwell's surviving relatives, she had delicate questions to ask them. On January 16, 1978, she met Mary Lou's sister Lena Martin at her home. Martin told Lee right away how little she thought of the Reverend Maxwell and how much she and her husband had worried about Mary Lou. Maxwell was "mean to her," Martin said, and "didn't treat her right." They shared the sense that he was dangerous, so much so that Essex Martin could remember for Lee exactly what he'd said after the Reverend called Lena to say that Mary Lou had been in an accident: "She ain't had no wreck; he just killed her."

The Martins insisted that the Reverend Maxwell had also killed his brother. On the night J.C. died, they told Lee, he had been in a car with the Reverend, who had let him out by Cottage Grove Cemetery, not far from where his body was later found. Their certainty sent Lee back to the evidence from John Columbus Maxwell's death, which included two insurance documents. The first was an application for a five-thousand-dollar policy on John Columbus Maxwell from the Crown Life Insurance Company of Illinois dated March 15, 1971, that named Willie J. Maxwell the beneficiary and used the Reverend's own mailing address. The second was the "Death Claim Notice" for that same policy, indicating that John C. Maxwell had died "from sickness" on February 6, 1972, asking that the check be sent to the same address. With the two forms side by side, it was obvious that the handwriting on both was identical: the Reverend Willie Maxwell had applied for the policy on his brother and then, less than a year later, been the one to request payment. The same signature also appeared on four other policies Maxwell held on his brother alone.

Lee's book was never going to be a *whodunit,* since the murderer was never a mystery. But while the *howhedunit* was as puzzling as ever, the *whyhedunit* had taken a turn for the obvious. Reverend Maxwell was an "elusive" figure, she once wrote to Rheta Grimsley Johnson, a journalist who knew Lee's family from her time at *The*

*Monroe Journal* and was hoping to interview Lee about the book she was writing. Declining an interview from her motel room in Alex City, Lee drew a horseshoe on the back flap of the envelope as a kind of homemade return address. "He might not have believed in what he preached, he might not have believed in voodoo," she wrote of the Reverend, "but he had a profound and abiding belief in insurance."

THE EXTENT OF THE REVEREND'S INSURANCE HOLDINGS RAISED a whole different set of questions about him, including exactly how much he had made from the policies and exactly how he had spent that money. District Attorney Tom Young had once claimed that Maxwell "always paid his debts and had excellent credit," and suggested that his neighbors disliked him for it: "Maybe that's why some people talked about him. That's a poor county, you know."

But Young was wrong. By January 1978, the Reverend's estate had been fully probated, and eighteen claims had already been filed against it, totaling almost sixty-five thousand dollars and ranging in size from a bill from Hardy Electric Company for thirteen dollars to some forty-five thousand dollars owed to the Bank of Dadeville. There were outstanding accounts at tire shops and country stores, and others for gas, groceries, and jewelry. The Reverend had been in serious debt at the time of his death, which meant he was also in debt at the time of the murder of Shirley Ann Ellington, much as he had been when his first wife was found dead.

That suggested a clear pattern of motive, yet Maxwell's finances were still baffling. Lee found that his insurance policy payouts exceeded his debts, and it wasn't obvious what he had done with all of that money, to say nothing of why he had worked so hard at so many legitimate jobs all those years: for Russell Mills, at the quarry, in the pulpwooding business, and in the pulpit. Like the law enforcement officers before her, Lee came to focus on the "lady friends" for whom the Reverend had been known around town—costly affairs, it now seemed.

Big Tom didn't know all that much about Maxwell's finances, but he was also more interested in talking about his new client than about his old one, having lately returned to the good graces of a community that only a few months before had considered him one of the Devil's own attorneys. Just as he had been congratulated in court for the verdict in the Burns trial, Radney was now getting congratulations all around town, and on January 20, 1978, he was officially named Man of the Year by the Chamber of Commerce. An editorial in the *Outlook* praised the decision: "Whether he's in the courtroom or the legislature or in politics, Mr. Radney always gives it everything he's got. And, on the record of his accomplishments, he's got plenty, and his efforts have paid big dividends for this community and this area."

Two days after that ceremony, Harper Lee went back to see Mary Ann Karr, the court reporter, and wrote her a check for one thousand dollars for the transcript of *State of Alabama v. Robert Lewis Burns*. She left with almost five hundred pages, double-spaced to leave room for annotations. She was also finally able to speak with Burns himself, because he was home from Bryce Hospital, already back to work, and more than willing to talk about shooting the Reverend.

Lee quickly found that Burns was nothing at all like Hickock or Smith, and also that interviewing a murderer in his living room was nothing like interviewing one in prison. Burns was a handsome, polite man, whose wife adored him and whose foster daughter—the one with special needs, who had been close to Shirley Ann Ellington— hung around his legs during their conversations just as she had during the recesses of his trial. During his two interviews with Lee, Burns repeated a lot of what he had heard about the Reverend and his voo- doo practice, adding a few details about clothespins Maxwell had sup- posedly worn on his ears and the bottles labeled with strange words that had allegedly been discovered when his house was cleaned out after his death. Burns told Lee that he was sure that the Reverend had murdered all five of his family members and that he had made Dorcas Anderson's husband drink some kind of poison, too. She listened attentively, he recalled, asking a lot of questions and sharing with him some of what she had already learned. "She knew all her stuff," Burns said, and she told him, "You'd be surprised at all the people that man's got insurance policies on."

The insurance was all very real, but the voodoo rumors were hard to substantiate. Still, Lee was interested in the allegations and in the culture that had produced them, because she'd grown up with the same kinds of superstitions in Monroe County and included some of them in *To Kill a Mockingbird*. "Before I remembered there was no such thing as hoo-dooing," Scout says of the soap figurines that Boo Radley carved to look like her and Jem, "I shrieked and threw them down." What Lee didn't already know from experience, she made a point of finding out, contacting an occult bookstore in New York to get a copy of its catalog and see what else she could learn about conjuring. The oldest shop of its kind in the country, Samuel Weiser Bookstore had opened on Book Row in 1926, but by the time Lee needed its assistance, it had moved to Broadway, established its own imprint, and racked up an inventory of over a hundred thousand books—everything from *African Folklore, Country Wisdom,* and *The Secrets of Superstitions* to *Occult America, Spirits and Spirit Worlds,* and *Vampires, Zombies, and Monster Men*.

Reading her way through the shelf's worth of voodoo books she ordered, Lee learned what her own life had already taught her: voodoo was an extensive and sincerely held system of belief, with practitioners all around the world. But, as far as she could tell, those practitioners did not include the Reverend Willie Maxwell. As much as Lee enjoyed the company of Tom Radney, her reporting on the rumors surrounding the Reverend made her far more inclined to agree with Tom Young, who had dismissed "all that voodoo stuff" as "based on natural superstition, surmise, conjecture, and reckless gossip." She couldn't find any evidence that Maxwell himself believed in voodoo, let alone that he could hex a jury or turn into a black cat. Nor was there any sign that he'd ever been to New Orleans at all, much less to study with the Seven Sisters.

The person who denied the voodoo business most vociferously was the Reverend's widow, who had always insisted on her husband's innocence. After securing an interview with the third Mrs. Maxwell, Lee experienced for herself what investigators who had worked on the earlier cases had told her about the widow's specialty, which was denying her previous statements and claiming she'd never said them. Lee herself would say, "I was disappointed by her lack of candor."

But what the widow wouldn't tell her, Lee would find out for herself. After the Reverend was murdered, she learned, Ophelia Maxwell had filed a lawsuit against the Gerber Life Insurance Company in the amount of fifteen thousand dollars. It was not for a policy in her late husband's name but for one on Shirley Ann Ellington. Gerber refused to pay on the grounds that the policy wasn't valid—partly because it was less than two years old and the girl hadn't died of natural causes, but also because Shirley's signature on the application had been forged.

After Gerber's reply, Ophelia Maxwell dropped the suit, but the act of filing it came straight from her husband's playbook, and it raised questions about what other policies the Maxwells might have held on Shirley. More disturbingly, it raised questions about whether Ophelia might have been the one to fulfill the role the Reverend had initially offered to the man from Eclectic. Ophelia's account of the day that her stepdaughter died had always been strangely vague; she had never been able to explain to anyone's satisfaction why her husband had been out scouting timber so late, or why the two of them had waited so long to look for the teenager after she supposedly set off, without a license, in their car.

That in itself might have been enough to raise Lee's eyebrows, but by then she also knew what most people around Lake Martin had forgotten: that Ophelia Maxwell had been a suspect in the death of the Reverend's first wife. When Lee reconstructed the crimes, as she had done many times with Capote, it became obvious that the Reverend needed transportation to or from at least some of the scenes where the bodies had been found. The testimony of the man from Eclectic had given credence to the widespread belief that someone had helped Maxwell; the question had always been who. Some had thought it was Fred Hutchinson, since he had already been convicted of homicide in an insurance scheme and it seemed unlikely that two such like-minded criminals would be operating independently in the same small town. But it is more likely that Lee suspected Ophelia Maxwell.

"I do believe that the Reverend Maxwell murdered at least five people," she wrote once in a summary of the case, "that his motive was greed, that he had an accomplice for two of the murders and an accessory for one." Well versed in criminal law and careful with her choice of words whether in a letter or a lede, she took care to distinguish between an accessory, someone present during a murder, and an accomplice, someone who assists before or after. To a writer living in Auburn who was interested in the case, she teased that the accomplice was not only alive, but living within a 150-mile radius.

On top of everything else that made researching the Reverend difficult, Lee now had to contend with a living accomplice. It wasn't so unlike those early weeks in Kansas before the Clutter murders were solved, when Jack Dunphy made Capote so worried for his own life that he asked Lee if she would carry a gun. She didn't then, and she wasn't now, but she did tell more than a few of her sources that she was concerned about threats to herself, her family in Alex City, and her older sister over in Eufaula. Whether she meant that the Reverend's accomplice might want to harm them or that someone else connected to the case might want to scare her off the project, she didn't say.

BUT IF LEE WAS NOW AFRAID OF THE SUBJECTS OF HER WORK, for the first time in a long time she was not afraid of the work itself. She had always loved mysteries, and this one, dark as it was, was combating her own darkness. Word had spread that she was digging into the Maxwell case, and her days were starting to fill with appointments and invitations. She accepted any that seemed likely to turn up new information on the Reverend, and in the early summer of 1978 she agreed to attend a cocktail party with the staff of the *Outlook*. By then, Al Benn had left to become the publisher of a newspaper in LaFayette, and Bill Hatcher, a hungry young editor from Cleveland, Tennessee, had been named his successor. Hatch, as everyone called him, had graduated from a small Wesleyan college, then gone to work for a newspaper in his home state before moving to Alabama to run *The Auburn Bulletin*. A gay man, he was not entirely at home in Alex

City, but he was at home in any newsroom, and although he was only half Harper Lee's age, he nearly matched her wit. The new editor in chief made some other hires, including Patty Cribb, who was named editor of the "Outlook on Living" section of the paper. Unlike Hatch, Cribb was a local; she had graduated from Benjamin Russell High School and returned to Alex City after college and graduate school in Florida. It was her mother who organized the cocktail party and invited Judge C. J. Coley, a local eminence who was equal parts Pliny the Elder and Thucydides.

Born in 1902, Clinton Jackson Coley was a native of Alex City and had grown in size and stature during the same years the town had. Ostensibly he was a banker and a probate judge, but for Lee's purposes he was the finest historian in the county and among the best in the state. Almost single-handedly, Judge Coley had convinced Congress to turn Horseshoe Bend into a national military park and convinced the U.S. Postal Service to honor Alabama native Helen Keller with a stamp. The rumpus room of his house was filled with knickknacks from every era of Alabama history, and Judge Coley was the kind of man who could, in one breath, tell you how many families got their mail at the Nixburg Post Office when Mrs. Crawford was postmistress there and, in the next, ask if you'd heard about the local boy who'd gotten into a knife fight with John Wilkes Booth before the latter left Alabama and started down the deadly path that would intersect with Abraham Lincoln. He had files full of clippings on regional history and shelves laden down with monographs, memoirs, and amateur genealogies, and he owned a copy of every pamphlet, poem, article, and chapbook ever written about the Battle of Horseshoe Bend. His great-grandmother had been buried in the cemetery on Highway 9 near where Shirley Ann Ellington had been found dead, and he could be counted on to tell the story of how, on the day of her grand, gaudy funeral, a sunny sky turned thunderous and lightning struck the silver shovel the grave digger was using, breaking it to bits—an admonition from the heavens, he insisted, about extravagance. It was talking with Judge Coley, Lee joked, that saved her from putting on five pounds at the cocktail party.

When Lee wrote to the Cribbs in June 1978 to thank them for hosting, she said, "You simply can't beat the people in Alex City," then added a cautionary note: "If I fall flat on my face with this book, I won't be terribly disappointed" since she had made so many friends in town. She sounded more confident, though, when she told them she would look forward to seeing them on her next reporting trip when she returned from New York that fall. "It was not good-bye," Lee said, "because I'll be coming back until doomsday."

# 22

# Horseshoe Bend

NOTHING WRITES ITSELF. LEFT TO ITS OWN DEVICES, THE world will never transform into words, and no matter how many pages of notes and interviews and documents a reporting trip generates, the one that matters most always starts out blank. In *The Journalist and the Murderer,* Janet Malcolm called this space between reporting and writing an "abyss." It is an awful place, and an awfully easy place to get stuck. Everyone told Harper Lee that the story she had found was destined to be a best seller. But no one could tell her how to write it.

When Lee returned to New York from Alabama, it was to 433 East Eighty-Second Street, where she had lived for over a decade. To the extent that a building can resemble a person, Lee's resembled her: unadorned and inconspicuous, it was in the middle of the city yet surprisingly removed from its bustle, and from the outside it revealed nothing. Almost no one knew that one of the most celebrated authors in America lived there, hidden in plain sight, with "Lee-H" listed on the buzzer board. For a while, she shared the first floor with two musicians, known then as Daryl and John but soon to become famous by their last names: Hall & Oates, who had no idea their neighbor was a novelist, much less Harper Lee.

Others in the building over the years knew who Lee was, but they also knew not to acknowledge her masterpiece, and except to ask about her travels northward or southward, they did not pry into her personal life. On the top floor were the Malkos, with whom she marveled about the superintendent's insistence on smoking while holding his oxygen tank and speculated about all the other neighborhood characters as well; below them on the third floor were the Bentleys, Sonya and Frank, whose children adored Lee, including their son who became her godchild; below them were Vivian Weaver and Elaine Adam, who had worked for the Council on Foreign Relations, and then as editors and typists for friends, including the writer Patrick Dennis, whose *Auntie Mame* was dedicated to them. "V.V. and Mme. A.," as they were known, liked turning their apartment into a salon and made conversation as easily as cocktails. Lee wasn't a recluse, but she socialized in other people's spaces or met them at museums and restaurants around the city. She was as protective of her interior space as her interior life, and many of her closest friends knew her for decades without ever setting foot inside her apartment.

For a woman of her means, that apartment was spartan, except for the private Bodleian Library she had managed to squeeze inside it. Once, after she'd had a nightmare about being evicted, she made an inventory of all her possessions for her friends Earl and Sylvia Shorris, who lived across the street. Should the dream ever come true, she warned them, the following would be dragged onto the sidewalk: "a dilapidated bed, a chair & table, about 3,000 books and the last two manual typewriters in the world—one of which won't work." In that event, she begged them, "rescue the typewriter." The books were her real companions, and she'd been collecting them since childhood. There was the poetry of Blake, Wordsworth, and Thomas Hardy, together with the contemporary American writers she admired—among them, Mary McCarthy, John Updike, Peter De Vries, John Cheever, and Flannery O'Connor—plus histories, crime stories, law books, and her five favorite novels: Samuel Butler's *Way of All Flesh*, Henry Fielding's *Tom Jones*, Proust's *Remembrance of Things Past*, Richard Hughes's *High Wind in Jamaica*, and Mark Twain's *Huckleberry Finn*.

When Lee unpacked the enormous leather briefcase that Tom Radney had given her, together with the rest of her luggage from Alabama, she found herself in the midst of a veritable mountain of Maxwelliana. In addition to the official paperwork and records, there were pamphlets, programs, and informational brochures from around Alexander City, photocopied pages from a history of Alabama, and her notes and cassette tapes from the interviews she had conducted with, among many others, the Reverend's neighbors and employers; his widow, Ophelia Maxwell; Robert Burns; the Reverend E. B. Burpo Jr., who had presided over Shirley's funeral and had testified at the Burns trial; Al Benn; Mary Lou Maxwell's sister Lena Martin; Mary Ann Karr; Sergeant Gray; Judge Jim Avary; and, of course, the Radneys.

When Lee had first read *In Cold Blood,* she would have been able to see clearly how it had been built from the work that she had helped with in Kansas. But reversing the process—looking at her own reporting notes and seeing the book inside them—was a very different matter. To begin with, she had to find a way to organize all her material. For Capote, she had sorted everything into ten tidy sections, but it wasn't entirely clear how best to divide the Maxwell case up into its many parts. The setting was straightforward, but the crimes, the victims, and the trials were all hard to disentangle. The easiest way to tell any story is chronologically, but because there were police investigations, criminal trials, and civil proceedings, some of them running concurrently, the time line of the Maxwell case crisscrossed like a game of cat's cradle.

Worse, she needed a protagonist to place at the center of her story, but it wasn't obvious who that might be. There was the Reverend Maxwell of course, but it was impossible to make a hero out of him, and much of his life, both before and after he was accused of murder, was underdocumented and alien to her. There was Robert Burns, but as showstopping as his funeral-home shooting had been, it was his sole contribution to the drama; he hadn't even lived in town for much of the time that it was unfolding. There were plenty of lawmen—too many, in fact, because the deaths were spread across seven years, two counties, and a handful of law enforcement agencies—but there was no Agent Dewey, heroically solving the case and hauling the killers into the courtroom in handcuffs; in point of fact, none of the cases had ever officially been solved. The crime doctor was interesting, but his crime crew hadn't solved any of the cases either, so they could hardly be considered heroic; even the general public's growing interest in forensic science couldn't justify making them the center of the story.

Then there were the various prosecutors and defense attorneys. Lee had been writing lawyers since she could write, and while the district attorneys wouldn't do, since no single one of them had been involved with all the cases, she liked a good defense attorney, and Tom Radney was a very good defense attorney. Moreover, Radney had represented the Reverend for ten years, and then represented his assassin, so he could easily carry the story from start to finish. He was also a complicated protagonist, the sort of morally complex character Tay Hohoff had encouraged her to avoid. Radney had profited immensely from his share of the insurance litigation, which had raised eyebrows around Tallapoosa County, and he had been essential to keeping the Reverend out of prison, which had drawn the ire of Coosa County, but Robert Burns's acquittal had restored his standing around Lake Martin.

Radney's legal talents were matched by his political ambitions, and choosing him would give Lee an opportunity to write about the role of race in the political machine of Alabama and the justice system of America. The difficulty was that the Maxwell case was not exactly an ideal parable about race and justice; she knew all too well that the story of a black serial killer wasn't what readers would expect from the author of *To Kill a Mockingbird*. While there are very good reasons to wonder if the investigations would have turned out differently had any of the Reverend's alleged victims been white, it's equally true that law enforcement officers in the South were often only too eager to convict African Americans for crimes, violent or otherwise. Moreover, the lawmen around Lake Martin couldn't be accused of negligence in the case of the Reverend Willie Maxwell; they had tried zealously to convict him and used every resource available to them, yet failed again and again.

Although Tom Radney wasn't a perfect protagonist, he was, like Agent Dewey in Kansas, an exceptionally convenient one. He was one of the few people from Alex City who called to see how Lee's book was going and he offered to do anything she needed to get it written: share memories, track down information, make connections for her, and lend her his service in any other way she needed. Lee found Big Tom generous with his time, but not an entirely reliable narrator of the events of the Maxwell case or his own life. That was often just out of carelessness, the way everyone sometimes misremembers things that happened years ago. "His memory for facts," Lee would later lament of Big Tom, "caused me much dismay."

But Lee was bothered less by what he told the world than by what he told himself. His "psychological processes," she would reflect, "were of clinical fascination to me." However good a lawyer he was, she understood right away that no matter whom he was representing, he was first and foremost representing himself. And she had talked with enough people around Alexander City to know that his charms weren't universally appreciated. She put the matter plainly a few years later, warning, "If accuracy is what you are after, check out everything he says; if a hero is what you want, invent one."

LEE DID WANT ACCURACY, BUT WHEN SHE TRIED TO START WRIT-ing, she found that facts were in short supply. To begin with, it was difficult to reconstruct the life of a sharecropper's son. History isn't what happened but what gets written down, and the various sources that make up the archival record generally overlooked the lives of poor black southerners. Lee could trace Tom Radney's entire career, along with his family's success and service, in *The Alexander City Outlook,* but when she went looking for anything about the Reverend Max-well, she found only his crimes. That was in keeping with the way black lives in the South and elsewhere had been treated—not merely criminalized but criminally neglected, including in her father's own newspaper, which had frequent mentions of the Lee family but only the occasional "Negro News" column. There were black newspapers, of course, but not even those had mentioned Maxwell until after his death; reporters from *The Afro-American* and *Jet* had covered the story only after the Reverend was gunned down. A writer trying to fix the life of the Reverend Willie Maxwell on the page was mostly at the mercy of oral history, which could be misremembered or manipulated or simply withheld from an outsider. There were also things no oral history could have told Lee except a confession from the Reverend.

Day after day, Lee sat down and tried to make a book out of, or around, those gaping holes. She had once fantasized about a kind of secular monastery for writers, where, supported by the government, they would be locked away with nothing but bread and water. Her own disciplines were less draconian: she liked to sleep late, start writing around noon, take a break for dinner, then carry on until deep into the night. She tended to write longhand first, and then, at the end of every day, she typed a fresh copy of her draft—"picking out the nut from the shell," she called it—on the Olivetti typewriter she'd finally bought to replace her faithful old Royal. "I work very slowly," Lee acknowledged. "A good eight-hour day usually gives me about one page of manuscript I won't throw away." But her necessities were few, "paper, pen, and privacy," she once joked, later amending the list only slightly: "A tremendous pot of coffee helps, but is not essential."

Lee liked to claim that other people, too, were not essential. "You depend entirely upon yourself and no one else," she had once said of writing, but in fact *To Kill a Mockingbird* had come into being through the extensive editorial direction of Tay Hohoff. "If the Lippincott editors hadn't been so fussy and painstaking," Maurice Crain once wrote, "we wouldn't have had nearly so good a book." But Crain and Hohoff were both dead, leaving Lee without the literary helpmeets who had once guided her from draft to publication. By the time she sat down to write her true-crime book, she had outlived her literary agency (Crain and Williams had passed along most of their clients to McIntosh & Otis, a firm started by one of Annie Laurie's friends) as well as her publisher (Lippincott had been acquired by Harper & Row, which would eventually become HarperCollins).

Lee valorized solitude, but the sociability of reporting was better for her, not least because it countered her depressive tendencies. But here she was, alone again with her typewriter and nothing to do but write. Every day, her to-do list consisted of the same single item: write a book. Even on days when she did manage to get something done, she could never cross it off. Making the story of the Reverend into the book she was now calling *The Reverend* wasn't turning out to be as straightforward as it seemed, and soon the optimism of "coming back" that she had expressed when leaving Alexander City faded into the pessimism of "doomsday."

Among the many already-written books keeping Lee company in her apartment was a copy of Daniel Defoe's *Robinson Crusoe,* which she had read, as she put it, umpteen times. Crusoe had been shipwrecked twenty-eight years, and Lee must have identified. The same number of years had passed since she had moved to New York, yet there she was surrounded by loneliness, struggling with a book that didn't seem to want to be written, on what must have felt, at times, like her own Island of Despair. Her father, like Crusoe's, had wanted her to stay home, but she had gone adventuring instead. Now she was alone in her apartment, notching her days.

WHAT LEE HAD LONG HIDDEN FROM THE WORLD, SHE COULDN'T hide from her family. Her sisters, as ever, watched over her, and three years into working on her new book, she accepted an invitation from the middle one, Louise Conner, to come stay with her in Eufaula, a hundred miles from Alexander City and not far from the Georgia line. Weezie was sixty-four and had lived in Barbour County since Nelle was ten. General Sherman started east of Eufaula on his march to the sea, so it still has one of the largest historic districts in the state, full of Gothic Revivals, Greek Revivals, classical revivals, and just about every other architectural style worth reviving. Back when it was settled, the town had been perched on the banks of the Chattahoochee River, but forty years after the Martin Dam tamed the Tallapoosa, the U.S. Army Corps of Engineers built a dam near Eufaula to make the Walter F. George Reservoir, and a year after that a wildlife refuge was established to protect the storks, falcons, bald eagles, and alligators displaced by the hydroelectric project. Between the refuge, the reservoir, and all of the historic buildings, Eufaula was, according to Harper Lee, "the loveliest town in the state."

Louise, who had opened her home on Country Club Road to Lee

many times before, was used to being "the sister of the author" and had long since reconciled herself to sharing her childhood with the entire world. She had given a few interviews right after *To Kill a Mockingbird* was published and had confided to some friends her shock at Nelle's instant celebrity. "My baby sister that we thought would have to be supported all her life could buy and sell us all at the drop of a hat," Louise wrote to one friend, marveling over how Nelle turned down work to avoid climbing income tax brackets and needed an unlisted telephone number to keep reporters and her legions of fans at bay.

By the time Nelle came to visit in 1981, though, Louise was already decades into the sort of life her little sister would never have. Her husband had died just two years before, after more than forty years of marriage, leaving Louise with two accomplished children. Both of her sons would become professors: Herschel H. Conner III, named for his father and known as Hank, taught telecommunications in the journalism department of the University of Florida; Edwin Lee Conner, named for his uncle, was already a fellow at Vanderbilt University and would go on to teach English literature at Kentucky State University. Louise had achieved something that neither of her sisters had: she had built a family. In consequence, she was used to being a disciplinarian, so aside from being able to help with the crosswords and reminisce about their family, she was capable of imposing some order on her baby sister's writing routines.

In January of that year, Lee wrote a letter to Gregory Peck and his wife, Veronique, to congratulate them on their twenty-fifth wedding anniversary, and to let them know how her work was going. "Louise guards my privacy like Cerberus," she said after dispensing with the felicitations, "and won't even let me go fishing until late afternoon, but keeps me shut up in one end of the house a la Collette's husband." Lee was being fed and housed and made to write, which was good for her, as was talking with Peck, her old collaborator.

Such conversations were rare for her. With the exception of Capote, Lee mostly shied away from other writers, even though she was surrounded by opportunities to befriend them. Indeed, her distance from literary circles bordered on the comical. As a postwar southern novelist, she was assumed to be close to and influenced by Carson McCullers, whom she barely knew and who resented her for "poaching on my literary preserves"; Flannery O'Connor, whom she never knew and who belittled *Mockingbird* as "a child's book"; and Eudora Welty, whom she adored but would later learn regarded her as a one-hit wonder. Even with those writers Lee tolerated, including the southern novelist and memoirist Reynolds Price and the editor and novelist Starling Lawrence, she rarely talked about her work. Like nearly all of her other friendships—which were numerous and varied, ranging from the professor across the street to the receptionist at the doctor's office—they were predicated on an understanding that she would never speak about her writing and they would never ask. Plenty of people knew Harper Lee for years without ever talking about "the Bird" or "the Book," and almost none of them ever asked her about what she had written since.

But in her letter that first week of 1981, she thanked Gregory Peck for his "willingness to talk" and wrote, "It is strange, but people not in our game (The Arts, uffle wuffle) have no concept of the intense loneliness of it." To give Peck a sense of what the last three years of trying to write about the Reverend had felt like, she quoted the journalist Gene Fowler: "Writing is easy; all you do is sit staring at the blank sheet of paper until the drops of blood form on your forehead." Writing hadn't come easy to her since those frenzied months when she had produced *Mockingbird;* now the very fact of having done so, triumphant as it was, was making her life more difficult. With her first novel, she told Peck, "nobody cared when I was writing it; now it seems that my neck is being breathed on, but I refuse to let this thing go until it approaches some standard of excellence." Her new mockingbird was starting to seem more like an albatross, and it weighed on her more heavily the more people knew about her work: "My agent wants pure gore & autopsies, my publisher wants another best-seller, and I want a clear conscience, in that I haven't defrauded the reader."

Lee was repulsed by the idea of writing anything lurid or pulpy, never mind that true-crime books were generally violent and best sellers were generally page-turners. However intriguingly bloodless some of the deaths in the Maxwell case were, any writer chronicling the story was obliged to begin and end with horrific scenes: a woman bludgeoned to death; a man shot in the face. She didn't want to disrespect the dead by making their deaths tawdry, but she also didn't want to disappoint her readers, or let down her publisher. Her first novel had relayed its most violent acts so indirectly that it was deemed appropriate for children, yet, almost impossibly, it had earned critical acclaim and outsold virtually every other book ever printed. Either of those feats, literary accolades or wild sales, would be difficult to pull off again, let alone both, and although people joked that Harper & Row would have published Lee's grocery list, she didn't want anything appearing under her name that wasn't as good as what she'd written before. If it were just a matter of getting another book out the door, after all, she could have handed over *Go Set a Watchman,* which was sitting in her family's safety-deposit box at the Monroe County Bank.

Instead, she wanted to write something new, whatever the challenges involved. Those challenges were not limited to the difficulty of writing, the confusion around the case itself, and the expectations surrounding a new book by Harper Lee. Two months later, she wrote to Gregory Peck again, this time from Monroeville, and confided a new concern she had about *The Reverend:* "Of course I'll probably be sued and lose my drawers over the book I'm working on now, and will have to sell my soul to keep my body, but we'll worry about that when the time comes to worry!"

Of all of Lee's concerns about her new book, this was perhaps the strangest. Capote had worried about a lawsuit when a rival writer claimed that Hickock and Smith had promised him their life stories, and the suit had given him some anxiety while he was writing *In Cold Blood,* but nothing ever came of it. (Capote *was* sued for defamation by Gore Vidal, after he claimed that his fellow writer had been thrown out of the Kennedy White House following some drunken transgressions, but that was a self-inflicted wound, and the two writers settled out of court.) Similarly, Lee herself had been threatened with legal action after *Mockingbird* was published. Although she liked to complain that everyone in Monroe County saw themselves in her novel, one family in particular really did—the Boulwares, of South Alabama Avenue—and they nearly sued her for it.

The legend around Monroeville went something like this: the Boulwares had a young son who had been caught breaking into a drugstore with two older boys. The teenagers were sent away to a reformatory school, but Mr. Boulware arranged with the sheriff to take custody of his son and thereafter kept him locked away in the family home. Like Boo Radley, Sonny Boulware was sometimes seen peeking out from behind their shutters, and when he got older, he was said to skulk around town at night. The Boulwares had an older daughter, and after *Mockingbird* was published, she had approached an attorney about suing Lee for her portrayal of their family. Lippincott rushed to the rescue with a carefully worded editorial explaining that the novel was a work of fiction and any resemblance to living persons was "coincidental," but it was after that scare that Lee had asked her father to stop calling himself Atticus in public.

It wasn't unreasonable, then, for Lee to contemplate the possibility of being sued. But she knew firsthand that publishers had legal teams review controversial projects before putting them in the world and that they assumed some of the liability upon doing so. Moreover, nearly everyone involved in the Maxwell case had seemed excited by the prospect of Lee's turning their lives into a book. Perhaps she worried that the Radneys would sue her if they didn't like her portrayal of them, but Big Tom was one of her biggest boosters: he still called once or twice a year to check on the book's progress, he came to see her in New York to talk about it, and whenever he was asked about her work on *The Reverend,* he expressed hope that she would publish it soon.

It was also possible Lee thought a member of the Maxwell family might sue her, because some of them had threatened legal action against the press after the Reverend's murder. But she had interviewed Ophelia Maxwell and knew exactly what the widow claimed had happened—and exactly what she had claimed hadn't happened—and she would have deployed the requisite "allegedly" and "supposedly" caveats of true crime. For his part, Robert Burns had an acquittal to his name, and anyway, he had never denied shooting the Reverend. Moreover, he had cooperated with Lee both times she interviewed him, and like Radney he always hoped that she would tell his story.

WHATEVER HAD LEE SPOOKED, SHE FOUND A FAMILIAR WAY OF handling that stress and all the others: the shortage of facts, the lack of an ideal protagonist, her unfamiliarity with the lives of African Americans, a certain uncomfortable moral muddiness concerning black criminality in a criminally racist society, and a related discomfort with her own deep delight in the self-serving mythologies of the southern gentry. Lee's drinking had become something of a scandal, not an overtly public one, but family and friends had long taken notice. The daughter of one of the driest men in Monroe County, whose oldest sister wouldn't even consume caffeine, had grown into a woman who couldn't say no to scotch or vodka, or failing that, to whatever happened to be on hand. When she drank too much, Lee had been known to blow raspberries at formal dinners in the presence of strangers and to return angrily to parties she'd been asked to leave to plead for just one more drink. Lee's friends understood that alcohol had the power to turn their brilliant Jekyll into an unpredictable Hyde, and a few of them—Truman Capote, Tom Radney, and, most transgressively, one of her pastors in Monroeville—had even committed what amounted to a cardinal sin in the Church of Harper Lee, by letting slip to the press that she had a drinking problem. Radney, in particular, had offered, on the record, too candid an explanation for the delayed publication of *The Reverend:* "I think she's fighting a battle between the book and a bottle of scotch. And the scotch is winning."

Like *Mockingbird,* and writing more generally, drinking was an off-limits topic for Lee, and broaching it could leave those formerly close to her excommunicated, or at least estranged. Lee had drifted away from one friend in New York, Isabelle Holland, after she became an evangelist for Alcoholics Anonymous. Holland's mother had been the last of seven generations to live in Tennessee; she sent her son to a boarding school in the old state but sent her daughter to one in the old country. Belle, as she was known, had expected to be a Henry James heroine in England but instead found no friends. When she came back to America, she moved to New York, where she became the publicity manager at Lippincott. Holland handled press for *To Kill a Mockingbird* and went on to write many novels of her own. Her own writing had improved in sobriety, and when she tried convincing Lee the same could be true for her, their friendship grew strained.

Lee had met another champion of Alcoholics Anonymous in Alex City. Along with bringing honor to the state of Alabama in the form of parks and postage stamps, Judge C. J. Coley, the once-sodden son of stern Presbyterian parents, had brought AA to his hometown, convening a meeting so filled with prominent men that it had its own cachet around town. "Anything worthwhile in my life," the judge said forty years into his sobriety, "can be traced to a decision to climb out of the bottle." For now, though, Lee was still deep inside it.

WHETHER OR NOT THEY TALKED ABOUT DRINKING, COLEY AND Lee most certainly talked about their shared love of Horseshoe Bend. In making the case to Congress to protect the battlefield, Coley had made himself into an expert on the Creek Wars; when Lee was in Alexander City, that battle was often on her mind, and not just because the motel she stayed in had been named for it. While working on *The Reverend,* she returned to the work of her favorite historian, Albert James Pickett, who wrote extensively about the Creek nation. Born in 1810, Pickett wrote newspaper essays for a living while gradually turning himself into a historian. He spent seventeen years collecting the material that would become his masterpiece: *History of Alabama, and Incidentally of Georgia and Mississippi, from the Earliest Period.*

Published in 1851, Pickett's book ran through a few editions before lapsing out of print. For amateur and professional historians alike, it was a grave loss, especially in the Lee household, where A.C. had revered its contents like scripture. Pickett was a pioneer of what we now call oral history, and because the events he was writing about were barely the past, he was able to interview many people who had been directly involved in them, including veterans and widows from both sides of the Creek Wars.

Lee adored Pickett's history, and—partly because she had been reading it anyway and partly to salvage an upsetting situation—she ended up talking about him at one of the only public lectures she ever gave. In February 1983, she wrote to Jim Earnhardt to confirm a rumor he'd heard: yes, it was true, she was on the docket for an event in Eufaula; no, she was not happy about it. Lee then explained how she had been dragooned into agreeing to give a lecture at the Alabama History and Heritage Festival. It had all started with a letter from her sister Louise, who had been asked to join a planning committee for the event, "since Eufaula reeks with History & Heritage." At the very first planning meeting, the academic organizers of the festival realized "Weezie is Harper Lee's sister, and it promptly hit the fan."

Most of the rules that Lee enforced on her family and friends were tacit; no one could quite say how they had learned not to mention *Mockingbird* or ask Lee what she was working on next. But in her letter to Earnhardt, Lee made clear both what some of those rules were and why people around her tended to follow them. Speaking of her oldest sister, she wrote, "It took all of Alice's powers of negotiation to get me to *speak* to Weezie after I received her letter. Betrayed by my own sister was what I felt." It was apparently genuine fury, not histrionics. Still, that Christmas, upon being made to understand the degree of arm-twisting her sister had suffered, Lee agreed to do the event. "I consented, on my terms, which consisted of NOTS: no evening platform speech, no interviews, no undue publicity, no Star Billing." One of her nephews, Louise's son Hank, had been present when she made her list of demands, and seeing how crestfallen the organizers were that she wouldn't even acknowledge *To Kill a Mockingbird,* he had agreed to read from his aunt's novel. She entreated Jim to pray for her and sulked: "If I didn't feel that I have to get my sister off the hook, I wouldn't go near it."

For all that, no one who attended Lee's lecture that spring would have been able to sense her consternation or her disdain. If anything, the famous author looked nervous, not annoyed. The title of her talk was "Romance and High Adventure," and she made good on its promise. After disparaging the American habit of throwing away the past either by erasing it or romanticizing it, particular dangers in the South, she shifted to her favorite historian. "It gives me the greatest pleasure," she said, although it likely did not, "to remind the members of my own generation (who have all read it) and report to the younger ones among us, that although it's the real thing, Pickett's *History of Alabama* is a work so fraught with romance and high adventure that even John Jakes would sit up and take notice."

Jakes, a wildly popular author of potboiling historical fictions, was nothing, Lee claimed, compared with Pickett and his actual history. His style, she said, "falls somewhere between Macaulay and Bulwer-Lytton," and his characters were better than anything on television. Lee populated the Little Theatre of the Eufaula High School, as Pickett had his pages, with the ghosts of Alabama history: Hernando de Soto clearing his way through the state's thickets for the first time in 1540, crossing the land that would become Lake Martin; the British brothers John and Charles Wesley preaching their way around the South; the wilderness woman who claimed to be the tsar of Russia's sister-in-law; James Adair, who lived with the Creeks for thirty years and emerged arguing that they were actually Jews; Chief Tecumseh, the Shawnee warrior who promised to prove the righteousness of his theology of resistance to white perfidy by threatening to make the earth shake, just before the New Madrid Fault unleashed its tremendous earthquake.

But then Lee paused to observe a curious fact: Pickett's history does not continue past statehood. It ends when Alabama joined the Union in 1819, pretty much when most Alabamians would have argued that things were just getting interesting. Lee, however, had a theory about why Pickett had stopped writing. "I do not believe that it was in him," she said, "to write of the eventual fate of the Creek Nation, of the Cherokees, of the Chickasaws and Choctaws, which was decided well within his own lifetime." Instead his narrative concluded with the "engagements" between Andrew Jackson's army and the Creeks, which, Lee said, "began to spell the end, which came, as we all know, in a few furious hours at Horseshoe Bend." Then Lee said something about the historian that was far more revealing than anyone in the high school auditorium might have realized: "I think Pickett left his heart at Horseshoe Bend."

IF SO, HE WASN'T THE ONLY ONE WHO HAD LEFT SOME CRUCIAL part of himself in Tallapoosa County. Lee left something there, too—if not her heart, then perhaps her nerve. For the first time in three decades, she was extraordinarily close to having another book: not an idea for one, not a rumor of one, but the actual meat and bones of it, the research, the reporting, the plot, the characters, even some of the prose. But she was still writing a *Watchman* that she did not yet know how to turn into a *Mockingbird,* and no new Maurice Crain or Tay Hohoff had walked into her life to help. In fact, another one of her lodestars was about to abandon her: soon she lost the very reason she had tried writing true crime, and one of the reasons she had ever started writing at all.

On August 25, 1984, a month before he would have turned sixty, Truman Capote died in Los Angeles. He had overdosed the year before in Montgomery while on his way home to Monroeville, but survived. Now the coroner in California who performed the autopsy noted the author's liver disease, but also the barbiturates, codeine, and Valium in his system; it seemed another overdose had killed him, although there was no way to know if it had been accidental or intentional. When Jim Earnhardt heard the news, he tried to phone Lee, and when she didn't answer, he sent a telegram. A few hours later, she returned his call but trailed off into a sad silence, saying, "My old friend . . ."

A month later, at the Shubert Theatre in New York City for his memorial service, Lee followed along in a program printed "Courtesy of Tiffany & Co." as William Styron, Leo Lerman, Joseph Fox, and Zoe Caldwell eulogized Capote and read excerpts of his work. The pianist and singer Bobby Short performed two songs, including one from a musical for which Capote had written the lyrics. In the final moments, a tape recorder played onstage, letting the author's famously strange voice fill the hall as he read from "A Christmas Memory," a short story about his childhood in Monroeville. His words rang the courthouse bell, cracked pecan shells, and made the theater smell of hominy and honey. For Harper Lee more than anyone else at the Shubert, the story was more than story: it was their life, as irretrievable now as he was.

When it was over, the hundreds of admirers and literati who had turned up made their way outside, and Lee joined Alvin and Marie Dewey, who had come all the way from Kansas, for dinner at the apartment of Sandy Campbell and Donald Windham on Central Park South. Their tiny mourning party ate chicken buttered according to Capote's own recipe and talked of their tortured friend. Capote had tried Antabuse to break his alcoholism and gone into rehab several times, but between those stints he could be found rambling incoherently onstage at Towson State University, popping pills and snorting cocaine at Studio 54, and arguing with a judge in Southampton after being arrested for drunk driving. He had gotten a face-lift and hair transplants, but no cosmetic work could disguise the damage he had done to himself. Harper Lee, who could still conjure him in his irrepressible boyhood, saw clearly what depression and addiction could do to people and to those who loved them. Capote, who had talked about *Answered Prayers* for over a decade, had never finished it. For years after his death, there were rumors that he had stashed it away in a bus station locker.

There were rumors about Lee's unfinished book, too, which is why, three years after Capote's death, a writer in residence at Auburn University contacted her to ask about the Maxwell case. Madison Jones was a year older than Lee and had published seven novels to her one. Like her, he had an interest in crime, and his last book, *Season of the Strangler,* consisted of a set of twelve interconnected stories based on a series of murders in Columbus, Georgia. Jones had called Monroeville to try to talk with Lee, and after her sister Alice relayed the message, Lee replied with a letter on June 5, 1987.

By then, Jones had talked with one of the Reverend's nephews, who had also tried contacting Harper Lee. "I know that a book on my uncle the late Rev. Will Maxwell will sell," Steve Thomason had written to her the month before. "I don't have any doubt," he insisted, because "people are still talking about him as if he were alive." Thomason invited Lee to his house in Alexander City, saying that "without you I'm going to have to take some no name writer or do it my self."

Lee wasn't sure if the two men were working together, so she replied to them separately. To "Mr. Thomason," she declined in three short sentences, thanking him for contacting her, indicating she was "not interested in buying information or entering into a financial transaction with anybody," and letting him know he was free to do whatever he wanted with his uncle's story. To "Madison Jones," she wrote a longer, more thorough reply that included both a tantalizing summary of the work she had done in Alexander City and a discouraging list of the difficulties she had encountered there. After all the time she had spent working on the story, she told Jones, she had learned five things:

(1) that I probably know more about the Reverend Maxwell's activities than does any other individual;

(2) that I have accumulated enough rumor, fantasy, dreams, conjecture, and outright lies for a volume the length of the Old Testament;

(3) that I do not have enough hard facts about the actual crimes for a book-length account;

(4) that the invitations I received for monetary contributions in exchange for information stretched from Cottage Grove to beyond Dadeville, some of them coming from incredible sources;

(5) that there is no cassette tape long enough to measure human vanity.

A decade had passed between when Lee first heard the story of the Reverend Willie Maxwell and when she finally let it go. Claiming that there were only legends left to be found, Lee told Jones to go ahead and look into it if he wanted. For her part, she was done.

# 23

# The Long Good-Bye

A T THE END OF THE PROFILE THAT HARPER LEE WROTE FOR
Truman Capote when he published *In Cold Blood,* she speculated
that "Kansans will spend the rest of their days at the tantalizing game
of discovering Truman." It was an odd claim; Capote loved publicity
so much that even before he died, there was little left to discover about
his time in Kansas, or anywhere else. Lee, by contrast, was so elusive
that even her mysteries have mysteries: not only what she wrote, but
how; not only when she stopped, but why.

For seventeen years after the publication of *To Kill a Mockingbird,*
readers wondered what Lee would write next; in the years during and
after she knocked on doors around Lake Martin, some knew exactly
what but wondered when. Many people knew the title. One woman
claimed to have seen a book jacket. Big Tom had heard from Lee more
than once that the book was on its way to the publisher or that the
galleys were already back from the printer. A friend of his remembered
Lee saying, one night at dinner, that she had written most of it but
was having trouble figuring out an ending. A friend of Lee's in New
York had a letter from her in which she said she'd written two-thirds
of it before giving up. Someone claimed Louise had read the whole
thing at her kitchen table in Eufaula and declared it better than *In
Cold Blood.* An English professor at the University of Alabama heard
from Lee's old friend Jim McMillan that she had written the whole
book but her publisher had rejected it because it was "too sensitive a
subject." McMillan's daughter had heard it was all written, too, but

locked away in a trunk, and would not be published until after Lee died.

Lee had arrived in Alexander City with such enthusiasm and chased her story with such determination that *The Reverend* seemed imminent, but her second book, like the Second Coming, appeared to be delayed. She spent years working on *The Reverend*, some of them under the watchful eye of her sisterly Cerberus in Eufaula. Three years after that stint in Barbour County, her new literary agent, Julie Fallowfield, said, "It's my understanding Miss Lee is *always* working." Nine years later, Fallowfield told another reporter the same thing: "She's always working on something."

That Harper Lee was always writing was obvious to anyone who knew her, if only because they were reminded whenever they opened their mail. Lee's correspondence constitutes its own archive, not only of her life, the heres and theres and sometimes the nowheres of her adventures, but also of her mind. She might have struggled sometimes with the prose in her books, but in her letters she wrote with the ear of Eudora Welty, the eye of Walker Evans, the precision of John Donne, the wit of Dorothy Parker, and, often, the length of George Eliot. Those letters came and went from friends and family around the country, while admirers and students around the world were thrilled to receive mail in response to their own.

Among other things, these letters revealed that Lee, a fan of small-stakes gambling, was a withering casino critic ("the worst punishment God can devise for this sinner is to make her spirit reside eternally at the Trump Taj Mahal in Atlantic City," she wrote to one friend in 1990), a capable sportscaster (ESPN could have hired her solely on the basis of her 1963 report on the "lallapalooza" that ensued when Wally Butts and Bear Bryant were accused of fixing a Georgia-Alabama football game), a dedicated chronicler of bar ballads from around the world (including Thomas Hardy's favorite, "Come Where the Booze Is Cheaper," with its rousing call to "Come where the pots hold more! Come where the boss is a bit of a joss! Come to the pub next door!"), and an amusingly sympathetic homicide reporter ("I know exactly why she did it," she explained in 1976 of Lizzie Borden: "Anyone burdened with long petticoats and having had mutton soup for breakfast on a day like that was bound to have murdered somebody before sundown"). Her letters were even known to include appendixes, some of them in verse. She once sent a friend in New York an Edward Lear–like guide titled "Some Sociological Aspects of Peculiarities of Pronunciation Found in Persons from Alabama Who Read a Great Deal to Themselves." After explaining how she came by her short *e*'s and soft *c*'s, she jests, "I was quite correct in every respect, down to wearing goloshes when rainy, / But was looked at askance—like I'd left off my pants—when I ventured to speak of Dunsany." (Forever a fan of Shakespeare, she'd been horrified in her younger days to have once mangled that place name from *Macbeth*.) The couplets go on like that for nearly a page, getting funnier at every line but suggesting her chronic failure to fit in, even where she should have: "For in this city the learned and the witty cannot be exactly called snobs— / It's not how you dresses but the fall of your stresses that tells the Brows from the slobs!"

Lee's writing voice catches like a briar; it doesn't tear its subjects, but sticks to them. Both her extensive field dispatches on life in Monroeville and Manhattan and her brief forays into journalism make it clear that Harper Lee could write nonfiction as ably as fiction. What she was writing, though, was always anybody's guess. "She continued to write," her sister Alice said of Nelle's work in the decades after *Mockingbird*. "I think she was just working on short things with an idea of incorporating them into something. She didn't talk too much about it."

Whatever she was writing, Harper Lee wasn't publishing any of it, but no "wonder" can be dismissed as "one hit" right away. It takes the passage of time for such language to feel applicable, and even then it is a strange and varied category, especially for writers of fiction. Lee wasn't like Napoleon or Mussolini, whose single novels came early but were eclipsed by other pursuits, and she wasn't like J. D. Salinger, whose one novel was accompanied by stories and novellas, or like Oscar Wilde, whose one novel hid in a thicket of plays, or like Dorothy Day and Thomas Merton, whose novels were but worldly pauses on their saintly processions, or like Lionel Trilling and Harold Bloom, who could be excused for just trying to practice what they preached in the one novel each that accompanied all of their literary criticism, or even like Emily Brontë and other literary wunderkinds who might well have produced additional novels had they not died first.

No, Lee wasn't like any of those. She was at some point, and then forever after, put in the same literary bushel basket as Margaret Mitchell and Ralph Ellison, who published wildly successful first novels but then were never heard from again. Ellison's *Invisible Man* appeared in 1952, and he worked on a second, "symphonic" novel for over forty years, but when he died in 1994, all he left behind was two thousand pages of notes. Mitchell had been a client of Annie Laurie Williams's and had won the Pulitzer Prize and the National Book Award for her first and only novel, an example that must have struck fear into Williams and Crain and possibly even into Lee herself once it was made known to her. Mitchell was killed in a car accident in 1949, but by then thirteen years had passed since *Gone with the Wind*. She, at least, had the excuse of "the jitters" brought on by World War II and her time volunteering with the Red Cross, not to mention pleurisy, eye problems, and a predilection for "the humbles," her term for her awe of other writers. But while Mitchell offered excuses and Ellison offered pages, Lee rarely even pretended to offer either.

Writer's block is a symptom, not a disease. It describes only the failure to write; it does not explain it. The disorder was invented by the English, or at least first described at length by the poet Samuel Taylor Coleridge, but one of the prevailing theories about her own version was distinctly American. Harper Lee came of age in one of the soggiest periods in American literature, when William Faulkner was claiming he couldn't write without a glass of whiskey nearby and Ernest Hemingway, upping the ante, said he needed a quart of it every day and also liked dry martinis and sweet mojitos whenever he could get them. Her acquaintance John Steinbeck and her friend Truman Capote both were known to drink to excess, and Lee's taste for coffee was matched by her taste for alcohol.

There's no question that Lee drank too much and grew difficult when she did so. But there's also no reason to believe that her drinking was a cause rather than an effect of her inability to write; the two might also have been concomitant symptoms of the same underlying discontent—or, for that matter, symptoms of different ones. Discontent, however, is not itself a sufficient explanation for failure to write either. Other writers, including many Lee knew, had written through their drinking and through their depression and through their perfectionism. No one of these struggles could explain Lee's failure to produce another book, even if every one of them made it harder for her to do so.

Nor could any one moment mark the time when, definitively, she no longer would. As Kierkegaard observed, we live forward but comprehend backward; in all likelihood, not even Harper Lee knew the specific moment at which she abandoned any of her books. Should a diary emerge—and there are rumors that Lee kept one—it's unlikely that there will be an entry on some Tuesday morning or Saturday night indicating that she had decided to give up on finishing her second book; even less likely is a thorough autopsy of the emotional or intellectual reasons that led to that decision, or her ongoing fidelity to it. Maybe, as Alice had said, a manuscript had been stolen from Nelle's apartment in Yorkville, but even if it had, such a theft, while devastating, would not have prevented her from reconstructing the draft. And burning any number of pages would not have barred her from writing new ones.

At one point in her life, after all, Harper Lee had been brimming with ideas. She had written Michael and Joy Brown a letter in 1958, the year after they held what she called "the mortgage on myself," since she'd insisted on repaying them every dollar of their Christmas gift plus interest, outlining what she believed would be the next fifteen years of her writing life:

(1) Race Novel
(2) Victorian Novel
(3) What Mr. Graham Greene calls An Entertainment
(4) I'm gonna tear Monroeville to pieces (1958 Monroeville)
(5) A Novel Of The United Nations
(6) India, 1910

All but one of those ideas were unfinished; it's not clear how many were even started. But unfinishedness, like love and loss, comes in degrees. Something can be more unfinished or less: it can be a third of the way done or halfway done, but also halfway done for two years or halfway done for twenty. In a strange inversion, the closer to done a book is, the more unfinished, in this sense, it feels. An idea, like "What Mr. Graham Greene calls An Entertainment," is evocative, and it's fantastically fun to imagine what kind of thriller Lee had in mind—say *The Confidential Agent,* but D. is sent to buy cotton in Alabama, or *A Gun for Sale,* but Raven returns home to Tuscaloosa. Even if Lee ever started such a book, it would still feel less unfinished than "I'm gonna tear Monroeville to pieces (1958 Monroeville)," which is what she started but abandoned in the draft of *Go Set a Watchman.*

That is why, of all of Lee's unfinished works, none feels as unfinished as *The Reverend.* It was an ambitious project undertaken in the prime of her life, one she didn't just mention in a private letter to friends but, uncharacteristically, talked about with colleagues and strangers. She spent time and money on the research and altered the geography of her life for long spells in order to do the reporting. Evident in all of that was the sincerity of her intention to write it, and evident in the events themselves was their potential to become a book.

Unfinishedness is an emotional category as much as a chronological and aesthetic one; plenty of artists keep revising and revisiting their work long after the critics and the public have deemed it done. Perfectionists, and Lee claimed to be one, often refuse to call it quits and have trouble handing off their work to editors, agents, and readers. "Do / you still hang your words in air, ten years / unfinished," Robert Lowell once asked in a sonnet for his friend Elizabeth Bishop, whose fastidiousness was famous; she was known to pin poems on her bathroom mirror and kitchen corkboard with spaces for single words she was trying to find, then leave them literally hanging for years.

It is possible that Harper Lee had decided to write for her own satisfaction or for posterity, not her peers, and that the feelings of incompletion and failure the public attributed to her were incongruous with her own experience. It is also possible she simply never dealt at all with her feelings about writing, or about anything else. "Self-pity is a sin," she told a reporter in 1963, already frustrated, only three years after *Mockingbird.* "It is a form of living suicide."

She was savage, not only with her own emotional needs, but with everyone else's, too. "I am impatient with people who use psychiatry as a substitute for boredom. It alarms me that women of my own generation decide they are whipped, then go to a psychiatrist—when all they need perhaps is a little more household help." It was a peculiar diagnosis of what women in the 1960s needed, and it betrayed an adolescent sense of class, mental health, and domestic life. In fairness, her comment came during the American rage for psychoanalysis, and she might well have just been chafing at the tendency to recommend it for everything and everyone, including writers struggling with their second novel. Still, it was a strikingly unsympathetic comment from the daughter of someone whose mental health had been fragile, and whose own emotional stability troubled those closest to her. And while maids had helped the Lee family manage, domestic workers were, for any number of reasons, not a viable substitute for psychological well-being.

As for Lee's take on domesticity: there are no nuclear families in *Mockingbird,* and Lee herself was skeptical of the institution. Her life was full of friendship and family, but if it ever included romantic partnership, she took tremendous pains to keep it private. When someone once suggested that she and Capote were a couple, she joked that the only thing they had in common was their interest in men—though whatever interest she had, or feigned, she appears never to have acted on it, including with Maurice Crain. At the same time, she forcefully denied insinuations that she was a lesbian, even though her close relationship with Marcia Van Meter over many decades led plenty of people close to her to suspect as much.

Lesbianism might have been the only rumor Capote spared her. Her childhood friend variously claimed that, among other things, she'd had a ruinous affair with a law professor at the University of Alabama and wanted to have another one with a married man; there doesn't seem to be any evidence for the former, and he later retracted the latter. But Capote's own notoriety continued to be a nuisance for her even after his death. "George Plimpton's minions are busy scouring the corners of the nation," Lee wrote in 1986, and soon enough they came looking for her in Monroeville. Lee wasn't there, so Plimpton couldn't talk to her, but that didn't stop him from including her in *Truman Capote: In Which Various Friends, Enemies, Acquaintances, and Detractors Recall His Turbulent Career.*

When Gerald Clarke's authorized biography of Capote came out in 1988, Lee wrote to historian Caldwell Delaney to advise reading it with a saltshaker in hand and to condemn, in particular, "Truman's vicious lie—my mother was mentally unbalanced and tried twice to kill me (that gentle soul's reward for having loved him)." She was also angry at Clarke's suggestion that Capote wasn't responsible for his life's course. "Drugs and alcohol did not cause his insanity, they were a result of it," she wrote, before going on to argue, either illogically or insensitively, that despite his insanity her friend should have taken responsibility for his life. "Most of us in the Western world make our own lives," Lee had said elsewhere. "Life doesn't make us. We create our events. Nobody asked us to be born, but while we're here we should do the best we can with what we have."

You don't have to have sinned as greatly as the Reverend Willie Maxwell for there to be a gap between your sermons and your actions. Paul had preached the dualism of body and soul to the Romans, and however much Harper Lee scoffed at the gloomy Protestant dogmas of her neighbors in Monroeville or joked about God being deafer than her sister Alice once her hearing went, she was born and raised in a faith that trained her to believe that moral perfection was not only possible but the product of discrete personal decisions. Yet it took a very long time for her to stop making one kind of choice and start making another. Somewhere along the line, she stopped doing two things destructive to her own well-being. One was drinking; the other was writing. By the time she responded to Madison Jones, telling the novelist that the Maxwell case was all his, she had freed herself from the expectations of writing about it. After three dark decades, her letters become more buoyant—no longer anguished, and absent almost any mention of trying to write.

"Books succeed, / And lives fail," Elizabeth Barrett Browning wrote, and indeed throughout Lee's life *To Kill a Mockingbird* succeeded. In 1993, she told her agent Julie Fallowfield that she wasn't interested in writing an introduction for an anniversary edition of her novel. "Please spare *Mockingbird* an Introduction," she wrote. "Although *Mockingbird* will be 33 this year, it has never been out of print and I am still alive, although very quiet. Introductions inhibit pleasure, they kill the joy of anticipation, they frustrate curiosity. The only good thing about Introductions is that in some cases they delay the dose to come. *Mockingbird* still says what it has to say; it has managed to survive the years without preamble." HarperCollins printed Lee's refusal as the foreword to its thirty-fifth anniversary edition.

The same year she wrote that note, Lee attended a ceremony honoring alumnae of the University of Alabama—even though she herself was not one, having dropped out before graduation. But she had also turned up around that same time to accept an honorary degree, and both appearances seemed to mark a new willingness to acknowledge that she had written a masterpiece, if only one. In 1997, she accepted another honorary doctorate, this time at Spring Hill College in Mobile, and not long after that, a filmmaker with financing from Universal Studios began shooting a documentary about the adaptation of Lee's novel. Charles Kiselyak interviewed many of those involved in the production of the film, including Gregory Peck, screenwriter Horton Foote, and director Robert Mulligan. He also spent time in Monroe County, assisted by Harper Lee, who was impressed by an essay he had written about Hank Williams. She accompanied his crew and suggested interview subjects, including neighbors who had known her and her family since childhood. Although she refused to appear on camera, Lee can be heard laughing offscreen during the interview with Ida Gaillard, one of her teachers at Monroeville High School. The documentary took its name, *Fearful Symmetry,* from her favorite bit of William Blake, and the narration sounded as if she might have written it: "Fame was a four-letter word, and boredom was for rich and dull-witted Yankees."

One of the subjects in that documentary was an English professor at the University of Alabama, a southerner who was more hot sauce than sweet tea. Claudia Durst Johnson had written some of the few scholarly articles on *To Kill a Mockingbird,* which she expanded into a critical study called *Threatening Boundaries*. There and elsewhere Claudia defended the novel when it was derided for being childish or middlebrow, attacked for its use of racial epithets, or accused of being insufficiently liberal. Lee had agreed to meet Claudia after her old friend Jim McMillan convinced the writer to at least sit in the same room with someone who had written admiringly about her work. Whatever Claudia said that first day she "interviewed" Lee in Tuscaloosa, it must have been Alabamian for abracadabra, because the writer, who had turned down more than a few would-be biographers, declared Claudia her Boswell. Virtually in the same breath, though, Lee all but doomed the project by making Claudia promise that she wouldn't get started until all of the dust was settled—the dust, in this case, being the kind usually accompanied by ashes.

The would-be biographer and subject exchanged letters every so often and talked on the telephone once Claudia moved to California, but Lee continued to insist that no work begin on a biography until she was dead, an insistence she maintained even after her sister Louise started showing signs of dementia. "Her memory is fragile these days," Lee explained in a letter to a family friend. Eventually, Weezie left Eufaula for Florida, where she spent her final years in an assisted living facility, the disease taking her further and further from those she knew; some days, she did not even recognize her sisters.

Lee, though, was still going back and forth to New York, albeit more slowly. She went for shows at the Cort Theatre, art exhibitions at the Met and the Frick, Mets games at Shea Stadium, lunches at Pearl Oyster Bar in the West Village, and drinks at Elaine's a few blocks up Second Avenue from her apartment. She had given up on the New York Public Library when it switched to computerized catalogs, but she still went regularly to read and borrow books at the Society Library near her apartment. Back in Monroeville, she stayed in her room with the built-in bookshelves in Alice's home, bought stationery at Walmart, retrieved her own mail from the same post office box she'd had for decades, and every so often played the penny slots at the Wind Creek casino in Atmore. She got her groceries at the Piggly Wiggly, ate supper at David's Catfish House, and, never mind that she was a millionaire many times over, carried her own laundry to the Laundromat. Alice, by then in her nineties, was still practicing law, and her most demanding client was still Nelle Harper Lee, whose contracts—domestic reprints and foreign editions, film royalties, stage rights, and any requests related to one of the most popular novels in the world—all flowed through Barnett, Bugg & Lee.

ON JANUARY 16, 2003, ALABAMA'S GOVERNOR, DON SIEGELMAN, declared an official Tom Radney Day. Harper Lee and everyone else in the state would have seen in the newspaper that the former senator Howell Heflin, the former congressman Ronnie Flippo, and dozens of other bigwigs turned up to watch Mr. Democrat receive the proclamation. Big Tom's four children all had families of their own by then, and a passel of grandchildren turned out to help him celebrate. An elder statesman and community giant, Radney had outlived any animosity that he had attracted in his younger days, but the Yellow Dog was still as busy as ever trying to turn the South blue. He had championed what became known as the Radney Rule, which prevented candidates from running as a Democrat if they hadn't supported the party's nominees in the previous four years.

That fall, when Nelle Harper Lee was seventy-seven years old and Alice Lee was turning ninety-two, the sisters celebrated by visiting the Alabama Department of Archives and History. The archives are in Montgomery, just across the street from the state capitol, where Big Tom had once taken family photographs for his final campaign, and once inside the Lees sat at a table on which the staff placed Albert James Pickett's notes, sketches, and maps. Nelle and Alice paged through the historian's papers, examining some of the source material that he had turned into the book they both loved so dearly. After that, they looked at the volume of legislative acts that included what Alice called "Daddy's prized bill," a law requiring counties to balance their budgets, and then at a hand-drawn map of Monroeville from 1930, which Alice could still populate house by house from memory.

The Lees' own childhood home on South Alabama Avenue had been replaced by an ice cream parlor in the 1950s, not long after their father sold it and moved to West Avenue. A section of the stone wall that separated Nelle from Truman is still standing, but what used to be the Faulk house on the other side is an empty lot. In the 1960s, when the set designers came to scout locations for *To Kill a Mockingbird,* they already found Monroeville too modern to pass for Maycomb. Like small towns around Alabama and across America, it had lost itself to fast-food and chain stores, franchises taking over the way kudzu had decades before. The Boulware house across the street had become a gas station; the oak tree with its ambry was filled with cement and then cut down to a stump.

In 2003, the same year the Lee sisters took their birthday visit to the archives, Al Benn, who was drafting his memoirs, brought some chapters to Alice's law office to see if her sister might not endorse them. A few days later, the excerpt arrived back with a note from Harper: "After a long career of responsible and at times courageous reporting, Al Benn brings his probity to his vivid memoirs." But while she was praising the autobiography of the former editor of *The Alexander City Outlook,* Lee was still refusing to write her own, or to let anyone else write about her life for her. When she heard tell of an unauthorized biography in the works, she warned her friends not to talk with the writer, Charles Shields, whose 2006 *Mockingbird* would be the first full-length biography of her. The Lee sisters, however, made a different choice and decided to talk with Marja Mills, a journalist from the *Chicago Tribune* who, after writing a profile of Harper Lee for the newspaper, moved in next door to write a book, ostensibly about Monroe County. Lee herself spent a lot of time with Mills, not only during that first visit, but in Alice's home and on adventures around the Black Belt throughout the journalist's stay in Monroeville. When the resulting memoir came out under the title *The Mockingbird Next Door: Life with Harper Lee,* Lee disavowed it, saying that she hadn't intended to cooperate with a biographical project.

Long accustomed to appearing unwillingly in print, Lee had also by then appeared unwillingly on stage and screen. Her dislike of Monroeville's annual production of a theatrical version of her novel had only increased as the audiences grew and the performances multiplied, and soon she had to contend with two competing films about the writing of *In Cold Blood,* both of which featured her as a central character, played first by Catherine Keener and then by Sandra Bullock. Lee saw both films, praised Philip Seymour Hoffman's Capote in *Capote,* and complained about the sartorial choices—socks with pumps—imposed on her in *Infamous.* For someone who had so assiduously avoided publicity for more than four decades, she must have felt as if the walls of Jericho were falling down around her, so much so that she mounted at least one uncharacteristic defense.

In April 2006, she wrote a letter to the editor of *The New Yorker* regarding the film *Capote.* It was the first time her byline appeared in those pages. "Of the screenwriter's many inventions," she complained, "his concept of William Shawn's activities during the creation of *In Cold Blood* is weirdly off." In only seventy-six words, she corrected two errors: first, she never spoke with Shawn on the telephone; second, Shawn never accompanied Capote to Kansas. Lee said nothing about who she was or why she might know better than the filmmakers, but her signature ("Harper Lee, Monroeville, Ala.") said everything. Or, as ever, nothing: even while correcting inaccuracies in the film version, she remained utterly silent about her friend's own transgressions in his book.

A WORSE CRISIS THAN CELEBRITY, THOUGH, FOUND LEE NEXT. Around midnight on Saturday, March 17, 2007, Lee suffered a serious stroke. It wasn't until Monday that two friends found her and rushed her sixteen blocks uptown to Mount Sinai Hospital, where doctors discovered that she was paralyzed on the left side. Some of her oldest and best friends in the city came by, including Joy Brown, bringing fried chicken and gossip, two of the things Lee liked most, but instead of convalescing in New York, she made arrangements to be moved to Birmingham. Lee came home to Alabama on the Amtrak Crescent that May, as she had for almost sixty years, only this time in the handicap room. The route was the same as it had been since she had first moved to New York: the train got to the nation's capital by supper, Atlanta by breakfast, and by lunchtime the next day she was back in Alabama.

She had lost more than twenty pounds, but after months of intensive physical therapy, she regained some mobility. By November 5, 2007, Lee had recovered enough that she was able to travel back up to Washington, D.C., stand up, and take President George W. Bush's arm as he awarded her the Medal of Freedom. It was her first visit to the White House since the Johnson administration. She still had a boyish haircut, not unlike the one from her earliest book jacket, and she looked just as surprised by all of the attention as she had forty years before.

It was the last time Lee would leave Alabama. When she got back, she settled into the Meadows of Monroeville, a one-story, sixteen-room assisted living facility on the Highway 21 Bypass. The fan mail found her there, as it always had no matter where she went, and one day it included a letter from a writer born in Alexander City. David Brasfield wanted to know what Lee knew about the Maxwell case, and on January 9, 2009, she replied to say that her own reporting had produced "a mountain of rumors and a molehill of facts." Brasfield ended up writing a pulpy, fictionalized version that borrowed Lee's title, *The Reverend,* and, apparently, borrowed Lee as well: one of the characters is a female novelist by the name of Hunter James who barely escapes being murdered.

A few months later, in June 2009, Alice Lee responded to another letter about Maxwell. This one was from a woman named Sheralyn Belyeu, whose husband had bought her an *Encyclopaedia Britannica* at the Salvation Army in Alexander City. Tucked beside the entry for Harpers Ferry, Belyeu had found a card from Harper Lee dated June 11, 1978: it was the note she had written thanking the Cribbs for the cocktail party she had attended just before leaving town. Belyeu wanted to know if Lee would mind if she made the letter public. Alice gave her permission, albeit in tragic terms. "Nothing you have done or will do in the future," she wrote, "will effect [*sic*] Harper Lee since she has no plans in the future [to write] about the experience. She is in frail health, nearly blind and paralyzed on the left side by a stroke."

Both Alice and her sister had serious vision deficits. Harper Lee's macular degeneration had gotten so bad that she could barely see a page of paper to write on it, and her letters, once Pentateuchal in their plots and Pauline in their syntax, were now short, scrawled by hand,

and absent anything but the occasional and often recycled literary allusion. In the years after her stroke, and especially in the years after her return to Monroeville, Lee's letters shortened to notes, and they were rarely more than dispatches from the war her body was fighting against old age—updates on her eyes, ears, and mind and what they were less and less able to do. Her hearing got bad enough that she couldn't talk on the telephone, and her memory, by most accounts, could reach back in time but not hold on to the present.

In October 2009, when Louise Lee Conner died in Gainesville, Florida, neither of her sisters was well enough to attend the services. Five years later, in November 2014, Alice Lee, who had practiced law into her triple digits, died at one hundred and three. By then, the family law office had moved from the Monroe County Bank and acquired an extra name on its shingle, Tonja Carter, who, after suing the author's former literary agent, had taken over her affairs. Three months after Alice Lee's death, it was Carter who declared her client's enthusiasm for a shocking piece of news: Harper Lee would be publishing another book.

That news went national almost instantly, and when it hit Alexander City, everyone in town assumed the book in question was *The Reverend*. Tom Radney had died on August 7, 2011, and for his family it was bittersweet to think that Lee was finally going to share his story with the world. A year before her stroke, his son, Thomas, had run into Harper Lee at the University of Alabama. When his father heard about the encounter, Big Tom wrote Nelle a note. "The years are getting by," he said, "and I would very much like to see you again before the grim reaper comes for either of us."

Lee responded to say, "It was a delight to see young Thomas—he has grown considerably since I last saw him!" He had indeed. Thomas, now a lawyer himself and practicing in the Zoo, had been only a few feet tall when Lee was reporting in Alex City, but by the time she sent that letter, he had children of his own. Together with their cousins and their aunts—who, like Thomas, had all stayed in Tallapoosa County—they could field two football teams, and did: every year, right before Christmas, the family gathered for a tradition known as the Radney Bowl. Three decades had passed since Lee had moved into a cabin on Lake Martin and Big Tom had won Robert Burns an acquittal. "Can't believe you've got high-school *grand*children," she wrote. "You and Madolyn must be walking on sticks now."

Lee said nothing in that letter about Willie Maxwell, nothing of the briefcase full of files Radney had given her all those years earlier, nothing of *The Reverend,* nothing of nothing. Whatever a writer might owe her sources, Lee hadn't delivered much of anything, even an explanation. She had, though, given the Radneys a mustard-seed-size reason to maintain their faith that she would write their story. After Big Tom died and the family sorted through his possessions, Madolyn Price, his oldest granddaughter—the daughter of his oldest daughter, Ellen—found that letter from Lee, along with, incredibly, what seemed like a chapter of *The Reverend.* Strangely, after all the time Lee had spent reporting the story, these four typed pages were fictionalized. Maxwell was still Maxwell, but Big Tom had become Jonathan Thomas Larkin IV, a lawyer who, as the chapter opens, gets a call from Maxwell saying that the police are accusing him of murdering his wife. The subsequent scenes sketch a history of Larkin's family, moving them from the shores of Ireland to a little patch of Alabama clay at the foothills of the Appalachian Mountains—the same basic technique that appears in the opening chapter of *To Kill a Mockingbird,* which took the Finch family all the way from Cornwall to the Creek Wars. The genealogy doesn't quite match that of Big Tom, and as big as he was in real life, he looms even larger in the chapter, destined to become "a lawyer and politician, the likes of which Alabama had not seen before." That discovery made Little Madolyn, as she was known, realize why her grandfather had always been so adamant that Harper Lee was going to write about him. And, of course, it made her wonder about what had happened to the rest of the book.

Little Madolyn tried writing to the author, hoping if nothing else to get back her grandfather's massive briefcase full of files, which she learned from her grandmother had never been returned. She got no direct response but eventually heard back from Tonja Carter that the aging author did not have the files and had no memory of her grandfather. At the time, that had struck the Radneys as heartbreaking, because it likely meant the author's memory was gone, and worse, that she had destroyed not only whatever she had written about the Maxwell case but all of her research, too. Now, though, they wondered if it had all been a mistake, and this new book was *The Reverend*.

It was not. On February 3, 2015, the world learned that the forthcoming book was actually the manuscript that Harper Lee had delivered to Maurice Crain fifty-eight years before—the original, unedited draft of *Go Set a Watchman*. Tonja Carter conveyed a statement from the author, still ensconced in the Meadows and never able to speak directly with the press, saying that Harper Lee was "happy as hell" about the publication.

The "new" book from Harper Lee turned out to be the oldest one she had written. The people of Alexander City made their peace with the fact that they might never get to read Lee's version of the life and death of the Reverend Willie Maxwell, and eventually the rumors about him quieted down, as they always had before. By then, after all, the Reverend had been dead for almost forty years, and his lawyer had been dead for five. And soon enough, the woman who tried to write about them both would be gone, too.

YOU CAN VISIT THEM ALL IN A SINGLE DAY IF YOU WANT. IN death, as in life, they stayed close to home, buried in the red dirt of Alabama. A wrought-iron archway and an American flag mark Peace and Goodwill Cemetery, where the Reverend's grave sits along the far right side, not far from many of his relatives. It is marked with a low stone and a plain brass plaque that reads, "Willie J. Maxwell," with no other detail beyond his army service. The years of his birth and death bracket a simple cross.

After you leave Peace and Goodwill, head northeast on Highway 22 until you come to the stop sign where the lawmen waited before the funeral of the Reverend. Keep going until the pines get thinner and the houses get thicker and you reach Highway 280; if you catch the stoplight there, you can look to the right and see what's left of the Horseshoe Bend Motel, now a Days Inn. Cross the intersection and Highway 22 becomes Lee Street. Follow it into town, and on your right you'll see the crumbling brick remains of Russell Mills—the textile industry has mostly moved to Latin America now—before coming up on the new annex to the Alex City courthouse, named for Judge C. J. Coley, and then to Court Square and the Zoo. Swing around the traffic circle and head out on Jefferson Street, where the House of Hutchinson Funeral Home was located before it burned down.

Cut west on Circle Drive, and you'll reach the Alexander City Cemetery. The grand front gates are open from dawn until dusk, and anytime between you can find your way to a long gray slab nearly as big as Big Tom. John Tomas Radney is memorialized on his headstone as "President Board of Trustees Alabama State University," for his service to a historically black college in Montgomery; as "Trustee of Huntingdon College," for his service to the Methodist Church; as "Captain U.S. Army JAG CORP," for his service to country; as "Alabama State Senator," for his service to state; and, at the top, where no one can miss it, "Mr. Alabama Democrat."

When you're ready to leave Alexander City, take Cherokee Road out of town, follow it all the way to Lake Martin, and cross over the waters at Kowaliga Bridge, just north of the Martin Dam. Continue south, past the town of Eclectic, and follow the road as it winds west past Wetumpka, where, eighty million years ago, a meteor the size of three football fields hurled itself from outer space into Alabama, changing the landscape of the state forever. Beyond that, you'll pass the place where the Tallapoosa River meets the Coosa River, and they continue on together to the coast. Drive on through Montgomery, the state capital, and head south; from there, any number of roads will take you west to Monroeville. If you see a sign for Burnt Corn, you'll know you're getting close. You're even closer when you can see the water tower and the cupola of the old courthouse, now a museum, where there's a piece of an old oak tree preserved behind glass.

In the early hours of the morning of February 19, 2016, at the age of eighty-nine, Harper Lee died in the Meadows, only a few streets away from the home on South Alabama Avenue where she had learned to read and write. Her funeral was private, and her body was interred in her family's plot in Hillcrest Cemetery. She is buried alongside her father, mother, and oldest sister. Look for the headstone that reads

"Lee," and the four modest markers in front of it. Many things could be carved into the one on the far left, but if you brush aside the pennies that always seem to accumulate on top of it, you'll find that the engraving doesn't say "Pulitzer Prize Winner" or "Author of *To Kill a Mockingbird*." It doesn't even say "Writer." It says only "Nelle Harper Lee."

# | Epilogue |

A T THE TIME THAT NELLE HARPER LEE DIED, SHE HADN'T said anything about the Maxwell case in years. For all that she loved facts, when it came to her own life and work, she made them very difficult to come by, and *The Reverend* remained as mysterious as the man whose life inspired it. In a strange symmetry of author and subject, Lee and her book became the object of as much "rumor, fantasy, dreams, conjecture, and outright lies" as Maxwell had once been.

Then, a year after her death, Lee's estate contacted the family of Tom Radney. A few weeks later, his oldest daughter, Ellen, drove from Alexander City to Monroeville, where I met her at the Monroe County Courthouse, and together we walked across the street to the Lee family law firm.

Waiting for us inside was an oversize leather briefcase. It was covered in a thick layer of dust and had been in Lee's possession since the fall of 1977. When we opened it, we found the red scrapbook of newspaper clippings that Jim Earnhardt's mother had made, along with file folders brimming with case records, depositions, letters, maps from around Lake Martin, photostatic copies of articles, the odd brochure, the warranty for a tape recorder, and two full court transcripts.

Inside a folder labeled "Mary," misfiled among all of the other documents, was a single page of Lee's typed notes from her reporting in Alexander City, identical to those that she had made for Truman Capote in Kansas, which are archived in the New York Public Library. The Radneys let me review the materials, then put them away with their chapter and went back to wondering what became of the rest of the book.

Other than what was in the briefcase, Nelle Harper Lee's estate is sealed. The entirety of her literary assets, including whatever else exists of *The Reverend,* remains unpublished and unknown.

# | *Acknowledgments* |

I am mindful that *Mockingbird* became the beloved book that it is through the tireless work of an agent and an editor, and I'm grateful to have found my own Maurice Crain and Tay Hohoff. Edward Orloff knew I had a book in me before I did, and while every writer deserves an agent who encourages her work, few are blessed to find one so loving and kind. For his part, Andrew Miller is the editor every writer dreams of: patient, steadfast, and encyclopedic about everything from Amtrak to Kierkegaard. Many of his colleagues at Knopf helped bring this book into the world, including Sonny Mehta, Zakiya Harris, Paul Bogaards, Chris Gillespie, Ruth Liebmann, Jessica Purcell, Rachel Fershleiser, Madison Brock, Bette Alexander, Ingrid Sterner, Lisa Montebello, Betty Lew, and Alabama's own Nicholas Latimer. I am moved by and grateful for their love for this book. The same goes for Jason Arthur at William Heinemann, who was a gentleman from the first time I heard his voice, and whose confidence in Nelle was contagious. I only hope I've honored his memory of his friend.

Special thanks go to the Radneys, for never losing faith. They've waited a long time for this story to be told, and I'm grateful they let me be the one to tell it. I'm very sorry that I missed Big Tom, but he left behind one of the warmest, most welcoming families in all of Alabama. I'm so thankful to Ellen for tending her father's memory, and to Little Madolyn for all her tireless work to tell her grandfather's story. Now and always, Roll Tide!

Jim Earnhardt taught me more about Harper Lee than almost anyone I met, not only because he shared his memories, but because his character taught me something about what she looked for in friends. He is also one of the finest journalists in Alabama, and I'm grateful for his friendship and encouragement along the way. Returning his scrapbook forty years after he loaned it to Harper Lee was one of my favorite experiences of reporting this book. Another journalist, Vern Smith, taught me an enormous amount about this case and many others in the Deep South. It's some kind of reporter who, forty years later, can still dig up his notes for a young cub.

Various librarians and libraries are acknowledged throughout the notes, but I'd like to specifically thank Heather Thomas and her colleagues at the Library of Congress, who managed, one "Ask a Librarian" at a time, to help me find every article ever written about the Reverend Maxwell, Tom Radney, and Harper Lee, plus an astonishing quantity of Alabama arcana.

Thanks to the living library of all things Alabama that is Diane McWhorter, who deleted one notable letter from this book and my life, but added more wisdom to both than I could ever repay.

Special thanks to Ben Phelan, fact-checker extraordinaire, whose knowledge of Alabama would impress Albert James Pickett, and who never tired of asking "How know?" Thanks also to David Haglund, Sasha Weiss, and Nicholas Thompson, without whom I would never have driven through the night to Alabama, or had half as much fun writing about what I found there; Becca Laurie, who is possibly the only "assistant researchist" to rival Nelle Harper Lee, not to mention a dear friend and beloved PI; Philip Gourevitch, who provided both the early nudge I needed and who, together with Larissa MacFarquhar, provided a model of deep, ethical journalism; David Grann, without whose books I couldn't have written this one, and whose early enthusiasm made all the difference; and Elliott Holt, who did so much for me and this book along the way and whose Alabama roots were an inspiration. Special thanks to Luppe Luppen for the Monroeville Mardi Gras and to the Jackson's Gap crew, Amanda Griscom Little and Laura Ruth Venable.

Jamaica Kincaid, Geneva Robertson-Dworet, Scoop and Kate Wasserstein, Francesca Mari, and Leslie Jamison have all made this book, and me, much better. To have one such friend is a blessing, but to have so many is more than anyone deserves.

For sharing their memories of "Aunt Dody," I am forever grateful to Ed Conner and Hank Conner. Ed, especially, brought her back to life with his humor, intelligence, sincerity, and sweetness; I delighted in our conversations and the early view of Ellenelle. I'm likewise grateful to Laura and David Byres for the antebellum grits, breakfast in a cup, and superhosting.

My mother and father, Sandy and Bill Cep, have loved me no matter what and deserve more thanks than I can give them here. They worked harder than anyone should ever have to in order to make sure their children could get an education and do whatever we wanted. I'm sure they never imagined raising a writer, but I'm also sure no writer could have better parents. I hope they know how proud I have always been to be one of their daughters.

My sisters, Melinda and Katelin, have tolerated my love of words and willingness to use too many of them for a very long time. One of them helped me learn to read, and the other was my first audience. Their laughter and love and faith have made my life rich and joyful, and their constant supply of legal pads, felt pens, mechanical pencils, and internet made this book better.

My partner in crime and everything else, Kathryn Schulz, deserves thanks for putting up with a hundred thousand miles of Wawa, Waffle House, whatifs, Patsy Cline, Hank Williams, Jason Isbell, taxidermy, and me. I couldn't have written this book, or anything else, without her.

# | *Notes* |

| PROLOGUE |

For the description of the trial, I relied on local, regional, and national news reports and the trial transcript, along with interviews I conducted with Mary Ann Karr, Robert Burns, Jim Earnhardt, Mary Lynn Blackmon, Alvin Benn, Leewood Avary, Madolyn Radney, and James Abbett. In particular, I am grateful for the archives of *The Alexander City Outlook, The Dadeville Record, The Coosa Press, The Montgomery Advertiser, The Afro-American, Jet,* and *The Anniston Star.*

| 1 | DIVIDE THE WATERS FROM THE WATERS

For the history of Lake Martin and its surrounding communities, along with the account of rural Alabama in the early twentieth century, I am indebted to *Heritage of Coosa County; Heritage of Tallapoosa County;* Schafer, *Lake Martin;* Walls and Oliver, *Alexander City;* Jackson, *Rivers of History;* Richardson, *That's Waht They Say;* Rosengarten, *All God's Dangers;* Agee and Evans, *Let Us Now Praise Famous Men;* Rogers, Ward, Atkins, and Flynt, *Alabama;* and Hamilton, *Alabama.* I also learned a great deal from some unpublished personal memoirs: Ben Russell's "The History of Benjamin Russell and Russell Lands Inc."; Ben Carlton's "Keno—Keyno: Keno Community Then and Yonder"; and the untitled memoirs of Inez Warren. For the Reverend Maxwell's early biography, I relied on regional newspaper coverage, local courthouse records, military service records, national census records, and trial transcripts. I am grateful to the staff of the Adelia M. Russell Library in Alexander City and the Horseshoe Bend Regional Library in Dadeville.

7 "the moral equivalent": William James, "The Moral Equivalent of War," *McClure's Magazine,* Aug. 1910, 463–68.

8 "Every loafing stream": "Montgomery Men Originators of Cherokee Development—Martin," *Montgomery Advertiser,* Nov. 8, 1925, 3.

9 "To gather the streams": *Mt. Vernon–Woodberry Co. v. Alabama Power Co.,* 240 U.S. 30 (1916).

14 "Our local Nordics": Langston Hughes, "Nazis and Dixie Nordics," *Chicago Defender,* March 10, 1945, reprinted in Hughes, *Langston Hughes and the "Chicago Defender,"* 78–80.

14 "There wouldn't be anybody": Frank Colquitt, interview by author, Feb. 3, 2016.

14 "You'd think that man": David M. Alpern and Vern E. Smith, "Seventh Son," *Newsweek,* July 4, 1977, p. 21.

## | 2 | MINISTER OF THE GOSPEL

For details of Mary Lou Maxwell's death, I relied on police reports, investigative notes, her autopsy file and death certificate, court transcripts, legal notes, and newspaper coverage. I am grateful to Dr. Richard Roper for reviewing her autopsy with me and offering his professional memories of the case as well as the crime lab. For the descriptions of the Reverend's work and the broader labor history of Lake Martin, I relied on Fickle, *Green Gold;* Allison, *Moonshine Memories; Heritage of Coosa County; Heritage of Tallapoosa County;* Flynt, *Alabama in the Twentieth Century;* local and regional newspaper coverage; the archives of *Alabama Forests;* and the assistance of Regina Strickland of the Horseshoe Bend Regional Library, Clara Williams, Alvin Benn, Jim Earnhardt, Patricia Wilkerson, Gladys Shockley, Vern Smith, Jacqueline Bush Giddens, Paul Pruitt Jr., Frank Colquitt, Benny Nolen, Clark Sahlie, Sam Duvall and Chris Isaacson at the Alabama Forestry Association, Lonette Berg of the Alabama Baptist Historical Commission, Andrew Childress and Richard Gilreath at the University of Texas at Austin's Briscoe Center for American History, and Karen C. Bullard of the Troy Public Library.

18 "The Reverend has been": Undated testimony by Dorcas Anderson, responding to questions from Charles Adair and Tom Radney, 5.

19 "I went back": Ibid., 4.

20 "He was one of the most outstanding": Vern Smith, Telefax reporting notes, "RE: THE REV. WILLIE MAXWELL," June 23, 1977, *Newsweek*

Clipping Archive, 1933–1996, Subject File CDL 1232, Briscoe Center for American History, University of Texas at Austin.

20 "When we cleaned": Ibid.

22 "I'd see after it all": Frank Colquitt, interview by author.

22 "minister of the gospel": Appeal to the Court of Civil Appeals of Alabama (301 So.2d 85), 13.

22 "He could pray a prayer": Vern Smith, Telefax reporting notes.

23 "She would often talk to me": Undated testimony by Dorcas Anderson, 5.

24 "recognize the said child": Declaration of Legitimation, 49:312, Probate Court of Tallapoosa County, Alabama.

24 "When she married, she married": Lena Martin, interview by Nelle Harper Lee, Jan. 16, 1978, from Lee's unpublished reporting notes.

26 "It is not our purpose to prove guilt": Paul Till, "These Crime Fighters Rarely See the Scene," *Advertiser-Journal Alabama Sunday Magazine,* July 2, 1972, 5.

27 "lady friends": Undated intake notes from Tom Radney's law firm.

28 "Dear Sir": W. M. Maxwell to Old American Insurance Company, Aug. 19, 1970, Defense Exhibit 3 from Maxwell Deposition on May 11, 1973.

| 3 | DEATH BENEFITS

For the history of life insurance, insurance fraud, and racial bias in the insurance industry, I relied on Sharon Ann Murphy, *Investing in Life;* Balleisen, *Fraud;* McGlamery, "Race Based Underwriting and the Death of Burial Insurance"; and Heen, "Ending Jim Crow Life Insurance Rates." For the details of Willie "Poison" Maxwell and Fred Hutchinson, I relied on newspaper coverage, police records, and the assistance of Colleen Hanko and the Clearwater Police Department. To reconstruct the Reverend Willie Maxwell's interactions with the insurance industry, I used newspaper coverage, court records, police records, state investigative files, trial transcripts, and the assistance of Sheree Chapman York, Stanley Lee Chapman, Ray Jenkins, David Story, John Denson, Jimmy Bailey, Ed Raymon, R. Stan Morris, Richard F. Allen, Dennis M. Wright, David Miller, Ashton Holmes Ott, Karen Strickland, and Terri Svetich, along with Willie Robinson and the Alexander City Police Department.

39 "told an altogether different story": Ray Jenkins, "Minister Slain After Giving Stepdaughter's Eulogy; He Is Called a Suspect in Her Death and Four Others," *New York Times,* June 21, 1977, 16.

40 "I have just about worn out": Radney to Robert Richard, Oct. 28, 1971.

| 4 |   SEVENTH SON OF A SEVENTH SON

For the history of voodoo, I relied on Puckett, *Folk Beliefs of the Southern Negro;* Hurston's "Hoodoo in America," *Mules and Men,* and *Tell My Horse;* Hyatt, *Hoodoo—Conjuration—Witchcraft—Rootwork;* Carmer, *Stars Fell on Alabama;* Raboteau, *Slave Religion;* Haskins, *Voodoo & Hoodoo;* Gates and Tatar, *Annotated African American Folktales;* Davis, *The Serpent and the Rainbow;* Chesnutt, *Conjure Tales and Stories of the Color Line;* Asbury, *French Quarter;* Roberts, *Voodoo and Power;* Davis, *American Voudou;* Pinn, *Varieties of African American Religious Experience;* and Tallant, *Voodoo in New Orleans.* I am grateful for the archival assistance of Jen Peters and Joe Festa with the Carl Carmer Collection at the Research Library of the Fennimore Art Museum and Patricia Tomczak with the Hyatt Folklore Collection at Quincy University. For the specific account of the Reverend Willie Maxwell, I relied on death certificates, trial transcripts, court records, local and regional newspaper coverage, the memoirs of Alvin Benn and E. Paul Jones, and interviews with Robert Burns, Vern Smith, Alvin Benn, and Jim Earnhardt.

43 "are too much given": Raboteau, *Slave Religion,* 76.

43 "the map of Dixie": Hurston, *Dust Tracks on a Road,* 104.

44 "Nobody knows for sure": Hurston, *Mules and Men,* 185.

45 "I got troubles": Carmer, *Stars Fell on Alabama,* 216.

47 "I went to New Orleans": J. T. "Funny Papa" Smith, "Seven Sister Blues" (1931).

| 5 |   JUST PLAIN SCARED

In addition to those sources already acknowledged, I am grateful for the assistance of Fred Gray, Nancy Powers, Norwood Kerr, and Scotty Kirkland at the Alabama Department of Archives and History, and Chad Carr of the Alabama Court of Appeals. I am indebted to the Radney family for allowing me to make use of Tom Radney's legal archive, and to the literary estate of Nelle Harper Lee for making available her reporting materials from the Maxwell case.

51 "He was a nice guy": Lou Elliott, "Five Tragic Deaths Preceded Minister's Shooting," *Montgomery Advertiser*, June 19, 1977, 7A.

52 "They said someone had": Ibid.

52 "neither he nor any members": Undated "Release Agreement" with Central Security Life Insurance Company, signed by Willie J. Maxwell, witnessed by Otis Armour of Armour Funeral Home.

54 "I'm going to get some fish": *Independent Life and Accident Insurance Company v. Willie J. Maxwell* (301 So.2d 85), 36.

56 "People really began to fear him": Vern Smith, Telefax reporting notes.

56 "They just didn't know": Phyllis Wesley, "Minister's Body Attracts Curious," *Montgomery Advertiser*, June 23, 1977, 2A.

56 "Most people were just plain scared": Vern Smith, Telefax reporting notes.

60 "the eerie evenings": Roth, *Patrimony*, 109.

60 "That insurance man came": *Independent Life and Accident Insurance Company v. Willie J. Maxwell* (301 So.2d 85), 158.

## | 6 |   NO EXCEPTION TO THE RULE

For the account of the murder of Shirley Ann Ellington and the murder of the Reverend Willie Maxwell, I relied on local, regional, and national newspaper coverage, police reports, autopsy records, trial transcripts, and interviews with Jim Earnhardt, Vern Smith, Robert Burns, Alvin Benn, James Abbett, David Story, Evelyn Gilley, and Dr. Richard Roper. I am also grateful for the assistance of Ray Jenkins, Elizabeth F. Shores, Kathryn Kaufman, Amanda McDonald, Dave Friedman, David M. Alpern, T. Michael Keza, Phyllis Alesia Perry, Paul Pruitt Jr., Alice Halsey at the Alabama Department of Forensic Sciences, and the Alexander City Police Department.

63 "I have prayed and thought": Elliott, "Five Tragic Deaths."

64 "He could not help it": Ibid.

65 "tell 'em a short version": Colquitt, interview by author.

67 "which would adequately account": Vann V. Pruitt Jr., "Memorandum to File" for the Department of Toxicology and Criminal Investigation, May 20, 1976.

67 "There will be no evidence": Lynda Robinson, email to author, Feb. 2, 2018.

67 "They must have wanted": Mary Dean Riley Hicks statement from the investigative files as quoted in Jones, *To Kill a Preacher*, Kindle loc. 789.

68 "asked me how dirty": Aaron Burton statement from the investigative files as quoted in Jones, *To Kill a Preacher,* Kindle loc. 721.

69 "Reverend Maxwell came to my house": Calvin Edwards statement from the investigative files as quoted in Jones, *To Kill a Preacher,* Kindle loc. 756.

71 "wasn't Shirley": Alvin Benn and Jim Earnhardt, "Death Probe Pushed," *Alexander City Outlook,* June 15, 1977, 4.

72 "They wouldn't let me": Ibid.

73 "All of us must go": Jim Earnhardt, "Maxwell Gunned Down at Funeral," *Alexander City Outlook,* July 20, 1977, 1.

73 "She didn't look the same": Vern Smith, Telefax reporting notes.

74 "You killed my sister": Earnhardt, "Maxwell Gunned Down," 1.

74 "They tore my chapel up": Ibid., 4.

74 "There's been a shooting": James Earnhardt, "The Scene / A Death Mourned . . . a Life Taken," *Alexander City Outlook,* June 20, 1977, 1.

74 "I thought someone was": Earnhardt, "Maxwell Gunned Down," 4.

75 "I was so scared": Ibid.

| 7 | WHO'S IN THE STEW?

81 "segregation now, segregation tomorrow": Frady, *Wallace,* 144.

81 "You know why I lost": This conversation was first recorded in ibid., but recounted in these exact words by Wallace's aide Seymore Trammell in McCabe and Stekler, *George Wallace.*

82 "low-down, carpet-baggin'": Frady, *Wallace,* 133.

84 "tie the Negro vote": Bentley, "Election of Tom Radney and the Transition Era of Southern Politics," 6.

84 "Negro support went": *Tuskegee News,* May 5, 1966, 1.

84 "You can easily see": H. H. O'Daniel, political advertisement, 1966.

85 "WHO'S IN THE STEW": H. H. O'Daniel's political advertisement.

86 "hard work, clean representation": Tom Radney, "An Open Letter to the Voters of Elmore, Macon, and Tallapoosa Counties," *Alexander City Outlook,* May 2, 1966.

| 8 | ROSES ARE RED

In addition to those newspapers already mentioned, for the context of Tom Radney's early political career, I relied on the archives of *The Southern Courier.*

It is thanks to the Vanderbilt Television News Archive that I was able to review Radney's interview with Dan Rather, and thanks to Laurie Austin of the John F. Kennedy Library that I could read his correspondence with the Kennedy family. I am grateful to the Radney family for letting me review all of Tom's press clippings, his speeches, and the correspondence that he received in the weeks after the 1968 Democratic National Convention. Madolyn Radney, especially, was candid and generous with memories of her husband's political career.

88  "had to spend more time": Mary Ellen Gale, " 'State's Pretty Jumbled Up,' Radney Tells Auburn People," *Southern Courier,* Nov. 11–12, 1967, 2.

89  "It's sort of a silly way": Sean Reilly, "JFK Refocused Lives in the Public Service," *Anniston Star,* Nov. 21, 1993, 12A.

89  "Edward Kennedy has shown": Senator Tom Radney, interview by Dan Rather, CBS News Special: "Democratic Convention," Aug. 26, 1968.

90  "Roses are red": Don F. Wasson, "Threats Move Radney to Give Up Politics," *Montgomery Advertiser,* Sept. 1, 1968, 1.

91  "I'd pick up the phone at 3 a.m.": Carolyn Lewis, "A Threatened Alabaman Bows Out: Supporter of Sen. Ted Kennedy Says He's Harassed," *Washington Post,* Sept. 28, 1968, E1.

91  "however, I do not believe": Wasson, "Threats Move Radney to Give Up Politics," 1.

92  "George Wallace has planted": Lewis, "Threatened Alabaman Bows Out," E2.

93  "At night": Ibid., E1.

93  "My wife and I have prayerfully decided": Wasson, "Threats Move Radney to Give Up Politics," 1.

93  "I only wish I could": Ibid.

93  "never again to be a candidate": "Radney Re-emphasizes Decision 'Never Again to Be Candidate,' " *Alexander City Outlook,* Sept. 5, 1968, 1.

93  "openly expressed position": "Freedom from Abuse," *Birmingham News,* Sept. 3, 1968.

93  "decision to leave politics": "Sen. Radney's Decision," *Alabama Journal,* Sept. 2, 1968, 4.

93  "Radney can hardly be faulted": "The Price of Politics," *Hammond Daily Star,* Sept. 18, 1968, 1A.

94  "I was proud of you": Esther Lustig to Radney, Sept. 4, 1968.

94  "your views are not mine": Margaret J. Vann to Radney, Oct. 6, 1968.

94 "There are a lot of people": Kenneth Noel to Radney, n.d.

94 "We so hope that these evil days": Jay Murphy to Radney, Oct. 5, 1968.

94 "I am a Negro": Edward L. Sample to Radney, Oct. 4, 1968.

94 "So bad were the telephone calls": E. B. Henderson to Radney, Oct. 2, 1968.

95 "picked up where": "The Southern Committee on Political Ethics," *Del Shields's Night Call*, Sept. 30, 1968.

95 "Well, we wanted": "Threats Against Radney Taper Off," *Birmingham Post-Herald*, Sept. 12, 1968.

| 9 |   THE FIGHT FOR GOOD

96 "There the common sense": Tennyson, "Locksley Hall," in *Selected Poems*, 59.

97 "I did not make it": Steve Taylor, "Radney's Retirement Is a Short-Lived One," *Anniston Star*, Sept. 28, 1969, 5.

97 "I am not defensive": Don F. Wasson, "Radney to Seek State's 2nd Spot," *Montgomery Advertiser*, Sept. 21, 1969, 1A–2A.

98 "This time I am in the fight": Taylor, "Radney's Retirement," 5.

98 "blood, sweat, and tears": David Marshall, "Our Problem Is Economic, Radney Says," *Birmingham News*, March 1970, 1.

99 "I yield to no man": Anne Plott, "Sen. Radney Says 'You Have to Pay Bill' for Education," *Anniston Star*, March 17, 1970, 3.

99 "I am proud of my Southern heritage": Mel Newman, "Radney Hits Those Who Talk of Closing the Public Schools," *Florence Times—Tri Cities Daily*, Dec. 5, 1969, 1.

99 "There'll be busloads of black children": Ellen Price, interview by author, Feb. 3, 2016.

100 "not defeated, only disappointed": Tom Radney, "Concession Speech," May 5, 1970.

| 10 |   THE MAXWELL HOUSE

For the history of courts and courthouses in Alabama, I relied on *Heritage of Tallapoosa County;* Schafer, *Lake Martin;* Walls and Oliver, *Alexander City;* Rumore's *From Power to Service* and *Lawyers in a New South City;* Feathers, "Catfights and Coffins"; and Dees, *Season for Justice.* I am grateful to all those former clients and colleagues of Tom Radney's who shared their stories, most especially Morris Dees, who once prevailed against Radney in a memorable legal case; I'm only sorry I couldn't tell the story of *Berry v. Macon County Board of Education.*

101 "the erection of a courthouse": National Society of the Colonial Dames of America in the State of Alabama, *Early Courthouses of Alabama, Prior to 1860* (Mobile, Ala., 1966), 52.
107 "with the memory like a Homeric bard's": Cash, *Mind of the South,* 28.
107 "jurymen seldom convict": Darrow, quoted in Sutherland, Cressey, and Luckenbill, *Principles of Criminology,* 411.

| 11 | PEACE AND GOODWILL

For the history of the insanity plea and challenges to it, I relied on J. R. Rappeport, "The Insanity Plea: Getting Away with Murder?," *Maryland State Medical Journal* 32, no. 3 (1983); James Gleick, "Getting Away with Murder," *New Times,* Aug. 21, 1978, 22–28; Mac McClelland, "They'll Be Here till They Die," *New York Times Magazine,* Oct. 1, 2017; and Friedman, *Crime and Punishment in American History.* I appreciate the assistance of Lauren McGuinn at the Federal Bureau of Investigation and Denita Pasley at the Central Alabama Community College.

110 "They might be coming": Wesley, "Minister's Body Attracts Curious," 2A.
111 "Voodooist Is Slain": *Baltimore Sun,* June 22, 1977, A3.
111 "Death of Voodoo Shaman": *Sumter Daily Item,* June 22, 1977, 6B.
111 "scared to death of him": "Slain Minister: As Mysterious in Death as He Was in Life," *Gadsden Times,* June 24, 1977, 2.
111 "it was like a burden": Vern Smith, Telefax reporting notes.
111 "There's no reason": Alvin Benn, "Will Maxwell," *Alexander City Outlook,* June 22, 1977, 4.
112 "living in a nightmare": Alvin Benn, "Mrs. Maxwell: 'It's Like I'm Living in a Nightmare,'" *Alexander City Outlook,* June 20, 1977, 1.
112 "I just hate all this publicity": "Slain Minister: As Mysterious in Death as He Was in Life," 2.
113 *"Their trouble and sorrow":* Funeral Program of the Reverend Willie Maxwell.
113 "we have nothing to hide": Jim Earnhardt, "Hundreds Attend Maxwell Funeral," *Alexander City Outlook,* June 24, 1977, 1.

114 "a murderer and a fugitive": Phillip Rawls, ". . . To Help Touch Somebody . . . ," *Montgomery Advertiser,* June 24, 1977, 1.

114 "The Devil couldn't take Moses": Ibid.

114 "I hope to hell not": Elizabeth F. Shores, "Minister Slain at Stepdaughter's Funeral Buried," *Birmingham Post-Herald.*

117 "Radney is silk": Alvin Benn, "Radney vs. Young," *Alexander City Outlook,* Sept. 28, 1977, 1.

117 "most trials resemble warmed-over grits": Alvin Benn, "Sometimes Drama Blooms," *Montgomery Advertiser,* May 10, 1981, 5A.

118 "You have mistreated my family": *State of Alabama v. Robert Lewis Burns,* 109.

118 "I had to do it": Ibid., 111.

118 "revolving door": This phrase appears in much of the coverage of the case and was repeated by District Attorney Tom Young during the trial; see ibid., 12.

| 12 | TOM V. TOM

All quotations are from the trial transcript.

| 13 | THE MAN FROM ECLECTIC

All quotations are from the trial transcript.

| 14 | WHAT HOLMES WAS TALKING ABOUT

Unless otherwise noted, all quotations are from the trial transcript. I am grateful to Steve Davis and Dianne Durbin at the Alabama Department of Mental Health for their help researching Bryce Hospital.

144 "Now, a cold-blooded murderer": Phyllis Wesley, "Trial Unfolds Like Film," *Montgomery Advertiser,* Sept. 29, 1977, 2.

144 "In a way . . . killing Willie Maxwell": Gleick, "Getting Away with Murder," 22–28.

145 "The first requirement": Holmes, *Common Law,* 41–42.

## | 15 | DISAPPEARING ACT

For the account of Nelle Harper Lee's life, I benefited from the work of ear-lier biographers, reporters, and researchers, most especially Keith, "Afternoon with Harper Lee"; Dannye Romine Powell, "Capote and Friend: More than a Gap in the Hedge?," *Odessa American,* Sept. 4, 1977, 5D; Drew Jubera, "To Find a Mockingbird: The Search for Harper Lee," *Dallas Times Herald,* Feb. 5, 1984; Kathy Kemp, "Mockingbird Won't Sing," *Raleigh News and Observer,* Nov. 12, 1997; Hazel Rowley, "Mockingbird Country," *Australian's Review of Books,* April 1999; Shields, *Mockingbird;* Madden, *Harper Lee;* Mills, *Mocking-bird Next Door;* and Crespino, *Atticus Finch.* For information in this chapter and throughout this section, I am grateful for the additional assistance and encouragement of Marja Mills, Drew Jubera, Dannye Romine Powell, Kerry Madden, Jane Kansas, Sue Cohen, Beth Ahearn Fisher, Della Rowley, Peter McIlroy, Allen Mendenhall, Rodney H. W. Cooper, Sharlyn Carter, Chip Cooper, and others who do not wish to be named. I'm grateful to the late Maryon Pittman Allen for recounting her conversation with Harper Lee so precisely and enlivening their shared history. Thank you to Youlanda Logan at the Jimmy Carter Presidential Library for locating the inscribed book.

150  "John . . . do you know where Nelle Lee is": Maryon Pittman Allen, inter-view by author, Feb. 19, 2017.

150  "What in the world": Ibid.

150  "It was like she was hiding": Ibid.

151  "To Rosalynn Carter": Inscription courtesy of the Jimmy Carter Presiden-tial Library.

151  "We are bound": Patricia Burstein, "Tiny Yes, but a Terror? Do Not Be Fooled by Truman Capote in Repose," *People,* May 10, 1976, 16.

## | 16 | SOME KIND OF SOUL

There is a great deal of misinformation about Harper Lee's life, and I have tried not to reproduce any of it here. She and her family expressed frustration with almost every written account of her childhood, but except for challenging the depiction of their mother's mental health in Clarke's *Capote,* they did not correct the record. I benefited from the interviews with Alice Lee conducted by Marja Mills and Mary McDonough Murphy, along with letters written by Louise Conner and an interview she gave to *The Sunday Ledger-Enquirer Magazine* not long after *To Kill a Mockingbird* was published. Beyond those, I relied mainly on the archives of *The Monroe Journal* and benefited greatly from an unpublished oral history of a neighbor of the Lee family, Marie Hubbird, who knew Nelle from age six until after she published *To Kill a Mockingbird*. I made use of Lee's college writings and the recollections of those who knew her during those years, and I am grateful to Eric Kidwell of the Houghton Memorial Library at Huntingdon College and the W. S. Hoole Library at the University of Alabama. There are too many current and former Monroevillians and Monroe Countians to thank, but I want to acknowledge Jane Busby, Susan Ward, Stephanie Rogers, Kathy McCoy, Marty Pickett, the Reverend Eddie Marzett, the Reverend Thomas Lane Butts, the Croft family, Dawn Hare, Tim McKenzie, and Janet Sawyer. Thank you to James Fishwick and Oliver Mahony of Lady Margaret Hall for their help looking into Lee's time at the University of Oxford, and Tom McCutchon of the Columbia University Rare Book & Manuscript Library for his help with the Annie Laurie Williams Papers.

153 "We must confer": Harper Lee to Annie Laurie Williams, June 4, 1959, Annie Laurie Williams Papers, Rare Book & Manuscript Library, Columbia University.

154 "nervous disorder": Marja Mills, "A Life Apart: Harper Lee, the Complex Woman Behind a 'Delicious Mystery,'" *Chicago Tribune,* Sept. 13, 2002, 1.

156 "entertained": "Misses Faulk and Lee Delightfully Entertain," *Monroe Journal,* Feb. 13, 1930.

156 "What Is the Cause of This Confusion?": "League Program for Next Sunday Night," *Monroe Journal,* Jan. 26, 1939.

157 "World's Foremost Man of Mystery": Clarke, *Capote,* 9.

158 they were both "apart" people: Gloria Steinem, "Go Right Ahead and Ask Me Anything (and So She Did): An Interview with Truman Capote," *McCall's,* Nov. 1967, 150.

158 "Master Truman Capote": *Monroe Journal,* June 13, 1935.

159 "She is one of the few teachers": "The Enduring Power of *To Kill a Mockingbird*," 47.

159 "What's that?": Plimpton, *Truman Capote,* 38.

160 "is something of a relief": Nelle Lee, "Idealistic Editor-Author Has Head in Clouds, Feet on Ground," *Huntress,* Jan. 17, 1945, 2.

160 "a place where diligent law students": Mary Williams, "'Little Nelle' Heads Ram, Maps Lee's Strategy," *Crimson-White,* Oct. 8, 1946, 1.

161 "Honey, I'm thuck": Nelle Lee, "Some Writers of Our Time: A Very Informal Essay," *Rammer-Jammer* 21, no. 3 (Nov. 1945): 14.

162 "A. C. Lee and Daughters, Lawyers": Elizabeth Otts, "Lady Lawyers Prepare Homecoming Costumes," *Crimson-White,* Nov. 26, 1946, 14.

| 17 | THE GIFT

For the account of Harper Lee's early years in New York, including the writing, editing, and publication of *To Kill a Mockingbird,* I relied on contemporary interviews with and correspondence from Harper Lee, Maurice Crain, and Tay Hohoff; the materials in the Annie Laurie Williams Papers at Columbia University; Harper Lee's autobiographical essay "Christmas to Me"; the commentary offered by Tay Hohoff in J. B. Lippincott Company, *Author and His Audience* and *The Literary Guild Review;* Jubera, "To Find a Mockingbird"; Walter, *Milking the Moon;* and later interviews with Joy and Michael Brown. Thank you to Charles Whaley and Petter Buttenheim for their remembrances of *The School Executive* and to Heather Thomas for locating all of the issues with Harper Lee on the masthead. I am grateful to Jonathan Burnham for allowing me to review the materials in the HarperCollins Collection and to Kathleen Shoemaker and Kira Tucker for their help at the Emory University Rose Library. I'm grateful also for the assistance of Jane Kansas, Steve Cuthrell, Louise Sims, Rachel McDavid, Clarissa Atkinson, and Justin Caldwell of Sotheby's.

165 "Nelle and I were instant friends": Brown, as quoted in Murphy, *Hey, Boo.*

167 "a mess": Nelle Lee to P. J. Cuthrell, n.d. (This letter is on stationery from Sabena Airlines, where Cuthrell worked with Lee until 1954.)

168 "Daddy is practical": Louise Conner, quoted in Tom Sellers, "Writing Giants from Small Beginnings Grow," *Sunday Ledger-Enquirer Magazine,* Dec. 4, 1960, 4.

169 "I am more of a rewriter": Hal Boyle, "Harper Lee Still Prefers Robert E. and Tom Jefferson," *Alabama Journal,* March 15, 1963, 11.

170 "no substitute": Harper Lee, quoted in Newquist, *Counterpoint,* 409.

170 "the gloomiest guy on this side": Michael Brown, "A Woman's New York," *Poughkeepsie Journal,* Dec. 5, 1951, 6.

171  "I've done things for him": Lee to Harold Caufield, June 16, 1956, Rose Library, Emory University.

171  "Francesca da Rimini": Lee to Harold Caufield, dated "Sunday," Rose Library.

171  "The Prisoner of Zenda": Lee to "Dears," dated "Sunday," Rose Library.

172  "Sitting & listening to people": Ibid.

172  "The Land of Sweet Forever": "Lee, Nelle Harper," Author Cardfile, box 210, Williams Papers.

172  "Old Woodenface": Unsigned letter from someone in the office of Annie Laurie Williams to Harper Lee, Jan. 7, 1961, Williams Papers.

173  "Why don't you write one": Harry Hansen, "Miracle of Manhattan—1st Novel Sweeps Board," *Chicago Sunday Tribune Magazine of Books*, May 14, 1961, 6.

173  "You have one year off": Harper Lee, "Christmas to Me," *McCall's*, Dec. 1961, 63.

174  "They'd saved some money": Ibid.

174  "don't care whether anything I write": "Alumna Wins Pulitzer Prize for Distinguished Fiction," University of Alabama *Alumni News*, May–June 1961, 15.

174  "The Cat's Meow": "Lee, Nelle Harper," Author Cardfile.

175  "an eye-opener for many northerners": Crain to Evan Thomas, April 10, 1957, HarperCollins Collection.

175  "childhood stuff": Crain to Lynn Carrick, June 13, 1957, HarperCollins Collection.

176  "the spark of the true writer": J. B. Lippincott Company, *Author and His Audience*, 28.

176  "dangling threads of plot": Tay Hohoff, "We Get a New Author," *Literary Guild Book Club Magazine*, Aug. 1960, 3–4.

176  "more a series of anecdotes": J. B. Lippincott Company, *Author and His Audience*, 28.

176  "She was a writer": Michael Brown, as quoted in Murphy, *Hey, Boo*.

177  "We talked it out": J. B. Lippincott Company, *Author and His Audience*, 29.

178  "the Quaker Hitler": Harper Lee to Doris Leapard, Aug. 25, 1990.

179  "She would go home": "The Enduring Power of *To Kill a Mockingbird*," 37.

179  "I was sitting here one night": Ibid.

| 18 | DEEP CALLING TO DEEP

For the details of Harper Lee's work with Truman Capote, I am indebted to Voss, *Truman Capote and the Legacy of "In Cold Blood"*; the University of Nebraska College of Journalism and Mass Communication's *Cold Blood: A Murder, a Book, a Legacy;* Clarke, *Capote;* and Plimpton, *Truman Capote.* I am grateful for the assistance of Ralph Voss and Glenda Brumbeloe Weathers; Rosemary Hope; Paul Dewey; Ron Nye; Douglas McGrath; Lawrence Grobel; David Ebershoff; Gerald Clarke; Alan Schwartz of the Truman Capote Trust; Carly Smith of the Finney County Public Library; Laura Graham of the Kansas Bureau of Investigation; Erin Harris at the Richard Avedon Foundation; and Tal Nadan, Kyle Triplett, and Cara Dellatte of the Brooke Russell Astor Reading Room for Rare Books and Manuscripts at the New York Public Library.

180 "assistant researchist": George Plimpton, "The Story Behind a Nonfiction Novel," *New York Times Book Review,* Jan. 16, 1966, 2.

180 "He said it would be": " 'In Cold Blood' . . . an American Tragedy," *Newsweek,* Jan. 24, 1966, 60.

181 "She had been thinking": Powell, "Capote and Friend," 5D.

181 "It was deep calling to deep": " 'In Cold Blood' . . . an American Tragedy," 60.

182 "I was jealous": Mills, *Mockingbird Next Door,* 166.

182 "At first it was like": Harper Lee, "Truman Capote," *Book-of-the-Month Club News,* Jan. 1966, 6.

182 "little gnome in his checkered vest": John Barry Ryan, as quoted in Plimpton, *Truman Capote,* 168.

184 "legitimate": "Office Memorandum to Mr. DeLoach," Dec. 21, 1959, Federal Bureau of Investigation file on Truman Capote.

184 "Absolutely fantastic lady": Nye, as quoted in Plimpton, *Truman Capote,* 170.

184 "If Capote came on": Dewey, as quoted in Dolores Hope, "The Clutter Case: 25 Years Later KBI Agent Recounts Holcomb Tragedy," *Garden City Telegram,* Nov. 10, 1984.

185 "Nelle sort of managed Truman": Ed Pilkington, "In Cold Blood, Half a Century On," *Guardian,* Nov. 15, 2009.

188 "nonfiction novel": Capote used this phrase frequently before, during, and after the publication of *In Cold Blood;* see, for example, Plimpton, "Story Behind a Nonfiction Novel," 1.

189 "Why they never look": Harper Lee's Notes, reel 7, box 7, folders 11–
14, Capote Papers, Manuscripts and Archives Division, New York Public
Library.

189 "To the Author of The Fire": Harper Lee's full dedication reads, "These
Notes Are Dedicated to the Author of The Fire and the Flame and the
Small Person Who So Manfully Endured Him," reel 7, box 7, folders 11–
14, Capote Papers.

190 "would probably have walked": Voss, *Truman Capote and the Legacy of "In
Cold Blood,"* 195.

| 19 | DEATH AND TAXES

For my account of the success of *To Kill a Mockingbird,* I relied on contemporary newspaper coverage of Harper Lee in *The Monroe Journal* and elsewhere,
Dolores Hope's extensive and ongoing documentation of Lee and Capote in
the *Garden City Telegram,* the agency correspondence to and from the Lee
sisters archived by Annie Laurie Williams at Columbia University, other letters
that Harper Lee and Truman Capote wrote during these years, and two extensive interviews with her conducted by Roy Newquist for his radio program
*Counterpoint* and Don Lee Keith for the *New Delta Review.* For their memories
of Nelle Harper Lee during this time, I am grateful to George and Elizabeth
Malko, Sonya Bentley Logan, Melissa Bentley, Alec Bentley, Harry Benson,
Bruce Higginson, Harry Mount, Beryl Barr, Jim O'Hare, and others close to
her who do not wish to be acknowledged by name. Thank you to Harry Benson for sharing his photographs of Lee and Capote, as well as recounting the
day he took them. Thank you to George M. Barnett for his memories of the
1976 Democratic National Convention, including the "Oscar W. Underwood
for President" party; I also relied on accounts of the party in *The New York
Times* and the *Alabama Journal.* Thank you to Rachel McDavid for sharing
memories of her father and some of Lee's other friends from the University
of Alabama. Thank you also to Dona Matthews, Dr. Felice Kaufmann, John
Carnahan, Irene Burtis, Maisie Crowther, Ken Lopez Bookseller, Jim Baggett
at the Birmingham Public Library, Margaret Harman at the Lyndon B. Johnson Library, Beth Davis of the Broadmoor, Toni Miller of the Pikes Peak
Library District, Jay Fielden and Alex Belth of *Esquire,* and Jeanne Walsh of
the Brooks Memorial Library.

192 "this is what is known": Dolores Hope, "The Distaff Side," *Garden City Telegram,* April 4, 1960, 4.

194 "Yes, Atticus was my father": Lee to Strode, March 6, 1961, Hudson Strode Papers, Hoole Library, University of Alabama at Tuscaloosa.

194 "Success hasn't spoiled": Bob Thomas, "No Complaints by Harper Lee on Hollywood," *Corsicana Daily Sun,* Feb. 9, 1962, 6.

194 "We can't stop them": Annie Laurie Williams to Alice Lee, Sept. 1, 1964, Williams Papers.

194 "If it sells more": Lee to Hamilton, Jan. 11, 2009, File 816.11.82, Virginia Van der Veer Hamilton Papers, Department of Archives and Manuscripts, Birmingham Public Library.

194 "in New York, where I became Famous": Lee to John Darden, n.d.

195 "First, catch your pig": Harper Lee, "Crackling Bread," in Barr and Sachs, *Artists' & Writers' Cookbook,* 251–52.

196 "The Gospel According to Nelle Harper": "Lee, Nelle Harper," Author Cardfile.

196 cycle of "reducing": Alice Lee to Annie Laurie Williams, Sept. 9, 1963, Williams Papers.

197 "Dear Nelle": Williams and Crain to Lee, telegram, July 12, 1961, Williams Papers.

197 "the second-novel doldrums": Lee to Bell, Aug. 17, 1960, MA 5134, Morgan Library & Museum.

197 "If I'd had any sense": Lee to Bell, Sept. 13, 1961, MA 5134, Morgan Library & Museum.

198 "not long ago she wrote": Capote to Andrew Lyndon, Sept. 6, 1960, in Capote, *Too Brief a Treat,* 292.

198 "Poor thing": Capote to Alvin and Marie Dewey, Oct. 10, 1960, in Capote, *Too Brief a Treat,* 299.

198 "I never dreamed": Vernon Hendrix, "Father of Novelist: Monroeville Attorney's Reactions Varied over Daughter's Book," *Monroe Journal,* Sept. 8, 1960.

199 "a junkyard dog": Edward Burlingame, as quoted in Jonathan Mahler, "Invisible Hand That Nurtured an Author and a Literary Classic," *New York Times,* July 13, 2015, C1.

200 "Dress Rehearsal": The title is referenced in the *Esquire* editor Harold Hayes's rejection letter to Lee, Oct. 27, 1961, Williams Papers.

200 "some white people": Lee to Harold Caufield, Nov. 21, 1961, Rose Library.

201 "I don't think this business": Bob Ellison, "Three Best-Selling Authors: Conversation," *Rogue,* Dec. 1963, 23.

201 "My book has a universal theme": Ramona Allison, "Nelle Harper Lee: A Proud, Tax-Paying Citizen," *Alabama Journal,* Jan. 1, 1962, 13C.

201 "be remembered as the one": Inscription courtesy of Morris Dees.

202 "I've been writing as long": Newquist, *Counterpoint,* 404, 408, 405, 410.

202 "Sometimes I'm afraid": Ibid., 405.

204 "I told her that I thought": Williams to Alice Lee, Oct. 8, 1965.

204 "To be a serious writer requires": Karen Schwabenton, "Harper Lee Discusses the Writer's Attitude and Craft," *Sweet Briar News,* Oct. 28, 1966.

205 "I'm tired of fighting": Lee to John Darden, Dec. 20, 1972.

206 "She was drinking at that time": George Malko, "Remembering Harper Lee," *Times Literary Supplement,* May 18, 2017.

207 "would drink and then tell somebody off": Jubera, "To Find a Mockingbird," 21.

207 "More tears are shed": Capote, as quoted in Inge, *Truman Capote,* 301.

208 "Allabhammah casts 20-foah votes": Ray Jenkins, "Alabama Delegation Feasts upon Nostalgia," *Alabama Journal,* July 12, 1976, 1.

208 "Kennedy broke the religion barrier": Alvin Benn, "Radney Sees Carter Breaking Region Barrier," *Montgomery Advertiser,* July 9, 1976, 9.

| 20 | RUMOR, FANTASY, DREAMS, CONJECTURE, AND OUTRIGHT LIES

For the history of crime writing and the account of the New Journalists, I relied on McDade, *Annals of Murder;* Knox, *Murder;* Wolfe and Johnson, *New Journalism;* Weingarten, *Gang That Wouldn't Write Straight;* Boynton, *New New Journalism;* and Priestman, *Cambridge Companion to Crime Fiction.* For the reactions to Capote's "nonfiction novel," I relied on Voss, *Truman Capote and the Legacy of "In Cold Blood";* Phillip K. Tompkins, "In Cold Fact," *Esquire,* June 1, 1966; Harper Lee's profile of Truman Capote for the Book-of-the-Month Club, along with her correspondence in the years after its publication. For their memories of Nelle Harper Lee in Alexander City, I am grateful to Madolyn Radney, Ellen Price, Robert Burns, Jim Earnhardt, Alvin Benn, Mary Ann Karr, Patricia Cribb, Ann Tate, Rheta Grimsley Johnson, Maryon Pittman Allen, Dr. Brooks Lamberth, Lynda Robinson, Gerald McGill, Ben Russell, and Catherine Burns. I also appreciated the remembrances offered by

Ben Burford and Chevy 6 of the Stable Club and Rob "Gabby" Withering-ton of Stillwaters. I am also grateful for the assistance of Diane McWhorter, Madison Jones IV, Ralph Voss and Glenda Brumbeloe Weathers, Curtis Smalls at the University of Delaware Library Special Collections, and Anne Marie Menta at Yale University's Beinecke Library.

210 *The Correct, Full, and Impartial Report*: McDade, *Annals of Murder*, 14.

211 "Journalism is the most underestimated": Plimpton, "Story Behind a Non-fiction Novel," 1.

213 "Truman Capote made a similar request": Patrick Smith, "Sisters, Family: Surviving Clutter Daughters Hope to Preserve Their Parents' Legacy," *Lawrence Journal-World,* April 4, 2005.

213 "Do you remember telling me": Capote to Alvin and Marie Dewey, Aug. 16, 1961, in Capote, *Too Brief a Treat,* 326.

214 "Truman's having long ago": Lee to Windham and Campbell, Sept. 28, 1984, YCAL MSS 424, box 11, Beinecke Library, Yale University.

214 "For over five years": Lee, "Truman Capote," 7.

214 "Truman did not cut me": Lee to Windham and Campbell, Sept. 28, 1984.

215 "the most important literature": Wolfe, preface to *New Journalism,* by Wolfe and Johnson.

215 "Of all the people": Capote, *In Cold Blood,* 85.

216 "There's a black boy dead": Lee, *To Kill a Mockingbird,* 369.

217 "are transfixed by a process": Trillin, *Killings,* xv.

217 "died and gone to Hell": Mary Ann Karr, interview by author, Feb. 13, 2017.

218 "You wouldn't think": Ibid.

219 "The Stable Club became": Alison James, "Local Store to Become Wal-greens," *Alexander City Outlook,* Dec. 1, 2012.

220 "If the Reverend was alive": Vern Smith, Telefax reporting notes.

220 "Around town the talk": Rheta Grimsley, "At His Own Murder Trial: Many Expected Maxwell," *Theopelika-Asburn News,* Sept. 27, 1977.

220 She complained: Lee to Madison Jones, June 5, 1987, box 12, folder 2, Madison Jones Papers, Rose Library.

221 "enough rumor, fantasy, conjecture": Ibid.

| 21 | COMING BACK UNTIL DOOMSDAY

In addition to those already acknowledged, I am grateful for the assistance of Faye Fox and Sheralyn Belyeu. I had the opportunity to review Tom Radney's files, as well as some additional materials from Harper Lee's investigation of the Maxwell case; these are cited when quoted, and also informed my account of her reporting. Not only did some subjects recall her using a tape recorder, but a warranty for a portable cassette tape recorder was found among her Maxwell files; so was a catalog from the Samuel Weiser Bookstore. The archives of *The Monroe Journal* and *The Alexander City Outlook* were helpful in contrasting the politics of Tom Radney and A. C. Lee; I relied on Isabel Wilkerson's *Warmth of Other Suns* for the account of the Great Migration. For the account of Lee's writing on race, I am indebted to some of the criticism of her work inspired by the publication of *Go Set a Watchman,* including that of Roxane Gay, Adam Gopnik, Michiko Kakutani, Kiese Laymon, Diane McWhorter, Jesmyn Ward, and Isabel Wilkerson. Thanks to Scotty Kirkland for letting me review Judge Coley's archives at the Alabama Department of Archives and History, and to Evelyn Puckett for sharing memories of her father.

222  "shy, reserved, matronly": Jubera, "To Find a Mockingbird," 21.

223  "the communist threat": "Tom Radney's Personal Background" on Radney campaign brochure, 1966.

223  "We the Jury find the defendant": Handwritten verdict slip from *State of Alabama v. Willie J. Maxwell* (Indictment No. 1494, Tallapoosa County Circuit Court, Fall Term 1971). From the files of Nelle Harper Lee.

224  "He seemed": Lee to Madison Jones, June 5, 1987.

225  "Never forget from whence you came": Appeared in various speeches by Tom Radney as recounted by Madolyn Radney.

226  "I never read anything by you": Jubera, "To Find a Mockingbird," 21.

226  "just sitting back": Madolyn Radney, interview by author, Feb. 25, 2015.

228  "nonfiction novels": Jim Earnhardt, *Montgomery Advertiser* " 'Literary Journalists' Goes Beyond Reporting the Facts," Nov. 18, 1984, 4B.

228  "politely correct a young man": Earnhardt, email to the author, May 18, 2017.

229  "My friend, an Alabamian": James Earnhardt, "Dust of Others Stirs Imagination," *Montgomery Advertiser,* Feb. 12, 1983, 1B.

229  "This is the way I like": Harper Lee to Earnhardt, Feb. 16, 1983.

229  "up to my neck": Lee to Rheta Grimsley Johnson, Feb. 21, 1978.

230 "mean to her": Lena Martin, interview by Nelle Harper Lee, Jan. 16, 1978, from Lee's unpublished reporting notes.

230 "She ain't had no wreck": Ibid.

230 died "from sickness": "Death Claim Notice" on Policy 529744 with Crown Life Insurance Company of Illinois, signed by Willie J. Maxwell.

230 an "elusive" figure: Lee to Johnson, Feb. 21, 1978.

231 "always paid his debts": Jim Stewart, " 'Voodoo Priest' Buried, but Whispers Live On," *Atlanta Constitution,* June 24, 1977, 23A.

232 "Whether he's in the courtroom": "Radney: Good Choice for Man of the Year," *Alexander City Outlook,* Jan. 23, 1978, 4.

232 "She knew all her stuff": Burns, interview by author, Feb. 13, 2017.

233 "Before I remembered": Lee, *To Kill a Mockingbird,* 80.

233 "all that voodoo stuff": Stewart, " 'Voodoo Priest' Buried, but Whispers Live On," 23A.

234 "I was disappointed": Lee to Madison Jones, June 5, 1987.

235 "I do believe that": Ibid.

237 "You simply can't beat": Lee to Louise and Patricia Cribb, June 11, 1978.

237 "It was not good-bye": Letter from Harper Lee to Louise and Patricia Cribb, June 11, 1978.

| 22 |   HORSESHOE BEND

It was an odd thing at the start of my reporting to go to 433 East Eighty-Second Street and stare at Harper Lee's name on the door buzzer. I benefited from Drew Jubera's recounting of his earlier experience at that building; thank you to Kate Richardson of Richlyn Marketing, LLC, John Oates, Dr. Michael Tanner, Bruce Higgison, Beth Forman, Sonya Bentley Logan, Alec Bentley, George and Elizabeth Malko, and Sylvia Shorris for their own memories of the building, its occupants, and their neighborhood. For the account of Lee's time in Eufaula, I relied on her letters from that period, the recollections of the Reverend Marcus Smith, Ann Smith, Jerry Elijah Brown, and others who do not wish to be named. For Lee's fears about litigation, I relied on her correspondence, the recollections of some who do not wish to be named, and the oral history of Marie Hubbird. I am honored to have been allowed to review and study the draft chapter that Harper Lee presented to Tom Radney, and am extremely grateful to his family for letting me do so; that unpublished manuscript informs my account of her turn from nonfiction to fiction. For the account of Albert James Pickett, I relied not only on his history but also on Lee's "Romance and High Adventure" and Owen's "Albert James Pickett, a Sketch." I am also grateful to Ari Schulman; Patrick Cather; Matthew Robinson of the Horseshoe Bend National Military Park; Betty Uzman of the Mississippi Department of Archives and History; Ashley Young and Sara Seten Berghausen of the David M. Rubenstein Rare Book & Manuscript Library at Duke University; Kristine Krueger of the Margaret Herrick Library of the Academy of Motion Picture Arts and Sciences; and the Virginia Center for the Creative Arts.

238 "abyss": Malcolm, *The Journalist and the Murderer,* 69.

239 "a dilapidated bed": Lee to Earl and Sylvia Shorris, Nov. 20, 1993.

242 "psychological processes": Ibid.

242 "If accuracy is what you are after": Ibid.

243 "picking out the nut": Joseph Deitch, "Harper Lee: Novelist of the South," *Christian Science Monitor,* Oct. 3, 1961, 6.

243 "I work very slowly": Ramona Allison, "'Mockingbird' Author Is Alabama's 'Woman of the Year,'" *Birmingham Post Herald,* Jan. 3, 1962.

243 "paper, pen, and privacy": Lee to Leo B. Roberts, Jan. 26, 1961, Archives and Information Center, Huntingdon College Library.

243 "You depend entirely": Vivian Cannon, "'Mockingbird' Author Wants to 'Disappear,'" *Mobile Register,* March 21, 1963, 1.

243 "If the Lippincott editors": Crain to Bonner McMillion, Jan. 1962, as quoted in Ari N. Schulman, "The Man Who Helped Make Harper Lee," *Atlantic,* July 15, 2015.

244 "the loveliest town in the state": Lee to Gregory and Veronique Peck, Jan. 6, 1981, Margaret Herrick Library, Academy of Motion Picture Arts and Sciences.

245 "My baby sister that we thought": Louise Conner to Anna Coine Cravey, Sept. 22, 1961, Huntingdon College Library.

245 "Louise guards my privacy": Lee to Gregory and Veronique Peck, Jan. 6, 1981.

246 "poaching on my literary preserves": Carr, *Lonely Hunter,* 433.

246 "a child's book": O'Connor to "A.," Oct. 1, 1960, in O'Connor, *Habit of Being,* 411.

246 "willingness to talk": Lee to Gregory and Veronique Peck, Jan. 6, 1981.

246 "Writing is easy": Lee slightly misquoted this line from Gene Fowler, which she had most likely encountered when it appeared in print a few

months earlier in Randolph Hogan, "Writers on Writing," *New York Times Book Review,* Aug. 10, 1980, 35.

246 "nobody cared when": Lee to Gregory and Veronique Peck, Jan. 6, 1981.

247 "Of course I'll probably be sued": Lee to Gregory and Veronique Peck, March 4, 1981, Herrick Library.

248 "coincidental": This is from Tay Hohoff's essay for *The Literary Guild Review,* which was reprinted as an editorial in various newspapers, including *The Eufaula Tribune,* May 26, 1960.

249 "I think she's fighting": Jubera, "To Find a Mockingbird," 21.

250 "Anything worthwhile in my life": Joe Patton, "Judge Coley: Active Life for 'Semi-retired' Banker," *Alexander City Outlook,* May 4, 1978, 3.

251 "since Eufaula reeks": Harper Lee to Jim Earnhardt, Feb. 18, 1983.

251 "It took all of Alice's powers": Ibid.

251 "It gives me the greatest pleasure": Lee, "Romance and High Adventure," 15.

252 "falls somewhere": Ibid.

252 "I do not believe that it was in him": Ibid., 19.

253 "My old friend": Earnhardt, email to author, May 31, 2017.

254 "I know that a book": Thomason to Lee, May 10, 1987, box 12, folder 2, Jones Papers.

255 "not interested in buying": Lee to Thomason, June 5, 1987, box 12, folder 2, Jones Papers.

255 she had learned five things: Lee to Jones, June 5, 1987, box 12, folder 2, Jones Papers.

| 23 |   THE LONG GOOD-BYE

In thinking about Harper Lee's later career, I benefited greatly from Posnock, *Renunciation;* Joan Acocella, "Blocked," *New Yorker,* June 14, 2004; Jamison, *Recovering;* Laing, *Trip to Echo Spring;* Kelly, *Book of Lost Books;* Dick Schlaap, "22 Invisible Mockingbirds," *San Francisco Examiner,* May 24, 1964; Lepore, *Joe Gould's Teeth;* Malcolm, *The Journalist and the Murderer;* and the *Unfinished* show at the Met Breuer. Many friends and acquaintances of Harper Lee's later years shared their time, memories, and letters with me. Some of them do not wish to be acknowledged, but I am grateful for the assistance of Sylvia Shorris, Sandy Mulligan, Hallie Foote, Cecilia Peck, Charles Kiselyak, Star Lawrence, Robert Weil, Claudia Durst Johnson, Marja Mills, Thomas Lane Butts, Cynthia Lanford, Kevin Howell, George Landegger, Wayne Flynt, Nancy Anderson, Penny Weaver, Fannie Flagg, Hugh Van Dusen, Deborah DiClementi, and Mary Higgins Clark. I am also grateful for the assistance of William Price, Drew Jubera, Alice Hall Petry, Mary McDonagh Murphy, Caroline Sparks, Michelle Dean, and Carolyn Waters at the New York Society Library.

256  "Kansans will spend the rest": Lee, "Truman Capote," 7.

256  "too sensitive a subject": Allen J. Going to William T. Going, July 11, 1987, as quoted in Alice Hall Petry, "Harper Lee, the One-Hit Wonder," in *On Harper Lee,* 159.

257  "It's my understanding": Jubera, "To Find a Mockingbird," 19.

257  "She's always working": "Harper Lee, Read but Not Heard," *Washington Post,* Aug. 17, 1990, C2.

257  "the worst punishment": Lee to Doris Leapard, Aug. 25, 1990.

257  "lallapalooza": Lee to "Dears," April 3, 1963, Williams Papers.

257  "Come Where the Booze Is Cheaper": Lee to Sylvia Shorris, Oct. 20, 1993.

257  "I know exactly why she did it": Lee to Mel Yoken, May 22, 1976.

258  "Some Sociological Aspects": Harper Lee, "Some Sociological Aspects of Peculiarities of Pronunciation Found in Persons from Alabama Who Read a Great Deal to Themselves," included with letter to Harold Caufield, n.d., Rose Library.

258  "She continued to write": Alice Lee, "Harper Lee: My Little Sister," *Guardian,* July 11, 2015.

259  "the jitters" and "the humbles": Brown and Wiley, *Margaret Mitchell's "Gone with the Wind,"* 11.

260  "the mortgage on myself": Lee to Claudia Durst Johnson, n.d.

261  "Do / you still hang your": Lowell, "For Elizabeth Bishop 4," in *Collected Poems,* 595.

261  "Self-pity is a sin": Boyle, "Harper Lee Still Prefers Robert E. and Tom Jefferson."

262  "I am impatient with people": Hal Boyle, "In the South We Are Still in the Victorian Age," *Pensacola News,* March 15, 1963, 4A.

262  "George Plimpton's minions": Lee to Donald Windham, Aug. 3, 1986, YCAL MSS 424, box 11, Beinecke Library.

263  "Truman's vicious lie": Lee to Delaney, Dec. 30, 1988, as quoted in Shields, *Mockingbird,* 270.

263  "Most of us in the Western world": Boyle, "Harper Lee Still Prefers Robert E. and Tom Jefferson."

263 "Books succeed, / And lives fail": Browning, *Aurora Leigh*, 243.

264 "Please spare *Mockingbird*": Mary B. W. Tabor, "A 'New Foreword' That Isn't," *New York Times*, Aug. 23, 1995, C11.

264 "Fame was a four-letter word": Kiselyak, *Fearful Symmetry*.

265 "Her memory is fragile": Lee to Gorman Houston, June 20, 2003, Alabama Department of Archives.

266 "Daddy's prized bill": Alice Lee to Family and Friends, n.d., Huntingdon College Library.

267 "After a long career of responsible": Alvin Benn, "Memories of Me and Nelle," *Montgomery Advertiser*, Feb. 20, 2016.

268 "Of the screenwriter's many": Harper Lee, "Mr. Shawn and Ms. Lee," *New Yorker*, April 10, 2006, 5.

268 Around midnight on Saturday: Alice Lee to Jim Earnhardt, July 30, 2007.

269 "a mountain of rumors": Lee to Brasfield, Jan. 9, 2009, as quoted in Varicella, *Reverend*.

269 "Nothing you have done": Alice Lee to Sheralyn Belyeu, June 22, 2009.

270 "The years are getting by": Radney to Lee, Feb. 2, 2006.

270 "It was a delight": Lee to Radney, Feb. 17, 2006.

271 "a lawyer and politician": "The Reverend" unpublished manuscript, 3, Radney Family Archives.

272 "happy as hell": Statement provided by HarperCollins, relayed from Tonja Carter, Feb. 5, 2015.

| EPILOGUE |

I am grateful to Ellen Price for asking me to accompany her to Barnett, Bugg, Lee & Carter, and to Little Madolyn, Anna Lee, and Cason for letting me be the first to review the contents of Big Tom's briefcase. As ever, they were generous and patient. I am especially grateful to the estate of Nelle Harper Lee for returning the briefcase in time for me to make use of it for my research.

# | *Bibliography* |

In addition to countless articles from newspapers and magazines, I relied on the following books, journal articles, and documentary films.

Agee, James, and Walker Evans. *Let Us Now Praise Famous Men*. Boston: Mariner Books, 2001.

Allison, Thomas R. *Moonshine Memories*. Montgomery, Ala.: NewSouth Books, 2014.

Asbury, Herbert. *The French Quarter: An Informal History of the New Orleans Underworld*. New York: Basic Books, 2008.

Ayers, H. Brandt. *In Love with Defeat: The Making of a Southern Liberal*. Montgomery, Ala.: NewSouth Books, 2013.

Baldwin, James. *The Evidence of Things Not Seen*. New York: Henry Holt, 1995.

Balleisen, Edward J. *Fraud: An American History from Barnum to Madoff*. Princeton, N.J.: Princeton University Press, 2017.

Barr, Beryl, and Barbara Turner Sachs. *The Artists' & Writers' Cookbook*. Sausalito, Calif.: Contact, 1961.

Bartram, William. *Travels Through North and South Carolina, Georgia, East and West Florida*. Savannah, Ga.: Beehive Press, 1973.

Benn, Alvin. *Reporter: Covering Civil Rights and Wrongs in Dixie*. Bloomington, Ind.: AuthorHouse, 2006.

Bentley, Charles A., Jr. "The Election of Tom Radney and the Transition Era of Southern Politics." Unpublished term paper, Fall 1967, Auburn University.

Berendt, John. *Midnight in the Garden of Good and Evil*. New York: Vintage Books, 1999.

Bloom, Harold, ed. *Modern Critical Interpretations: Harper Lee's "To Kill a Mockingbird."* Philadelphia: Chelsea House, 1999.

Boynton, Robert S. *The New New Journalism: Conversations with America's Best Nonfiction Writers on Their Craft.* New York: Vintage Books, 2005.

Brown, Ellen F., and John Wiley Jr. *Margaret Mitchell's "Gone with the Wind": A Bestseller's Odyssey from Atlanta to Hollywood.* New York: Taylor, 2011.

Browning, Elizabeth Barrett. *Aurora Leigh.* New York: Oxford University Press, 1998.

Bunch-Lyons, Beverly. "'Ours Is a Business of Loyalty': African American Funeral Home Owners in Southern Cities." *Southern Quarterly* 53, no. 1 (Fall 2015): 57–71.

Capote, Truman. *The Grass Harp: Including A Tree of Night and Others Stories.* New York: Vintage Books, 1993.

———. *In Cold Blood: A True Account of a Multiple Murder and Its Consequences.* New York: Vintage Books, 1994.

———. *Other Voices, Other Rooms.* New York: Signet Books, 1948.

———. *Too Brief a Treat: The Letters of Truman Capote.* Edited by Gerald Clarke. New York: Vintage Books, 2005.

Carmer, Carl. *Stars Fell on Alabama.* Tuscaloosa: University of Alabama Press, 2000.

Carr, Virginia Spencer. *The Lonely Hunter: A Biography of Carson McCullers.* Athens: University of Georgia Press, 2003.

Cash, W. J. *The Mind of the South.* New York: Vintage Books, 1991.

Cason, Clarence. *90° in the Shade.* Tuscaloosa: University of Alabama Press, 2001.

Chesnutt, Charles W. *Conjure Tales and Stories of the Color Line.* New York: Penguin Books, 1992.

Clarke, Gerald. *Capote: A Biography.* New York: Ballantine Books, 1988.

Crespino, Joseph. *Atticus Finch: The Biography.* New York: Basic Books, 2018.

Davis, Rod. *American Voudou: Journey into a Hidden World.* Denton: University of North Texas Press, 1998.

Davis, Wade. *The Serpent and the Rainbow: A Harvard Scientist's Astonishing Journey into the Secret Societies of Haitian Voodoo, Zombis, and Magic.* New York: Simon & Schuster, 1985.

Debo, Angie. *The Road to Disappearance: A History of the Creek Indians.* Norman: University of Oklahoma Press, 1979.

Dees, Morris. *A Season for Justice: A Lawyer's Own Story of Victory over America's Hate Groups.* With Steve Fiffer. New York: Touchstone, 1991.

Dewey, A. A. "In Cold Blood Country." *New Letters* 43, no. 2 (Winter 1976): 105–12.

Dyer, Geoff. *Out of Sheer Rage: Wrestling with D. H. Lawrence.* New York: Picador, 1997.

"The Enduring Power of *To Kill a Mockingbird.*" *Life,* June 26, 2015.

Faust, Drew Gilpin. *Republic of Suffering: Death and the American Civil War.* New York: Vintage, 2008.

Feathers, Anne Herbert. "Catfights and Coffins: Stories of Alabama Courthouses." *Alabama Review* (July 2008): 163–89.

Fickle, James. *Green Gold: Alabama's Forests and Forest Industries.* Tuscaloosa: University of Alabama Press, 2014.

Flynt, Wayne. *Alabama in the Twentieth Century.* Montgomery: University of Alabama Press, 2006.

———. *Mockingbird Songs: My Friendship with Harper Lee.* New York: HarperCollins, 2017.

Forney, John. *Above the Noise of the Crowd: Thirty Years Behind the Alabama Microphone.* Huntsville, Ala.: Albright, 1986.

Frady, Marshall. *Wallace.* New York: Random House, 1996.

Friedman, Lawrence M. *Crime and Punishment in American History.* New York: Basic Books, 1994.

Gates, Henry Louis, Jr., and Maria Tatar, eds. *The Annotated African American Folktales.* New York: Liveright, 2018.

Goodman, James. *Stories of Scottsboro.* New York: Vintage, 1995.

Gosse, Philip Henry. *Letters from Alabama, U.S., Chiefly Relating to Natural History.* Mountain Brook, Ala.: Overbrook Press, 1983.

Gray, Fred. *Bus Ride to Justice: Changing the System by the System: The Life and Works of Fred D. Gray, Preacher, Attorney, Politician.* Montgomery, Ala.: NewSouth Books, 2002.

Greenhaw, Wayne. *Alabama on My Mind: Politics, People, History, and Ghost Stories.* Montgomery, Ala.: Sycamore Press, 1987.

Grobel, Lawrence. *Conversations with Capote.* New York: Plume, 1985.

Hamilton, Virginia Van der Veer. *Alabama: A History.* New York: W. W. Norton, 1977.

Haskins, Jim. *Voodoo & Hoodoo: Their Tradition and Craft as Revealed by Actual Practitioners.* Lanham, Md.: Scarborough House, 1990.

Heen, Mary L. "Ending Jim Crow Life Insurance Rates." *Northwestern Journal of Law and Social Policy* (Fall 2009): 360–99.

Hemphill, Paul. *Lovesick Blues: The Life of Hank Williams*. New York: Penguin Books, 2006.

*The Heritage of Coosa County, Alabama*. Louisville, Ky.: Heritage Publishing Consultants, 2000.

*The Heritage of Monroe County, Alabama*. Louisville, Ky.: Heritage Publishing Consultants, 2000.

*The Heritage of Tallapoosa County, Alabama*. Louisville, Ky.: Heritage Publishing Consultants, 2000.

Hohoff, Tay. *Cats and Other People*. Garden City, N.Y.: Doubleday, 1973.

———. *A Ministry to Man: The Life of John Lovejoy Elliott*. New York: Harper & Brothers, 1959.

Holland, James W. *Andrew Jackson and the Creek War: Victory at the Horseshoe*. Tuscaloosa: University of Alabama Press, 1968.

Holmes, Oliver Wendell, Jr. *The Common Law*. Mineola, N.Y.: Dover, 1991.

Hughes, Langston. *Langston Hughes and the "Chicago Defender": Essays on Race, Politics, and Culture, 1942–62*. Edited by Christopher C. De Santis. Chicago: University of Illinois Press, 1995.

Hurston, Zora Neale. *Dust Tracks on a Road*. New York: Harper Perennial Modern Classics, 1996.

———. "Hoodoo in America." *Journal of American Folklore* no. 174 (Oct.– Dec. 1931): 317–417.

———. *Mules and Men*. New York: Harper Perennial Modern Classics, 2009.

———. *Tell My Horse*. New York: Harper Perennial Modern Classics, 2008.

Hyatt, Harry Middleton. *Hoodoo—Conjuration—Witchcraft—Rootwork: Beliefs Accepted by Many Negroes and White Persons, These Being Orally Recorded Among Blacks and Whites*. 5 vols. Hannibal, Mo.: Western, 1970.

Inge, M. Thomas, ed. *Truman Capote: Conversations*. Jackson: University of Mississippi Press, 1987.

Jackson, Harvey H., III. *Inside Alabama: A Personal History of My State*. Tuscaloosa: University of Alabama Press, 2004.

———. *Rivers of History: Life on the Coosa, Tallapoosa, Cahaba, and Alabama*. Tuscaloosa: University of Alabama Press, 1995.

Jamison, Leslie. *The Recovering: Intoxication and Its Aftermath*. New York: Little, Brown, 2018.

Johnson, Claudia Durst. *Reading Harper Lee: Understanding "To Kill a Mockingbird" and "Go Set a Watchman."* Santa Barbara, Calif.: Greenwood, 2018.

———. *"To Kill a Mockingbird": Threatening Boundaries.* New York: Twayne, 1994.

Jones, E. Paul. *To Kill a Preacher.* New York: Page, 2018.

Kasprzak, Perry. "Don Lee Keith Is Dead: A Student's Acquaintance with a Maverick New Orleans Journalist." *Southern Cultures* 12, no. 1 (Spring 2006): 92–103.

Keith, Don Lee. "An Afternoon with Harper Lee." *Delta Review* (Spring 1966): 40–41, 75, 80–81.

Kelly, Stuart. *The Book of Lost Books: An Incomplete History of All the Great Books You'll Never Read.* New York: Random House, 2006.

King, Florence. *Confessions of a Failed Southern Lady.* New York: St. Martin's Press, 1985.

Kiselyak, Charles. *Fearful Symmetry: The Making of "To Kill a Mockingbird."* Universal City, Calif.: Universal Home Video, 1998.

Knox, Sara L. *Murder: A Tale of Modern American Life.* Durham, N.C.: Duke University Press, 1998.

Laing, Olivia. *The Trip to Echo Spring: On Writers and Drinking.* New York: Picador, 2013.

Lee, Harper. *Go Set a Watchman.* New York: HarperCollins, 2015.

———. "Romance and High Adventure." In *Clearings in the Thicket: An Alabama Humanities Reader: Essays and Stories from the 1983 Alabama History and Heritage Festival,* edited by Jerry Elijah Brown, 13–20. Macon, Ga.: Mercer University Press, 1985.

———. *To Kill a Mockingbird.* New York: Warner Books, 1982.

Lepore, Jill. *Joe Gould's Teeth.* New York: Random House, 2016.

J. B. Lippincott Company. *The Author and His Audience: With a Chronology of Major Events in the History of J. B. Lippincott Company.* Philadelphia: J. B. Lippincott, 1967.

Lloyd Parry, Richard. *Ghosts of the Tsunami: Death and Life in Japan's Disaster Zone.* New York: MCD/Farrar, Straus and Giroux, 2017.

Lowell, Robert. *Collected Poems.* New York: Farrar, Straus and Giroux, 2003.

Madden, Kerry. *Harper Lee.* New York: Viking, 2009.

Malcolm, Janet. *The Journalist and the Murderer.* New York: Vintage, 1990.

Martin, Thomas W. *The Story of Horseshoe Bend National Military Park*. Birmingham, Ala.: Southern University Press at Birmingham Publishing Company, 1959.

McCabe, Daniel, and Paul Stekler. *George Wallace: Settin' the Woods on Fire*. [Alexandria, Va.]: PBS Home Video, 2000.

McDade, Thomas M. *The Annals of Murder: A Bibliography of Books and Pamphlets on American Murders from Colonial Times to 1900*. Norman: University of Oklahoma Press, 1961.

McGlamery, J. Gabriel. "Race Based Underwriting and the Death of Burial Insurance." *Connecticut Insurance Law Journal* 15, no. 2 (2008–2009): 531–70.

McWhorter, Diane. *Carry Me Home: Birmingham, Alabama: The Climactic Battle of the Civil Rights Revolution*. New York: Simon & Schuster, 2013.

Meacham, Jon, ed. *Voices in Our Blood: America's Best on the Civil Rights Movement*. New York: Random House, 2003.

Mills, Marja. *The Mockingbird Next Door: Life with Harper Lee*. New York: Penguin Press, 2014.

Moates, Marianne M. *Truman Capote's Southern Years: Stories from a Monroeville Cousin*. Tuscaloosa: University of Alabama Press, 2008.

Monroe County Heritage Museum. *Images of America: Monroeville*. Charleston, S.C.: Arcadia, 1999.

*The Monroe Journal Centennial Edition, 1866–1966*. Monroeville, Ala.: Monroe Journal, 1966.

Murphy, Mary McDonagh. *Hey, Boo: Harper Lee and "To Kill a Mockingbird."* First Run Features, 2010.

———. *Scout, Atticus, and Boo: A Celebration of Fifty Years of "To Kill a Mockingbird."* New York: Harper, 2010.

Murphy, Sharon Ann. *Investing in Life: Insurance in Antebellum America*. Baltimore: Johns Hopkins University Press, 2010.

Newquist, Roy. *Counterpoint*. New York: Simon & Schuster, 1964.

O'Connor, Flannery. *The Habit of Being: Letters of Flannery O'Connor*. Edited by Sally Fitzgerald. New York: Farrar, Straus and Giroux, 1988.

Opal, J. M. *Avenging the People: Andrew Jackson, the Rule of Law, and the American Nation*. Oxford: Oxford University Press, 2017.

Owen, Marie Bankhead. "Albert James Pickett, a Sketch." *Alabama Historical Quarterly* 1, no. 1 (Spring 1930): 113–15.

Petry, Alice Hall, ed. *On Harper Lee: Essays and Reflections*. Knoxville: University of Tennessee Press, 2008.

Pickett, Albert James. *History of Alabama and Incidentally of Georgia and Mississippi, from the Earliest Period.* Tuscaloosa, Ala.: Willo, 1962.

Pinn, Anthony B. *Varieties of African American Religious Experience: Toward a Comparative Black Theology.* Minneapolis: Fortress Press, 1998.

Plimpton, George. *Truman Capote: In Which Various Friends, Enemies, Acquaintances, and Detractors Recall His Turbulent Career.* New York: Nan A. Talese, 1997.

Posnock, Ross. *Renunciation: Acts of Abandonment by Writers, Philosophers, and Artists.* Cambridge, Mass.: Harvard University Press, 2016.

Priestman, Martin, ed. *The Cambridge Companion to Crime Fiction.* Cambridge, U.K.: Cambridge University Press, 2003.

Puckett, Newbell Niles. *Folk Beliefs of the Southern Negro.* New York: Negro Universities Press, 1926.

Raboteau, Albert J. *Slave Religion: The "Invisible Institution" in the Antebellum South.* New York: Oxford University Press, 1978.

Richardson, Paul. *That's Waht They Say: A History of East Alabama, Chambers, Randolph, Tallapoosa, and Lee Counties.* Lafayette, Ala.: Solo Press, 2011.

Roberts, Kodi A. *Voodoo and Power: The Politics of Religion in New Orleans, 1881–1940.* Baton Rouge: Louisiana State University Press, 2015.

Rogers, William Warren, Robert David Ward, Leah Rawl Atkins, and Wayne Flynt. *Alabama: The History of a Deep South State.* Tuscaloosa: University of Alabama Press, 1994.

Rosengarten, Theodore. *All God's Dangers: The Life of Nate Shaw.* Chicago: University of Chicago Press, 1974.

Roth, Philip. *Patrimony: A True Story.* New York: Vintage Books, 1996.

Rumore, Pat Boyd. *From Power to Service: The Story of Lawyers in Alabama.* Montgomery: Alabama State Bar Association, 2010.

———. *Lawyers in a New South City: A History of the Legal Profession in Birmingham.* Birmingham, Ala.: Association Publishing Company, 2000.

Schafer, Elizabeth D. *Lake Martin: Alabama's Crown Jewel.* Charleston, S.C.: Arcadia, 2003.

Shields, Charles J. *Mockingbird: A Portrait of Harper Lee.* New York: St. Martin's Press, 2006.

Sutherland, Edwin H., Donald R. Cressey, and David F. Luckenbill. *Principles of Criminology.* 11th ed. Lanham, Md.: General Hall, 1992.

Tallant, Robert. *Voodoo in New Orleans.* Gretna, La.: Pelican, 2012.

Tennyson, Alfred. *Selected Poems.* New York: Penguin Classics, 2007.

Trillin, Calvin. *Killings.* New York: Ticknor & Fields, 1984.

Varicella, Christamar. *The Reverend*. Self-published, 2012.

Voss, Ralph F. *Truman Capote and the Legacy of "In Cold Blood."* Tuscaloosa: University of Alabama Press, 2011.

Walls, Peggy Jackson, and Laura Dykes Oliver. *Alexander City*. Charleston, S.C.: Arcadia, 2011.

Walter, Eugene, as told to Katherine Clark. *Milking the Moon: A Southerner's Story of Life on This Planet*. San Francisco: Untreed Reads, 2014.

Weaks, Mary Louise, and Carolyn Perry, eds. *Southern Women's Writing: Colonial to Contemporary*. Gainesville: University of Florida Press, 1995.

Weingarten, Marc. *The Gang That Wouldn't Write Straight: Wolfe, Thompson, Didion, Capote, and the New Journalism Revolution*. New York: Crown, 2005.

Wilkerson, Isabel. *The Warmth of Other Suns: The Epic Story of America's Great Migration*. New York: Random House, 2010.

Windham, Donald. *Lost Friendships: A Memoir of Truman Capote, Tennessee Williams, and Others*. New York: Morrow, 1987.

Wolfe, Tom, and E. W. Johnson, eds. *The New Journalism*. New York: Harper & Row, 1973.

| ABOUT THE AUTHOR |

Casey Cep is a writer from the Eastern Shore of Maryland. After graduating from Harvard College with a degree in English, she earned an M.Phil. in theology at Oxford as a Rhodes Scholar. Her work has appeared in *The New Yorker*, *The New York Times*, and *The New Republic*, among many other publications. *Furious Hours* is her first book.

| A NOTE ON THE TYPE |

This book was set in Adobe Garamond. Designed by Robert Slimbach, the fonts are based on types first cut by Claude (ca. 1480–1561). Garamond is believed to have followed the Venetian models and it is to him that we owe the letter we now know as "old style."

Composed by North Market Street Graphics,
Lancaster, Pennsylvania

Printed and bound by Berryville Graphics,
Berryville, Virginia

Designed by Betty Lew